Residential Architecture in Bhoja's Samarāṅgaṇasūtradhāra

Residential Architecture in Bhoja's Samarāṅgaṇasūtradhāra

Introduction, Text, Translation and Notes

FELIX OTTER

MOTILAL BANARSIDASS PUBLISHERS
PRIVATE LIMITED • DELHI

First Edition: Delhi, **2010**

ISBN: 978-81-208-3447-7

MOTILAL BANARSIDASS
41 U.A. Bungalow Road, Jawahar Nagar, Delhi 110 007
8 Mahalaxmi Chamber, 22 Bhulabhai Desai Road, Mumbai 400 026
203 Royapettah High Road, Mylapore, Chennai 600 004
236, 9th Main III Block, Jayanagar, Bangalore 560 011
Sanas Plaza, 1302 Baji Rao Road, Pune 411 002
8 Camac Street, Kolkata 700 017
Ashok Rajpath, Patna 800 004
Chowk, Varanasi 221 001

Printed in India

By Jainendra Prakash Jain at Shri Jainendra Press,
A-45 Naraina, Phase-I, New Delhi 110 028
and published by Narendra Prakash Jain for
Motilal Banarsidass Publishers Private Limited,
Bungalow Road, Delhi 110 007

Contents

Preface

This book is a revised version of my M.A. thesis submitted to the Department of Foreign Languages of Philipps-Universität, Marburg (Germany) on 8 February 2005. To the best of my knowledge, it was at that time the first translation of any part of the *Samarāṅgaṇasūtradhāra* into the English language; I trust that it remains a useful study of the sections devoted to residential architecture in the *vāstuśāstra* commonly ascribed to the renowned Paramāra king Bhoja of Dhārā.

Public interest in the traditional science of Vāstuvidyā has been increasing over the past two decades or so – primarily in India, but to a somewhat lesser degree in Europe and the US as well. On the whole, the indological community has been slow to react to this trend: Few *vāstuśāstra*s have been translated into Western languages, and many important texts remain unedited. Consequently, there is to date no reliable comprehensive history of the origin and development of Vāstuvidyā. It is hoped that this book will be received as a small contribution to this daunting task.

Throughout the process of writing and revising this book, I have received help and support from a number of individuals and institutions that must not go unacknowledged: I would like to thank my colleagues at the Universities of Marburg and Halle an der Saale for their support and encouragement – in particular, Prof. Rahul Peter Das, Prof. Michael Hahn, Dr. Ulrike Roesler, Dr. Jayandra Soni, Dr. Luitgard Soni, Dr. Roland Steiner, and Martin Straube, M.A.; Dr. Dragomir Dimitrov for desperately needed technical (as well as moral) support; the graduate school *Asia and Africa in World Reference Systems* (Halle); and, of course, my family – especially my wife Mandy and my son Paul, for their love, support, and patience.

There is one more person to whom I owe a great debt of gratitude: My late grandfather Heinz-Peter Hahn (1920-1997), to whose cherished memory I dedicate this book.

Abbreviations

ABORI	Annals of the Bhandarkar Oriental Research Institute
ACM	Hemacandra: *Abhidhānacintāmaṇi*
ADhR	VIJAYARĀJENDRASŪRI: *Abhidhānarājendra*
AK	Amarasiṃha: *Nāmaliṅgānuśāsana (Amarakośa)*
ALB	Adyar Library Bulletin
ArchOr	Archiv Orientální
AOS	American Oriental Series
ARM	Halāyudha: *Abhidhānaratnamālā*
Br̥S	Varāhamihira: *Br̥hatsaṃhitā* [ed. TRIPĀṬHĪ]
Br̥SṬ	Utpala: *Vivr̥ti* (*Br̥hatsaṃhitāṭīkā*)
CC	AUFRECHT: *Catalogus Catalogorum*
CV	*Cullavagga*
DET	BURROW, EMENEAU: *A Dravidian Etymological Dictionary*
DNA	Buddhaghosa: *Sumaṅgalavilāsinī (Dīghanikāya-Aṭṭhakathā)*
DNM	Hemacandra: *Deśīnāmamālā*
EI	*Epigraphia Indica*
EWA	MAYRHOFER: *Etymologisches Wörterbuch des Altindoarischen*
GOS	Gaekwad's Oriental Series
HIL	GONDA: *History of Indian Literature*
HJM	Haribhaṭṭa: *Jātakamālā*
IA	Indian Archaeology
IJHS	Indian Journal for the History of Science
JAOS	Journal of the American Oriental Society
Jāt.	*Jātaka*
JORM	Journal of Oriental Research, Madras
JRAS	Journal of the Royal Asiatic Society
KA	Kauṭilya: *Kauṭilīyārthaśāstra*

KEWA	MAYRHOFER: *Kurzgefaßtes etymologisches Wörterbuch des Altindoarischen*
KS	Vātsyāyana: *Kāmasūtra*
KSṬ	Yaśodhara: *Jayamaṅgala (Kāmasūtraṭīkā)*
MhV	*Mahāvaṃsa*
MM	*Mayamata*
MP	*Matsyapurāṇa*
MS	*Mānasāra*
MV	*Mahāvagga*
NGMPP	Nepal German Manuscript Preservation Project
NM	Bhoja: *Nāmamālikā*
OLZ	Orientalistische Literatur-Zeitung
PCM	Merutuṅga: *Prabandhacintāmaṇi*
PD	BÖHTLINGK, ROTH: *Sanskrit Wörterbuch* ('Petersburg Dictionary')
pd	BÖHTLINGK: *Sanskrit-Wörterbuch in kürzerer Fassung* ('Shorter Petersburg Dictionary')
PED	RHYS DAVIDS and STEDE: The Pali Text Society's Pali-English Dictionary
PSM	SHETH: *Pāiasaddamahaṇṇavo*
SBB	Sacred Books of the Buddhists
SIAL	Sources of Indo-Aryan Lexicography
SKĀ	Bhoja: *Sarasvatīkaṇṭhābharaṇa*
ŚKD	DEVA: *Śabdakalpadruma*
ŚMK	Bhoja: *Śṛṅgāramañjarīkathā*
VP	*Viśvakarmaprakāśa*
WZKSO	Wiener Zeitschrift für die Kunde Süd- und Ostasiens
YK	Bhoja: *Yuktikalpataru*
ZDMG	Zeitschrift der Deutschen Morgenländischen Gesellschaft
ZII	Zeitschrift für Indologie und Iranistik

A Note on the text

Original sources are invariably quoted by chapter (or act) and stanza according to the division found in the respective printed edition; a '+' indicates the prose passage following a stanza, e.g. Mr̥cch 03.06+ refers to the prose passage following the 6th stanza in the 3rd act of the play. In the critical appáratus, the abbreviations used by AGRAWALA have been retained; the readings of SASTRI's and AGRAWALA's edition have been indicated by Śa, those of SHUKLA (1965a) by Śu.

The transliteration of Sanskrit follows international practice, vocalic 'r' being indicated by r̥ rather than ṛ (which is reserved for the retroflex 'r' of NIA). In the transliteration of Hindi text, silent 'a' has not been indicated except where the Hindi text obviously quotes words from Sanskrit – not as *tatsama*s, but as genuine foreign words.

1. Introduction

1.1 General Introduction

The *Samarāṅgaṇasūtradhāra* (SAS), a treatise on *vāstu* ascribed to king Bhoja of the Paramāra dynasty who ruled in Mālava in the first half of the eleventh century,[1] has received little scholarly attention so far.[2] The text of SAS, which has not been transmitted in its entirety, was first edited from three mss[3] by T.S. Ganapati SASTRI in two volumes in 1924/25; a second revised edition by V.S. AGRAWALA was published in November 1966 as GOS No. 25. AGRAWALA was also preparing a study of the text, including an index of technical terms, which was to be published as GOS No. 32,[4] but his untimely death in July 1966 prevented the completion of this work which, had it ever been published, would surely have helped to throw some light on the more obscure passages of the work, and would probably have rendered much of this study superfluous.

The degree of dissent regarding the nature and importance of SAS can perhaps best be illustrated by juxtaposing two statements by D.N. SHUKLA, author of the two-volume *Vāstu-Śāstra* – in effect a study of *vāstu* literature, based on the text of SAS –, and P.K. ACHARYA, author and editor of the *Manasara Series*.

1) In his *Vāstu-Śāstra Vol. I: Hindu Science of Architecture* (1958: 143), SHUKLA makes his case for the originality and independence of SAS:

> In the end, I may touch on the pertinent problem of the sources from which it has drawn and the originality it can claim. I am of the definite view that the whole work is a master-piece of original contribution. Even some of the preliminary chapters (i.e. Mahadādisarga, Bhuvanakośa and Sahadevādhikāra etc. etc.) though drawn from the Purāṇas, are independent and original in sense [sic!] that they are not reproductions. [...] The House architecture is its special contribution. The S.S may be deemed as the founder of the civil architecture among the ancient classics of this branch of lore.

2) ACHARYA on the other hand did not seem to hold SAS in very high esteem; after providing its table of contents in his *Hindu Architecture in India and Abroad* (1946b:178-181), he states that

> [t]his outline of the contents of a modernized text [?] will clearly show its compilation in a confused manner. There is no logical sequence or order in the arrangement of the chapters. The contents of the same chapter have been unnecessarily described in several chapters. The patron being a king, and the primary object being the royal palaces, some twenty-one chapters (XLIX– LXX) have been devoted to the same subject. Because the compilation was largely, if not wholly, based on the *Mānasāra*, however, some thirteen chapters at the end have been devoted to the subjects of sculpture and painting, as has been done in the *Mānasāra*, although the treatment is less methodical. The preliminary chapters dealing with the origin of the world and arrival of the heavenly architect are the only original, but entirely non-architectural, matters.

Obviously, both of these statements require some explanation. First of all, SHUKLA's idea that the separate treatment of residential architecture was the original contribution of SAS cannot hold good if one takes into consideration the 52nd *adhyāya* of Varāhamihira's *Bṛhatsaṃhitā* (BṛS) entitled *vāstuvidyā*,[5] the 254th and 255th chapters of the *Matsyapurāṇa* (MP), and the 2nd, 4th, and 7th *adhyāya*s of the *Viśvakarmaprakāśa* (VP), which on closer examination prove to be if not SAS' chief sources for residential architecture, then at least the basis of its exposition thereof. Indeed, many passages in the 19th, 22nd, and 24th *adhyāya*s of SAS are hardly intelligible without recourse to the text of – and commentary on – BṛS 52;[6] for the sake of illustration, consider the following stanza from the text of SAS (19.16):

> *śreṣṭham aṣṭaśataṃ rājñām etāni tu yathākramam |*
> *catuḥṣaḍaṣṭahānyā syuḥ pañcamaṃ ca pṛthak pṛthak ||*

> 'The biggest [house] for kings [shall have a width of] one hundred and eight [cubits],[7] but these [following houses] in due order shall be diminished in steps of four, six, and eight, and [there shall be] a fifth [house] one after the other.'[8]

Taken on its own, this stanza is hard to make any sense of; its meaning becomes apparent if one compares its contents with that of BṛS 52.04:

> *uttamam aṣṭābhyadhikaṃ hastaśataṃ nṛpagṛhaṃ pṛthutvena |*
> *aṣṭāṣṭonāny eva pañca sapādāni dairghyena ||*

> 'The biggest house of a king shall be one hundred cubits in width augmented by eight; [the other] five [shall be] diminished [in successive steps of] eight, [and] augmented by one fourth in length.'

According to Utpala's commentary, a king intending to have a palace built for himself has a set of five ground plans of different dimensions to choose from, the most spacious of which has a width of 108 cubits; the respective sizes of the remaining four ground plans are arrived at by gradual diminution of this figure in steps of eight cubits, yielding a length of 100, 92, 84, and 76 cubits respectively.[9]

Thus, while the treatment of residential architecture found in SAS is not the earliest example of such an exposition (being, as it is, preceded by BṛS, MP, and VP, as well as those authorities quoted by Utpala in his commentary), it cannot even be said to be the most exhaustive specimen either; for instance, the treatment accorded the residential buildings (the *eka-*, *dvi-*, *tri-*, and *catuḥśālas*) in the text of the *Mayamata* (MM) is just as comprehensive and in-depth by any standard;[10] apart from this, there is of course a number of treatises that deal with residential architecture exclusively, the best known of which is probably the relatively recent *Manuṣyālayacandrikā* (MĀC).[11]

But if SHUKLA's enthusiasm cannot stand up to scrutiny, neither can ACHARYA's wholesale dismissiveness. It is true that the text of SAS (at least where it is concerned with residential architecture) abounds in repetitions and inconsistencies, a problem which we will discuss later;[12] but it is certainly not true that SAS is primarily concerned with royal palaces; the chapters quoted by ACHARYA in support of his claim all deal with temple architecture exclusively.

Apparently, the editor of MS made the mistake of translating *prāsāda* 'temple' as 'palace,' a meaning it never has in the usage of SAS.[13] His further claim that 'the compilation was largely, if not wholly, based on the *Mānasāra*' is positively preposterous; first of all, MS is definitely one of those *śāstra*s justifying SHUKLA's claim that treatises on *vāstu* did not distinguish between sacred and secular architecture, a distinction which SAS carefully maintains;[14] furthermore, even a superficial comparison of the technical vocabulary contained in the two texts in question will reveal a considerable degree of divergence;[15] and last but not least did ACHARYA grossly exaggerate the age of MS,[16] the compilation of which was probably not completed before the 15th century – insofar as compilations of *śilpaśāstra*s are ever 'completed' at all.[17]

1.2 The text of SAS

In its present form, SAS consists of roughly 7,430 *śloka*s[18] in 83 *adhyāya*s; since none of the surviving mss is complete, it is impossible to say how extensive the original text really was, and whether indeed it was ever finished.

1.2.1 Structure of *adhyāyas*

The structure of the individual *adhyāya*s follows the same basic model in more or less every instance: First, there is an introductory stanza in the *anuṣṭubh* metre indicating the topic of the *adhyāya*, and bearing witness to the nature of the entire work as a sequence of answers given by Viśvakarman to the enquiries of his sons into the nature of architecture by the use of such phrases as '*atha brūmaḥ*,' '*atha pravakṣyāmaḥ*,' '*athocyate*' etc.; the entire chapter is usually composed in the *anuṣṭubh* metre with the exception of the concluding stanza (or stanzas), which are invariably composed in a longer metre, most commonly *upajāti* or *vasantatilakā*.[19] The strict adherence to this convention gives a certain amount of structure and internal arrangement to the text.[20] The same method is followed in MM.[21]

Below (1.3.2.2), we shall see that the colophons of the individual *adhyāya*s are not original, but were added subsequently; this assumption is also supported by the evidence provided by the 39th *adhyāya*: the colophon gives its title as *dvāraguṇadoṣaḥ*, 'merits and defects of the doors.' The introductory stanza, however, runs thus:

> *gr̥hāṇy uktāni sarveṣām evaṃ karmopajīvinām |*
> *varṇināṃ ca gr̥hasthānāṃ kathyante 'taḥ paraṃ yathā ||*

'The houses for [the use of] all professionals have been thus declared; and the houses for [those] *gr̥hastha*s [who are] *varṇin*s are now declared.'

An indication of the topic mentioned in the colophon is only given in 39.35ab:

> *guṇadoṣān pravakṣyāmi dvārāṇāṃ sarvavāstuṣu |*

'I will [now] proclaim the merits and defects of the doors with reference to all *vāstu*s.'

The stanza directly preceding it, moreover, is composed in the *upajāti*-metre. It is thus highly likely that before the insertion of the colophons, 39.01-34 constituted a thematic unit of its own, as distinct from the rest of what is now the 39th *adhyāya* as from any other portion of the text – in other words, that the scribe in question forgot to insert a colophon in this place. It is on these grounds that of the 39th *adhyāya*, I have felt justified to restrict my translation to the first 34 stanzas.

1.3 Authorship and related problems

The authorship of the works attributed to Bhoja is a contentious issue; There is a tradition ascribing no less than 84 works from the most diverse branches of science and literature to the Paramāra king, all of which are said to have been named after Bhoja's own *biruda*s or titles.[22] AUFRECHT (CC I:418) was quick to dismiss the possibility of Bhoja actually having written any of the 21 works recorded in CC under his name, saying that it was 'almost superfluous to add that none of the following works were actually written by himself, but belong to authors who either lived during his reign, or some time after.' It is not clear whether AUFRECHT's dismissal was prompted by his disbelief that a medieval Indian king could have been able to divert sufficient time and energy from the burdens of office to make any serious contribution to literary as well as political and military history,[23] or by the philologist's instinct to be on his guard when presented with a list of works ascribed to so hallowed and legendary a figure as Bhoja's. Be that as it may, there is some consensus among scholars that at least three works from the list, viz. *Sarasvatīkaṇṭhābharaṇa* (on poetics), *Śṛṅgāraprakāśa*, and the first five books of the *Campūrāmāyaṇa* can be attributed to Bhoja.[24]

As indicated above, an intimate study of some two hundred stanzas out of more than seven thousand is hardly the place to answer the question of Bhoja's authorship conclusively – if indeed it ever can be. But in order to approach that question we would first have to ascertain whether SAS is the work of an individual author at all, rather than a compilation; the work of a single author would naturally be expected (1) to betray a greater degree of stylistic unity and coherence than a compilation; (2) to be relatively free of unnecessary repetitions and redundancies; and (3) to contain no material that can be shown to be in direct contradiction to other parts of the text.

With these thoughts in mind, I shall now present the evidence furnished by the text passages under consideration in the context of this study, viz. *adhyāyas* 10, 16, 18-25, 28, 39, and 48.

1.3.1 The language of SAS

In the preface to the second edition, AGRAWALA (1966:xiii) characterises the style of SAS as follows:

> I wish to endorse fully the remarks of the previous editor about the beautiful style of Sanskrit found in the Samarāṅgaṇa Sūtradhāra which it is a pleasure to go through and relish its classical flavour: "Generally the language of extant Śilpa works is ungrammatical, but the present work is free from grammatical solecisms and written most[ly] in a sweet and beautiful style."[25]

It is certainly true that the Sanskrit of SAS is generally superior e.g. to that of AP, MS or ŚRK to mention only a few, and is far removed from the now proverbial 'most barbarous Sanskrit' of the 'books of masons and carpenters, which give the rules for building houses' so severely dealt with by BÜHLER.[26] Although the metrical structure of the text is rather uniform bordering on the monotonous (cf. 1.2.1 above),[27] the metre is generally correct and one does not get the impression that the rather tight truss of the *anuṣṭubh* seriously impeded the author's ability to express his ideas.[28] The strict application of the *pathyā* in the 18th *adhyāya* may serve as an example: of 57 stanzas in the *anuṣṭubh* metre, there are only 12 deviations from the regular form, most of which are *ma-* or *na-vipulās*; the caesuras between the individual *pāda*s are observed in every instance, and there is only one occurrence of a caesura within a compound (18.56cd).

As against this, of the 57 1/2 *anuṣṭubhs*[29] contained in the 21st *adhyāya* there are 22 *vipulās*, and the same number of compounds bisected by the caesura.

Of course, it should be taken into account that those passages most likely to have caesuras within a compound are the lengthy and rather tedious exercises in *prastāra* (1.5.7 below), which enumerate all the mathematically possible arrangements of certain architectural objects within a building; this is done by assigning consecutive numbers to the potential positions of e.g. the *mūṣā*s[30] – cf. 19.166:

yasminn ādyāṣṭamīṣaṣṭhī¹pañcamyo muṇḍam eva tat |
dvipañcamyaṣṭamīṣaṣṭhyo ¹ *mūṣā mātaṅgasaṃjñite* ||

'In which [*catuḥśāla* there are] the first, eighth, sixth, [and] fifth [*mūṣā*], that is [called] *muṇḍa*; the second, fifth, eighth, [and] sixth *mūṣā* [are found] in [the *catuḥśāla*] called *mātaṅga*.'

There is a strong possibility that the author chose to variate the position of the long compound within each half-stanza in order to break the monotony of the rather tiring *prastāra* passages at the (relatively low) cost of abandoning a strict observance of the caesuras;[31] this variation in itself is thus no sufficient evidence for a different authorship in the case of *adhyāya*s 19-23 and 25 on the one hand and 18 on the other.

There is, however, at least one case of a violated caesura, viz. 22.08ab:

mṛtyudaṃ mahiṣīgāvī¹bhyāṃ bhaved yamasūryakam |

'[A *dviśāla* being constituted] by [the *śālā*s known as] *mahiśī* and *gāvī* shall be the death-bringing *yamasūryaka*.'

In addition to this, there are two cases on record of an elision of *sandhi* at the caesura, viz. 20.02cd:

vāmā vā dakṣiṇā vāpi agrataḥ pṛṣṭhato 'pi vā ||

'The left hand [*śālā*] or the right hand [*śālā*], in front or in the back.'

and 39.03ab:

māhendre 'rke 'tha satye vā āryake vā niketanam |

'The dwelling [shall be situated] in [the *pada*] of Mahendra, [that of] Arka or Satya, or Āryaka.'

In all four instances it is difficult to see how the mistakes, or rather: irregularities should have crept in in the course of textual transmission; it is more likely that the stanzas in question were composed as we find them in the printed edition.[32]

1.3.1.1 Variations of gender

There are three words on record the gender of which varies throughout the text, viz. (1) *alindaḥ/-ā*; (2) *kaṇṭhaḥ/-ā*; (3) *gṛhaḥ/-am*.

1.3.1.1.1 *Alindaḥ/-ā*

This word, denoting the verandah either in front of the dwelling or facing the (interior) courtyard,[33] is masculine throughout the text; in 18.23b, however, it occurs in the feminine as *alindā*:

> *śālāgre valabhī yā syād alindeti vadanti tām* |
>
> 'The *valabhī* that may be situated in front of the house – that they call *alindā* [...]'

None of the dictionaries have *alindā*, f., and it is not found in the *kośa*s either; it is also the only occurrence within the text of SAS. Since it is also the only occurrence of *alindaḥ/-ā* in the 18th *adhyāya*, it might be taken to be indicative of the fact that this chapter is the work of a different author (as we shall see below, this is the most likely explanation); alternatively, one might speculate whether *alindā* is feminine on account of its being a particular type of *valabhī*, also feminine. But the *valabhī* in its turn is explained as a particular type of *prāsāda*, masculine; and the grammatical gender of the object defined generally has no impact on the gender of the descriptive term by which it is defined. A third possibility, viz. a semantic difference between *alindaḥ* and *alindā*, can be safely ruled out on the grounds that *alindaḥ* can also refer to the kind of front porch described in 18.23ab – cf. 1.5.2 below.

1.3.1.1.2 *Kaṇṭhaḥ/-ā*

The masculine form occurs in 18.42b, where it refers to a wall,[34] as well as in 28.26d, 39b, 44c, where it refers to some type of moulding.[35] The feminine *kaṇṭhā* occurs in 18.15d and 18.26c, referring to a kind of low wall or parapet in the former, to the wall of a house in the latter instance.[36]

The readings of the mss in 18.15 are ambiguous; Kha Ga Da have *kaṇṭhā ... yā*, Ka has *kaṇṭho ... yaḥ*. This leaves some room for the speculation that the original reading might have been *kaṇṭhā* (*visarga* dropped before *h*) ... *yāḥ*; but the reading *yā ... kaṇṭhā* in 18.26 is attested in all mss.

As we have seen, both *kaṇṭhaḥ* and *kaṇṭhā* can translate as 'wall,' whereas the meaning 'a kind of moulding' seems to be peculiar to *kaṇṭhaḥ*. The semantic difference does not seem to depend on gender – unless we emend **kaṇṭhā* ... **yā* in 18.42, in which case we would have *kaṇṭhā* 'wall or parapet' and *kaṇṭhaḥ* 'a kind of moulding.' Either way, it should be noted that *kaṇṭhaḥ/-ā* has the meaning 'wall or parapet' in the 18th *adhyāya* exclusively, whereas *kaṇṭhaḥ* 'a kind of moulding' – arguably the more conventional meaning – is only used in the 28th; and neither the masculine nor the feminine (which is not recorded in the dictionaries at all) can usually refer to a wall. It seems that this meaning is peculiar to the 18th *adhyāya*.

1.3.1.1.3 *Gṛhaḥ/-am*

It is hardly surprising that the word *gṛha* is one of the most frequently used technical terms in the passages of SAS selected for this study; wherever it occurs in an inflected form that is not common to masculine and neuter, the latter is invariably used – with the exception of 18.04:

grāmaḥ syān nigamād ūno grāmakalpo gṛhas tv asau |

'A village shall be smaller than a *nigama*, a house, though, [shall be] similar to a village [but smaller].'

In this case, the use of the masculine form cannot be considered to be a peculiarity of the 18th *adhyāya*, as 18.09, 12, 19 have the nominative singular neuter *gr̥ham*; the question arises whether there is any semantic difference between the two.

In 18.04, *gr̥ha* is the last link in a series of settlements enumerated in descending order with reference to their size or importance: (1) *rājadhāni* 'royal residence' – (2) *śākhānagara* 'suburb or urban settlement in general' – (3) *karvaṭa* 'market town' – (4) *nigama* 'small market town' – (5) *grāma* 'village' – (6) *gr̥ha* 'house;' *gr̥ha* is defined as *grāmakalpa-* 'similar to a village (but smaller).'[37] Normally one would expect *gr̥ha* to be defined as that which a *grāma* is made up of; but the context of the enumeration suggests that *gr̥ha* must be distinct from *grāma*. One might wonder if *gr̥ha* m. refers to a sort of farmstead as against *gr̥ha* n. 'house (in general);' but isolated farmsteads away from the village do not seem to have been a regular feature of the ancient or medieval Indian landscape.[38] It is more likely that, given the encyclopaedic character of the 18th *adhyāya*, the word *gr̥ha* was only added to the list of settlement types for the sake of completeness.

If the variation of gender is not indicative of any semantic difference, the only likely explanations are (1) a spelling error in 18.04; or (2) an interpolation in the same stanza. As the title of this section suggests, there is a third possibility, viz. a different authorship of the 18th *adhyāya*; we shall pick up this thread in our concluding discussion under 1.3.5 below.

1.3.2 Internal arrangement

1.3.2.1 Sequence of *adhyāyas*

As indicated above, the internal arrangement of SAS seems to leave much to be desired; although the spheres of residential and sacred architecture are kept strictly separate as far as the individual *adhyāyas* are concerned,[39] it is hard to make out any guiding principle in their order: the royal palace is the topic of the 15th, 30th, and 51st *adhyāyas*; the doors in their various aspects are discussed in the 24th, 28th, 39th, 43rd, and 48th *adhyāyas*; and a description of the architect and the eight limbs of architecture, though introductory in character, are only furnished in the 44th and 45th *adhyāyas* respectively.[40] SHUKLA (1958:32 sq.) thought that

> because the author being a king, the compilation and the arrangement might have been left to some of his assistants, or it might be a later mishap that the present arrangement is faulty and gives the impression that the work, especially the first 48 chapters of it, lack coherence, logical sequence and order.

This prompted him to attempt a restoration of the 'original' sequence of the *adhyāyas*;[41] the result is as arbitrary as it is unconvincing.[42]

Yet it is very much open to discussion whether indeed the sequence of *adhyāyas* is as incoherent and illogical as ACHARYA thought; rather, the work allows for a broad division into four sections, viz.:

1) introductory, including the layout of the *vāstupuruṣamaṇḍala* (*adhyāyas* 01-14);
2) town-planning, residential architecture, and miscellaneous matters (*adhyāyas* 15- ca. 51);[43]
3) temple architecture (*adhyāyas* 52-69);
4) sculpture and painting (*adhyāyas* 70-83).

Within the first two sections, there is again a certain number of blocks of consecutive *adhyāyas*, sometimes with one or two intervening chapters, forming a thematic unit, viz.:

1) *adhyāyas* 01-07;
2) *adhyāyas* 11-14;
3) *adhyāyas* 19, 21-23, 25;
4) *adhyāyas* 30-32;[44]
5) *adhyāyas* 44-45.

At the same time, there are certain *adhyāya*s that seem out of place, or contain subject matter that has already been discussed elsewhere; some of these have been quoted above, others will be examined more closely under 1.3.3 and 1.3.4 below. For our present purpose, it will suffice to point out that, while the internal arrangement of SAS seems to follow some kind of logical sequence, there are still enough inconsistencies to warrant the working hypothesis that the text is not the work of a single author.

1.3.2.2 The colophons

We may now consider the evidence furnished by the colophons and the numbering of the individual *adhyāya*s, which contain some inconsistencies:

1) The colophons of the 1st to 57th and the 59th *adhyāya*s are modelled on the following scheme in all mss:

> *iti mahārājādhirājaśrībhojadevaviracite samarāṅgaṇasūtradhārāparanāmni vāstuśāstre* <title> *nāma* <number> *adhyāyaḥ* |

The colophons of the next eight *adhyāya*s (60 - 67), as well as the 73rd, insert *parameśvara* and drop *apara*:

> *iti mahārājādhirājaparameśvaraśrībhojadevaviracite samarāṅgaṇasūtradhāranāmni vāstuśāstre* <title> *nāma* <number> *adhyāyaḥ* |

The colophons of the remaining *adhyāya*s (68 - 72, 74 - 82) have neither *parameśvara* nor *apara*; ms Da, however, retains *parameśvara* in the colophons of *adhyāya*s 70, 75, 78 - 81.

The colophon of the 58th *adhyāya* seems to be missing altogether in mss Ka Kha and Ga; Da merely has *prāsādastavanaṃ nāma*, without author and title of the work, nor number.

2) The colophon in *adhyāya* 55 reads *pañcamo 'dhyāyaḥ* instead of **pañcapañcāśo 'dhyāyaḥ* in all mss; similarly, the colophon in 71 simply reads *saptamaḥ* instead of **ekasaptatitamo 'dhyāyaḥ*; the 57th *adhyāya* is erroneously referred to as *ṣaṭ-pañcāśo 'dhyāyaḥ*; Da reads °*aṣṭapañcamo 'dhyāyaḥ*.

3) From the 72nd *adhyāya* onward, the numbering in the colophons is confused; the number 72 has been assigned both to the 72nd and the 73rd *adhyāya* in all mss, so that the number of each successive *adhyāya* is lower by one.[45]

These findings are relatively easy to account for: as we have seen above, we may safely assume that the autograph did not contain any colophons or numberings of *adhyāya*s at all, both having been added only later by scribes and/or redactors of the text; the most likely explanation for the faulty numberings of the 55th and 71st *adhyāya*s is a scribal error; and the faulty numbering of the 57th *adhyāya* and from the 73rd *adhyāya* onwards is obviously due to the fact that whoever inserted the numberings in the first place erroneously assigned the same number to two consecutive *adhyāyas*. This is further corroborated by the fact that after the 72nd *adhyāya*, the correct order is not taken up again, but the wrong numbering is carried through to the end.

The three groups of colophons identified above are not congruent with any thematic divisions, and there is no evidence that they represent different layers of textual transmission; rather, they merely seem to reflect the arbitrariness with which the colophons were introduced into the text.

1.3.3 Repetitions

A number of passages devoted to subject matter already treated in one or more different chapters have been identified:

1) In 24.35-42, the names and auspicious properties of residential houses are given as depending on the position of the front door with reference to the *pada*s of the *vāstupuruṣamaṇḍala*, as well as the names of the respective *śālā*s:

35. That building, though, that faces east [and whose] door is connected with [the *pada* of the *vāstupuruṣamaṇḍala*] belonging to Mahendra – that house is called *bhadra*, and the *śālā* shall be [called] *hastinī*.
36. [The house called] *bhadra* causes happiness for the master [of the house, and] increases [his] fame and power; and the works of him who lives in the house called *bhadra* are accomplished.
37. The dwelling faces south, and its door [is situated in the field associated with] Gṛhakṣata – that house [is called] *nandapīṭhaka*, and the *śālā* shall be [called] *mahiṣī*.
38. One knows the house of the type of *nandapīṭha* to cause bliss at all times; [it is] endowed with all qualities of prosperity, [and] causes increase of wealth and grains.
39. The dwelling faces [the direction] of Varuṇa, and its door [is situated in the *pada* associated with] Kusumāhvaya – that [building] the wise shall know as *saurabha*, and the *śālā* shall be [called] *gāvī*.
40. The masters of the house residing in [a house of the type of] *saurabha* experience joy at all times, fruitful plowing and commerce, and [they shall have] obedient sons.
41. The dwelling faces north, the door is connected with [the *pada* belonging to] Bhallāṭa – that [house] is called *puṣkara*, and the *śālā* shall be [called] *chagalī*.
42. [Residing] in [a house of the type of] *puṣkara*, [the master shall be] virtuous, content at all times, a friend to [his] friends and [all] good people, of good fortune, and endowed with many sons and wealth.[46]

In 39.02-09, the same positions of the front doors are given:

02. The best dwelling for a brahman shall be [located] in [the quarters of the *vāstupuruṣamaṇḍala* associated with] Bhallāṭa, Dhanada, Caraka, or Pṛthivīdhara, with its door in [the quarter] belonging to Mahendra.

03. The abode that is auspicious for a *kṣatriya* shall be made in [the quarter of] Mahendra, Arka, Satya, or Āryaka with its door in [the field of] Gṛhakṣata.
04. The abode of a *vaiśya* shall be made in [the quarter] belonging to Yama, Vivasvant, or Gandharva, [or in the field associated with] Gṛhakṣata; the door is auspicious in [the field of] Puṣpāhvaha.
05. The best dwelling for a *śūdra* shall be made in [the quarter] belonging to Varuṇa or Puṣpadanta, or Mitra, or Asura with its door in [the quarter associated with] Bhallāṭa.
06. The *vāstu* of the brahmans faces east, the house shall be facing south; at all times he prospers with wealth and grains, and with sons and grandsons.
07. The *vāstu* faces south, the abode faces west; a *kṣatriya*'s wealth, grain, and valour increase here.
08. The door of the *vāstu* faces west, [that] of the abode faces north; there thrives the *vaiśya* with wealth, grains, sons, cattle and so on.
09. The *vāstu* shall have its door in the north, and the house is facing east; and [there] the livelihood of a *śūdra* prospers with wealth and grains.[47]

It should be noted that there is no complete congruence of the auspicious properties (*phalas*) mentioned in 24.35-42 and 39.02-09; in the latter passage, there seems to be some agreement between the *phala* of the houses and the *varṇa* of their respective masters, while the former passage makes no mention of the houses' suitability for any particular *varṇa* at all.

The names of the *śālā*s given in 24.35-42 have already been mentioned in 23.38:

> And that [the total number of *ekaśālas*, 23.37] has been declared in due order, according to their positions and names: *hastinī, mahiṣī, gāvī,* and *chāgalī* in due order.[48]

These names are also used in 22.07-10 to describe the six basic setups of a *dviśāla*; we shall examine this passage more closely under 1.3.4 below.

2) 39.11-17 contains a description of four basic constellations of the main entrance to the compound and the door of the *śālā*:

> 11. *Utsaṅga* and *hīnabāhu*, next *pūrṇabāhu*; and *pratyakṣāya* has been proclaimed as the fourth [type of] dwelling.
> 12. [It is called] *utsaṅga* because the two doors of *vāstu* and abode [respectively] face one [and the same] direction; it brings about destruction of good fortune, increase of progeny, wealth, and grain.
> 13. Where the house of the *vāstu* is [situated] on the left of the door – that *vāstu* is called *hīnabāhuka* by the experts on *vāstu*.
> 14. He who dwells there has few possessions, very few friends, [and] few relatives; he shall always be at the mercy of women, and tormented by various diseases.
> 15. That house which may be [situated] to the right of the entry of the *vāstu* – that shall be known as *pūrṇabāhuka* on account of the fact that entry takes place in clockwise direction.
> 16. Certainly there the men who reside in that *vāstu* always aquire sons and grandsons, and the happiness of wealth and grains.
> 17. If the door of the *vāstu* is situated at the back of the house – that is the ill-reputed *pratyakṣāya* with its entrance in counter-clockwise direction.[49]

This passage is repeated almost verbatim (albeit in a different order) in 48.25-31:

> 25. *Utsaṅga* and *pūrṇabāhu*, next *hīnabāhu*; [and] *pratyakṣāya* – thus are proclaimed the four [types of] entrance.
> 26. Where the door of the house is facing [that] of the *vāstu* – that is called *utsaṅga*, *pūrṇabāhu* [if it is situated] in clockwise direction [from the entrance of the *vāstu*].
> 27. [Where the entrance to the house is situated] to the left [of the entrance to the compound] – that shall be [called] *hīnabāhu*, *pratyakṣāya* [shall be called that which is] in the back [of the house]; thus has been declared the fourth [type of] entrance of a *vāstu* by the learned.
> 28. In the case of an entrance called *utsaṅga*, there may be loss of progeny for the master of the house; or he may experience loss of wealth and grain, or his death shall certainly occur.

29. In the case of [an entrance of the type of] *pūrṇabāhu*, there are always sons and grandsons, and the happiness of wealth and grain for the householder residing in that *vāstu*.
30. In the case of [an entrance of the type of] *hīnabāhu*, the master of the house has got few friends [and] very few relatives; he shall be of few possessions, at the mercy of women, or tormented by diseases.
31. If the entrance [of the type of] *pratyakṣāya* has been laid out in a dwelling – then the men dwelling there shall surely suffer loss of wealth.[50]

Two things should be noted in this context: (1) that 39.11-17 does not contain any detailed information about the *phala* of a *pratyakṣāya*-type entrance, which might indicate that one stanza was lost between 39.17 and 39.18; (2) that in 39.12d I have emended °*kṣaya*° on the basis of Da °*bhaya*° (for °*jaya*°); otherwise the contents of 39.12 and 48.28 would have been diametrically opposed.

3) There is a rather curious case of a repetition within one and the same *adhyāya*, in the space of only a few lines; 20.11-12 run thus:

11. One *alinda* shall be built in front or on the right; if [it is situated] in front, [it leads] to the king's favour, if [it be built] on the right, [the result shall be] increase of wealth.
12. A single *alinda* shall not be built on the left, nor in the back; [if it is built] on the left, [it leads] to destruction of wealth, [if it is built] in the back the householder will die.[51]

The same rules are given again in 20.19-20:

19. We will now pronounce the result of an *alinda* built in the back, on the left, in front, or on the right in due order.
20. [If an *alinda* is built] in the back, [it leads] to loss of a wife, to acquisition of wealth [if it is built] on the right; [if it is built] in front [it leads] to the king's favour, [if it is built] on the left, [its result is] destruction of wealth.[52]

4) 21.02-05ab gives the names and orientations of the four principal types of *triśāla*:

> 02. Of these, there are four principal [types], they are called by name: *hiraṇyanābha, sukṣetra, cullī*, and *pakṣaghna*.
> 03. The *hiraṇyanābha* is laid out as lacking the northern *śālā*; it shall be wealth-bestowing for the master; the *sukṣetra* is without the eastern [*śālā*].
> 04. The *sukṣetra* is endowed with [auspicious] marks, it causes increase of wealth for the owner; the *cullī* is without the southern *śālā*, it destroys the possessions.
> 05. The *pakṣaghna* is without the western [*śālā*], it causes enmity and destroys the household. [...][53]

The same names are given in 20.24-26, albeit in a much condensed manner:

> 24. There, one shall describe the [buildings of the type of] *triśāla* [which are] of many diverse types; of all types, those two that have no southern [or] western [*śālā*] are to be frowned upon.
> 25. In the one, [there is] death for the master [of the house], in the other, [there is] loss of wealth; those two that have no eastern [or] northern [*śālā*] are auspicious, and their [respective] designations according to their type [are now enumerated].
> 26. They shall be – [according as they are] lacking the northern, eastern, southern etc. *śālā*, in this order – *hiraṇyanābha, sukṣetra, cullī*, [and] *pakṣaghna* by name.[54]

5) The six basic types of *dviśāla* are described in 22.07-10ab:

> 07. That dwelling in which there are the two *śālā*s [called] *hastinī* and *mahiṣī*: that is known as *siddhārtha*, [and] it causes increase of wealth.
> 08. [One that is constituted] by [the *śālā*s known as] *mahiśī* and *gāvī* shall be the death-bringing *yamasūryaka*; the *daṇḍa* shall [consist] of the *śālā*s [known as] *chagalī* and *gāvī*, it causes danger of punishment.
> 09. The *vāta* is connected with *kareṇu* and *chagalī*, it causes alarm; the *cullī*, [constituted] by *mahiṣī* and *ajā*, causes alarm [and] destroys the wealth.
> 10. The *kāca*, [constituted] by *kareṇu* and *gāvī*, destroys the affection of [one's] friends. [...][55]

The same names are given in 20.28-32:

28. The *dviśāla*s [are situated] in the intermediate directions, one shall specify [their *phala*s] in those [directions] across from their [inner] angles; two [of them have wings] facing each other, all in all one shall know these six:
29. [the *śālā*s of a building of the type of] *siddhārtha* [are situated in] the south [and in] the west, here is found fulfilment of worldly goals; [the *śālā*s of a building of the type of] *yamasūrya* [are situated in] the north [and in] the west, always [there is] mortal danger there.
30. But in case [the *śālā*s are situated in the directions of] east and north, it shall be [called] *daṇḍa*, always there shall be punishment there; but in case [the *śālā*s are situated in the directions of] east and south it is called *vāta*, that *vāstu* [causes] the worst kind of strife.
31. If it faces north and south, the *dviśāla* [is known as] a *vāstu* [of the type of] *kāca*; there, there shall be enmity with close relatives, never shall that [type of house] be built.
32. But [that building] which faces east and west – [that] one shall know as a *vāstu* [of the type of] *cullī*; there, [there is] terrible loss of wealth, never shall one cause that [type of house] to be built.[56]

6) Directions for writing a *prastāra*[57] have been given in two separate places; a *prastāra* of eight is described in 19.35cd-37:

35. [...] First, write down eight *guru*s, then, below the first *guru*:
36. write down [one] *laghu*, then distribute the rest as above; fill in the first [*laghu*] with *guru*s until all may have become *laghu*s.
37. In the first position [of each line, there shall be] one *guru* and one *laghu* alternately; then, there shall be twice that number in each consecutive position.[58]

23.02-03 gives the same rule as 19.35cd-36, only for a *prastāra* of four:

02. First, write down four heavy syllables [?] according to regulations; from these arise sixteen divisions of dwellings.
03. First, write down one *laghu* underneath the *guru*, the rest as above; afterwards, fill in with *guru*s until all may have become *laghu*s.[59]

Note the almost complete agreement between 19.36cd and 23.03cd; the phrase *gurūn varṇān* in 23.02ab seems to suggest that the single line was taken more or less directly from a work on *chandas*.

7) In 20.02-03, the negative consequences of excessive measurements are described:

02. Where the *śālā* may be excessive in its [individual] building elements, its width, height, or length – either the left or the right hand [*śālā*], or [the one] in front or in the back –
03. [there a *śālā*] excessive in [size or number of its individual] elements destroys the property, [one that is] excessive in width [destroys] the household; [one that is] excessive in height [destroys] the *pūjā*, [one that is] excessive in length [destroys] the lineage.[60]

The same consequences are given in 48.132:

Excess of building elements destroys the property, excess of width the household; excess of height, the *pūjā*, excess of length, the lineage.[61]

8) The positive and negative consequences of uneven building ground have been made the topic of 20.04-07:

04. That *vāstu* the ground on the left of which may be depressed [and the ground] on the right [of which may be] an elevation – that is indeed full of faults, [and] brings about the destruction of sons and grandsons.
05. [That *vāstu*] the ground on the right [of which] is depressed, and [the ground] on the left [of which] is an elevation – even if it were built with care, [will bring] little reward for the master [of the house].
06. Where the ground may be depressed in the back, [and] more massive in front [of the *vāstu*] – that house brings about [fulfilment of] all desires for all *varṇa*s.
07.If the abode were low in front and high in the back, it quickly leads to loss of equanimity for the master [of the house].[62]

The respective *phala*s of declivities have also been discussed in 48.02-04:

02. Ground which is depressed in the direction of Rakṣas, Ambunātha, Kīnāśa, Marut, [or] Dahana, or in the middle – that brings about disease, poverty, and epidemics.

03. Depressed in the direction of Vahni, it leads to danger from fire, death, [if] it is depressed towards the south; sickness, [if] depressed in the direction of Rakṣas, depressed towards the west it leads to destruction of wealth and grains.
04. It brings about strife, absence from home, and disease [if] depressed in the direction of Marut; that ground, though, which is depressed in the middle – that leads to destruction of everything.[63]

The obvious difference is that in 20.04-06, the *phala*s depend on the orientation of the building, not on the cardinal and intermediate directions. It is surprising that the two related topics were not discussed in the same place. A complementary rule to 48.02-04 is given in 08.65cd-66ab:

> [Such ground is] recommended [that is] not saline, abounding in grass, smooth, inclined towards the north; inclined towards the east or northeast, or inclined towards all directions [from the centre], and "mirror-bellied."[64]

9) 20.11-18 concerns itself with the positive and negative results of the position of one or two *alinda*s with reference to the front door of a *śālā*; the correspondence with 23.04-12ab will be discussed at length in the note on 20.11-12 below.

10) The formula for computing the dimensions of the front door are given in 24.26-27; the same formula is given in 28.02. These stanzas are not given here as they will be discussed at some length in the note on 24.26-27 below.

11) 28.55-56 enumerate certain building elements that should not be employed in a dwelling:

55. *Siṃhakarṇa*, *kapotāli*, *ghaṇṭākarṇa*, [and] *ardhapakṣaga* [?]; and [representations of] banners, parasols, and princes [or: young men] shall be avoided in [residential] houses.
56. Neither Garuḍa [?], banner, *siṃhakarṇa*, [representations of] princes, bells, and *marālapallī*;[65] nor *praskhalārdha*s [?], nor indeed leaves shall he who wishes for happiness employ in [the decoration of] dwellings.[66]

Cf. 48.106:

[Representations of] *karṇāvāt* [?], Garuḍa, bells, banners, parasols, [and] princes, *siṃhakarṇa* [and] *kapotāli* shall be avoided in dwellings.[67]

12) Another curious repetition occurs with reference to the kinds of trees unfit for use as building material; they are first described in 16.05-15, 19-21:

05. Growing in cities, cemeteries, villages, by *lakes, *caitya*s [or] in hermitages; growing in fields, groves, on the borders [of the realm],[68] in uneven places, [or] in low places;
06. and growing in soil that is acrid, sour, bitter, [or] salty; riddled with holes, and growing in hard soil – these trees one shall avoid.
07. Having examined the colour, softness, bark etc. of the trees thoroughly, one shall ascertain their age, and avoid the young ones and the old ones.
08. The maximum age of trees is known to be three hundred years; one shall take those over sixteen and under one hundred and fifty.
09. Because of the effects of [old] age, saplessness as in men has been said to occur in trees, and their leaves [have] holes as well.
10. Brittle they may be, and hollow, with holes the shape of boar's eyes, and with rough bark; therefore, one shall avoid them, also trees that are withered at the top.
11. Crooked, dried up, scorched, and stunted trees one shall avoid, also [trees] with broken or only one or two branches.
12. [Trees which are] crowded in on by other [trees], damaged by lightning, wind, or water; with knotty wood [?], where bees and snakes have taken their abode;
13. [trees which are] entangled, fallen, [or] surrounded by mighty bees, and sullied by birds that feed on meat and impure things;
14. [trees which are] covered with cobweb, rubbed against by the beings of the forest, damaged by elephants; [that are] too massive at the 'shoulder' for their foot, and that have been marked to indicate the way;
15. [trees which] bear flowers and fruit out of season, and which have been affected by diseases; that have become the abodes of owls – these one shall avoid, and all others of this description. [...]

19. *Karṇikāra, dhavaplakṣa, kapittha, viṣamacchada; śirīṣa, udumbara, aśvattha, śelu* [?], *nyagrodha, campaka;*
20. *nimba, āmra, kovidāra, akṣa*, and *vyādhighāta* have been declared unfit; they are undesirable in house-construction, because they bring about what is undesired.
21. Undesirable are [trees] with thorns or sweet fruit, also *kṣīradrumas*; and those which emit a sweet smell, surely they cause the cattle to perish.[69]

Cf. 48.112-116:

112. One shall avoid those trees which have been struck by a biped, a horse, fire, water, or wind; that are the abode of a multitude of birds, frequented by crows and owls.
113. [Trees that are] spoilt by bees, evil spirits, and snakes, growing near *caityas* or in the cemetery, at the crossroads, in a place where three roads meet, at the confluence of great rivers, [or] by the road;
114. [trees that] grow near temples, that are withered at the top, whose leaves are destroyed; that are enveloped by creepers, that are riddled with holes, hollows, and knots;
115. that have fallen towards the south or east [when being felled] – those one shall avoid, also thorny [trees]; *kapittha, udumbara, aśvattha, śirīṣa, vaṭa, campaka*;
116. *kovidāra, dhava, ariṣṭa, śleṣmātaka, vibhītaka*; also *saptacchada, kṣīravṛkṣas*, and trees which yield fruit – these one shall avoid.[70]

It is obvious that these two passages are not completely congruent; there are slight deviations in the names of the trees, and some defects are mentioned only in the one place and not in the other.[71] It is difficult to decide whether these differences are necessarily indicative of separate authorship.

1.3.4 Inconsistencies and contradictions

1) We have already considered the repeated treatment of the six basic types of *dviśāla* in 20.28-32 and 22.07-10ab; we have also seen that the latter description is made rather cryptic by the reference to the individual *śālās* as *hastinī/kareṇu*, *mahiṣī*, *gāvī*, and

chagalī/*ajā*. The definitions of these four terms as given in 23.38 and 24.35-42 (see above) are also ambiguous; in the former instance, only their order (presumably in clockwise direction) is given, but without a starting point; and in the latter instance, it is not clear whether the names given there refer (1) to the *śālā* situated on the eastern etc. side of the *vāstu*, (2) to a *śālā* the door of which faces the specified direction, or (3) to the *śālā* within a *vāstu* that has its door in the respective cardinal direction. In that latter case, we would have to take into account the rules regarding the relative position of *vāstu*-door and *śālā*-door as given in 39.11-17 and 48.25-31: There it is stated that the latter should be situated to the right of the former, so that entry may take place in clockwise direction; this constellation is known as *pūrṇabāhu*.

There are thus four mutually exclusive possibilities:

(1) the names of the individual *śālā*s with reference to the cardinal directions as used in 22.07-10ab are in accordance with 20.28-32; this would be incompatible with the specifications of 39.11-17:

hastinī – south
mahiṣī – west
gāvī – north
chagalī – east;

(2) the *śālā*s of 24.35-42 are situated in the cardinal direction mentioned in the same stanza:

hastinī – east
mahiṣī – south
gāvī – west
chagalī – north;

(3) the *śālā*s of 24.35-42 have their door in the specified direction; as the entrance of the *śālā* always faces the courtyard, we arrive at the following:

hastinī – west
mahiṣī – north
gāvī – east
chagalī – south; or

(4) the cardinal directions in 24.35-42 refer to the door of the *vāstu* rather than that of the respective *śālā*. By applying the principle of *pūrṇabāhu* we get:

hastinī – north
mahiṣī – east
gāvī – south
chagalī – west.

Since the six types of *dviśāla* as described in 20.28-32 are in accordance with the specifications of BṛS, MP, and VP (and can thus be considered to be 'canonical' to some degree), the first possibility would appear most likely. But if that were the case, then the constellation of *vāstu*- and *śālā*-door as given in 24.35-42 would be *hīnabāhu* – a constellation that is expressly forbidden. Conversely, if we apply the names as defined in 24.35-42 to the six basic types of *dviśāla* observing the principle of *pūrṇabāhu*, we would get the following:

siddhārtha – NE
yamasūrya – SE
daṇḍa – SW
vāta – NW
cullī – EW
kāca – NS.

While the latter two agree with the specifications of 20.28-32 (and by the same token, also with those of BṛS, MP, and VP), it is obvious that the other four are diametrically opposed to them. While the exact nature of the relationship of the 20th, 22nd, 24th, and 39th *adhyāyas* cannot be ascertained, it is obvious that there is no way to reconcile the specifications of all four passages.[72]

2) Mention has already been made of the list of settlements given in 18.02-04ab (under 1.3.1.1.3 above); they are, in descending order, *rājadhānī – śākhānagara – karvaṭa – nigama – grāma – gṛha*. If we assume that the first two can be subsumed under the hyponym *nagara*, and that *gṛha* was only added for the sake of completeness (see above), we get an order of four settlements, viz. *nagara – karvaṭa – nigama – grāma*; SAS 10.79-82 gives a different set: *nagara/pura – kheṭa – grāma*.[73] One might argue that 18.02-04ab merely distinguishes between larger and smaller *kheṭas*, and calls the former *karvaṭa* and the latter *nigama*; but as the 18th *adhyāya* is basically a *kośa*, and as such aiming at comprehensiveness, one would rather expect the term *kheṭa* to be included in the list as well.

3) There is another disagreement between the technical terms of the 10th and 18th *adhyāyas*, concerning the defences of the city; they have been given in tab. 1. The fact that the latter *adhyāya* records more synonyms is easily accounted for by the lexicographical character of that chapter. But the most serious discrepancy between the two passages in question concerns the city gate; 18.52cd clearly refers to it as *gopura*,[74] whereas the 10th *adhyāya* has *pratolī* throughout. In 18.25ab, this is defined as a structure that can be inhabited like a tunnel.[75] It will not be necessary here to dwell on the widely different meanings that have been variously assigned to the term *pratolī* as they will be discussed at some length in the note on 18.25 below. Suffice it to say that the differences noted here make a common source for the 10th and 18th *adhyāyas* rather unlikely.[76]

1.3.5 Conclusion

We have seen that on closer examination, the 'sweet and beautiful style' of SAS is not as uniform as one might expect of a single-author work; the handling of the metre varies from chapter to chapter, and so does the gender of certain words. Yet, there is still an overall sense of stylistic unity; the technical vocabulary – with certain exceptions, see below – is basically the same in all chapters.

Tab. 1 – the city defences according to the 10th and 18th *adhyāyas* of SAS		
	SAS 10	SAS 18
'moat'	*parikha*	—
'wall'	*vapra*	*caya, prākāra, sālā*
'parapet'	*prākāra*	
'gate'	*pratolī*	*gopura*
'door-bolt'	*argala, indrakīla, parigha*	*parigha, phaliha, gajavāraṇa*
'tunnel' (?)	—	*pratolī (suraṅgā)*
'watchtower'	*aṭṭālakā*	*aṭṭa, aṭṭālakā, aṭṭālī, aṭṭālikā*
'battlement'	—	*upakārya*
'road coming from the wall' (?)	*carikā (?)*	*anupala*
'road along inner side of wall'	*ghaṇṭāmārga*	*upaniṣkala*

While the stylistic differences may not carry enough weight to warrant any doubts regarding SAS' authorship, the variations of gender all have a single *adhyāya*, viz. the 18th, as their smallest common denominator. Since the vast majority of technical terms introduced in this chapter do not occur elsewhere in the text, there is ample ground for the assumption that is was written by a different author. But that still would have no implications for the basic question whether SAS is the product of a single author, or a multi-author work; one interpolated *adhyāya* out of 83 would be no great matter.

If the stylistic evidence alone is not sufficient to make any qualified statements about SAS' authorship, the sometimes chaotic sequence of *adhyāya*s proves to be more relevant; as we have seen (1.3.2.1 above), traces of an inherently logical arrangement are apparent, and the question arises whether this was disturbed by frequent interpolations, or by a somewhat negligent compilator. We shall return to this question after examining the remaining evidence, viz. the frequent repetitions and the incompatibilities discussed in the preceding two paragraphs.

It will not have escaped the attention of the discerning reader that some *adhyāya*s have been mentioned disproportionately often in this section: the 18th, which seems to be rather isolated in the text of SAS, and the motley collection of miscellanea that is the 20th *adhyāya*. In fact, nearly all of its 36 stanzas contain material that has also been discussed elsewhere.[77] I am inclined to believe that this chapter is one of the earliest composed; its brevity, especially where it touches upon matters discussed at greater length elsewhere – cf. the discussion of the basic types of *dvi*- and *triśāla*s – makes it look like a core around which the more elaborate descriptions of the 22nd, 23rd, and 48th *adhyāya*s were built. Conversely, what reason would there have been to incorporate into a chapter mostly devoted to the various possible positions of the *alinda* the basic types of *dvi*- and *triśāla*s already discussed at much greater length in the following two *adhyāya*s?[78]

Be that as it may, the most conclusive evidence for a multiple authorship is furnished by the inconsistencies regarding the 20th,

22nd, 24th, and 39th *adhyāya*s discussed in the preceding paragraph. While there can be no final certainty as to which of the passages in question is secondary, I am inclined to believe that the passage in the 22nd *adhyāya* is unrelated in origin to the other three, for the following reason:

As we have seen, both 23.38 and 24.35-42 maintain a certain degree of ambiguity regarding the exact position of the four *śālā*s referred to as *hastinī*, *mahiṣī*, *gāvī*, and *chagalī* – either deliberately or accidentally. One possible explanation is that the author of those lines was not sure himself; but AP 92.10 gives exact positions of the four *śālā*s,[79] which suggests that they had some currency among *śāstrakāra*s in Western India at the time, as the stanza in question, unlike the *prastāra* tables, was not copied directly from SAS. It is much more likely that the ambiguity of 23.38 and 24.35-42 is simply a matter of style: a certain degree of obliqueness is certainly not unusual for a treatise on *vāstuvidyā*.[80] But whatever the reason for this ambiguity, it is not inconceivable that it actually lead to the misunderstanding on the part of the author of 22.07-10ab.

To sum up: the text of SAS, at least where it deals with residential architecture, is beset with a number of inconsistencies with regard to style, organization, vocabulary, and contents; taken on their own, neither the stylistic differences nor the frequent repetitions amount to much; taken together, and combined with the other inconsistencies just enumerated, they become difficult to account for if we accept the authorship of a single person. This leads us back to the question whether SAS was originally conceived as a compilation, with a redactor rather than an author, or whether the inconsistencies discussed above are rather due to a number of interpolations in an otherwise uniform text. The answer, I believe, is twofold: some cases, as for instance the *internal* inconsistencies of the 10th *adhyāya*, are best explained as interpolations; the same is true of the bulk of the 31st *adhyāya*.[81] At the same time, we have seen that the vocabular inconsistencies confine themselves to isolated instances in the 10th and 18th *adhyāyas*; and a comparison of that latter chapter with the rest of the text is made rather difficult by its radically different character as a lexicographical work. Unless we ascribe the relative unity of the technical vocabulary to the fact that the entire SAS is the work of a single author – and I hope to have shown that this is not likely to be the case –, there remain two basic possibilities: (1) the hand of a skilled redactor who replaced 'foreign' terms with more usual ones, or (2) a common background of the several authors.

It does not seem wise to attempt an answer on the basis of our relatively scarce evidence; as has been pointed out before, this is hardly the place to settle the question of Bhoja's authorship of SAS with anything even remotely approaching definitiveness. To that end, it would also be necessary to consider the question whether the hand of Bhoja himself, known to us through the works his authorship of which has come to be generally accepted, can be discerned anywhere in the text of SAS (although there is ample ground for the assumption that SAS has been associated with the historical personage of the Paramāra king from a relatively early date, as we shall see in the following section). Yet I hope to have presented the evidence contained in the passages under consideration faithfully, and that the exploits contained in these pages will be found helpful to a certain extent in an eventual reappraisal of the works ascribed to Bhoja.

1.4 The title *samarāṅgaṇasūtradhāra*

In the introduction to the first edition of 1924, SASTRI maintains that the word *samarāṅgaṇasūtradhāra* 'means, literally, an architect of human dwellings;'[82] This is further explained by AGRAWALA:[83]

The name Samarāṅgaṇa Sūtradhāra is worthy of attention. The word Sūtradhāra literally means 'thread-bearer', *i.e.* an architect who takes his measurements by means of the plumbline. Here is a pun on the word '*samara*' which means both a battlefield and a mortal human being (*sa* + *mara*) (destined to die). Thus the title as applicable to Bhoja would signify firstly that he was the architect of the fortunes on the battlefield, *i.e.* who planned the course of battle leading to victory, and secondly, who was the architect of human dwellings, i.e. civil architecture on an extensive scale.

SHUKLA (1958:307) has subjected the compound to a pseudo-classical analysis of his own devising:

samyañci arāṇi samarāṇi (tathā bhūtāni) aṅgaṇāni (etādṛśāni bhavanāni śālabhavanānīty artha), athavā samarāṇi saṃyuktāni aṅgaṇāni, yeṣāṃ tāṇi, (bhavanānīty arthaḥ) teṣāṃ sūtradhāra.[84]

PAREEK (2002:16), on the other hand, believes that the title is derived from the fact that the treatise 'was compiled by Sūtradhāra Samarāṅgaṇa under the patronage of the Paramāra king Bhojadeva of Dhārā,' unfortunately without quoting any source. The following section shall be devoted to a closer examination of the title and its potential meaning(s).

1.4.1 *Samara*

This term is not often ecountered as denoting 'mortal (beings);' none of the dictionaries consulted have it, its conventional meaning being 'battle(-field), strife.' KEWA (s.v. *samaráḥ*) derives it from *saṃ-ṛ* 'to meet, encounter; to clash.'

Among the five other titles besides SAS recorded in CC beginning with *samara*°,[85] there is one work called *Samarakāmadīpikā* which is classified as 'erotic;' it is rather unlikely that *samara* here translates as 'battle(field).' If we accept the rendering 'mortal being,' the whole title could roughly be translated as 'the lamp or elucidation of the passion of mortals, or: of mortal passions.' This would suggest that there is in fact a Sanskrit word *samara* 'mortal (being),' apparently with the etymology suggested by AGRAWALA (< *sa-mara*). But since it is not attested anywhere else (and since our translation is a mere conjecture), it seems to have been of little currency; alternatively, *samara* (from *saṃ-r̥*) could legitimately be interpreted as 'meeting, encounter, hence: sexual congress.' The absence of any information on the date of the *samarakāmadīpikā* adds to the uncertainty; on the whole, a rendering of *samara* as 'mortal (being)' remains doubtful.

1.4.2 *Aṅgaṇa*

Both SASTRI and AGRAWALA, and SHUKLA seem to have taken *aṅgaṇa* as referring to the human dwelling, which is not a meaning it can usually have, its basic meaning being 'courtyard.' It will not be necessary here to delve into the etymology and development of the word, as it will be discussed at some length under 1.5.1 below; it will be sufficient for our present purpose to consider the case for a synecdoche.

Supporting evidence is scarce indeed; there can be no doubt that the courtyard forms an integral part of *śāla*-architecture, and is indeed the only thing distinguishing an *ekaśāla* from a *śālā* (i.e., a hut without an adjoining courtyard); the fact that in a *catuḥśāla* it covers the central or *brahmapada* of the *vāstupuruṣamaṇḍala*, and is even referred to as *garbhagr̥ha*, a term more commonly associated with the inner sanctum of a temple, also testifies to its (ritual) importance.[86] But it is very much open to doubt whether these rather fine points were common property to a sufficient extent to make the equation *aṅgaṇa* = *veśman* universally (if at all) acceptable. As RHYS DAVIDS (1898) has shown, the word *aṅgaṇa*/*aṅgana* can also refer to a forest clearing or any open space; moreover, *samarāṅgaṇa* 'battlefield' is well attested.[87] We shall pick up this thread again in our concluding discussion under 1.4.4 below.

1.4.3 *Sūtradhāra*

Before we examine the term *sūtradhāra* with regard to its meaning in the architectural context, we should perhaps note that the usual designation for 'master builder' or 'architect' adopted in SAS is not *sūtradhāra*, but *sthapati*;[88] I have not been able to locate the former term in SAS at all, and neither does it occur in MS (which has, however, the equivalent *sūtragrāhin*), MM, or ŚRK.[89] The only work consulted where the chief architect is indeed consistently referred to as *sūtradhāra* is AP.[90]

DHAVALIKAR (1971:216), evaluating the epigraphical records of *sūtradhāra* and *sthapati*, remarks that

> [t]he word *sūtradhāra* does not occur in early Indian inscriptions, that is, those which belong to the pre-Gupta period. The earliest occurrence of the word *sūtradhāra* is in a fifth century inscription in Ajanta Cave No. 15. Earlier we sometimes or rather rarely come across the mention of *sthapati*, the architect, as in the case of the Peshawar Museum inscription of Vaṇhaḍaka. But from the fifth century onwards the word *sūtradhāra* begins to occur in epigraphical records and continues for a long time till about the Vijayanagar period when the Muslims dominated the greater part of the country.

We may thus assume that the word *sūtradhāra* '(chief) architect' still had some currency at the time SAS is supposed to have been written or compiled, even though the *vāstu* texts, as we have seen, hardly use it at all.[91]

1.4.4 *Samarāṅgaṇa-sūtradhāra*

As we have seen, there is little room for the interpretation of the compound *samarāṅgaṇasūtradhāra*: 'architect of human dwellings' suggested by SASTRI. Leaving aside the semantic problems connected with **samara* 'mortal being' and **aṅgaṇa* 'dwelling,' there is also the problem of SAS' contents: of the roughly 7,430 stanzas of the text, only an estimated 1,519 are devoted exclusively to civic architecture in the widest sense,[92] the rest being either of a general nature, or dealing with temple architecture.[93] The residential building in the stricter sense – the dwellings of *karmopajīvin*s and *varṇin*s – are discussed in no more than 1154 stanzas, of which 213 are dedicated to the royal palace alone.[94] If *samarāṅgaṇasūtradhāra* really had the meaning assigned to it by the editors, one would expect residential architecture to figure much more prominently in the text than it actually does.

Of course, there is still the possibility that SAS was originally designed as a treatise on residential architecture, and that most or all of the material on temples was interpolated by later redactors of the text; but one gets to wonder what that *Urtext* would have looked like, taking into account the fact that not all of the material dedicated to the residential building seems to have come from the same pen.

One important clue is contained in the colophons of the 1st to 57th and the 59th *adhyāya*s (cf. 1.3.2.2 above): there, SAS is referred to as 'the *vāstuśāstra* whose other name is *samarāṅgaṇasūtradhāra* (*samarāṅgaṇasūtradhārāparanāma vāstuśāstram*).' It seems that the original SAS, whatever its shape and extent, had no distinct title at all; there is no dearth of texts bearing no other title than *Vāstuśāstra*[95] or *Vāstuvidyā*.[96]

Where then does the title *samarāṅgaṇasūtradhāra* come from? As we have seen above, there is a tradition that the works of Bhoja were given his own *biruda*s as titles (the reliability of that tradition need not concern us for the moment); and as the panegyric name of a king, the word *samarāṅgaṇasūtradhāra* is quite easy to construe: The 'stage manager (*sūtradhāra*) of the battlefield (*samarāṅgaṇa*),' the king who directs his armies against his enemies.[97]

As for the relationship of the tradition cited above and the title of SAS, there are two basic possibilities: Either Bhoja's (still hypothetical) *biruda* was applied to a *vāstuśāstra* composed in part by him or under his patronage in the first place, giving rise to the tradition; or the tradition came first, possibly started by the application of Bhoja's praise name *sarasvatīkaṇṭhābharaṇa* 'neck ornament of Sarasvatī' to a poetological work written by him.[98] In the latter case, it would have been left to posterity to apply the panegyric *samarāṅgaṇasūtradhāra*, rightly or wrongly associated with the historical personage of Bhoja, to an as yet untitled treatise on architecture, a *vāstuśāstra* associated with the Paramāra king, under the impact of the tradition.

If that were indeed to have been the case, it would be of secondary importance whether or not the application of Bhoja's *biruda*s to the texts produced at his court was really the standing practice of his own days; it does not have any bearing on the question of authorship, for even if Bhoja's *biruda*s were really applied to texts written in his lifetime and at his court, they need not necessarily have been composed by the monarch himself. If the application was performed posthumously (as I believe to be the case, at least with reference to SAS), then the texts in question might have been written by anyone with a sound knowledge of Sanskrit and the respective subject matter.

In absence of any further evidence, we are left to speculate, and to accept what seems most likely to us. I am inclined to believe (1) that the composition of SAS was in fact closely associated with Bhoja himself[99] – whether or not individual *adhyāya*s are the king's own or not is a moot point as long as no convincing parallels in style or contents with other works attributed to him can be established –; (2) that the multi-author work was originally untitled, and added to over the years by various authors; and (3) that a traditional association between Bhoja's *biruda*s and the titles of the works written at his court prompted a later copyist or redactor to apply a title associated with the monarch and containing the ambiguous word *sūtradhāra* to the architectural treatise. This latter assumption is made even more likely by the tentativeness with which the colophons of more than half of the individual *adhyāya*s quote the title of the work. That the title is not original is also suggested by the fact that the term *sūtradhāra* does not occur in the text itself – see 1.4.3 above.

1.5 The vocabulary of SAS

In the following section, a few of the technical terms occuring in SAS with reference to the residential building will be examined in brief. It should be pointed out that the basic meaning given for any of the terms listed below is that supplied by the textual evidence of SAS, which in some instances will be found to be in contradiction to the meaning supplied by other texts, both from the sphere of *vāstu* and general literature alike. Given the absence of a single authoritative source for Sanskrit architectural terminology (in spite of ACHARYA's protestations to the effect of the MS being one);[100] the regional diversification of architectural styles in the subcontinent; and the sheer age and changing character of the language in which the vast majority of *vāstuśāstra*s is composed, this should hardly be surprising. In fact, it seems that the meaning of architectural terms in Sanskrit is not as fixed as it is in most modern languages; as we shall see below (1.5.2), the word *alinda* has been used by different authors to refer to a front porch, a passage around an interior courtyard, a corridor provided with lattice windows, and a gallery. There has been much throwing about of brains as to which of these meanings is 'correct' – a pointless endeavour, since each of these meanings is attested in Sanskrit and Pāli literature; the ambivalence is real, and cannot be resolved by arbitrarily determining one meaning that would fit all instances. Rather, each occurrence must be taken on its own and compared with the attested uses of the word in order to decide which meaning is intended in the given passage.[101]

1.5.1 *Aṅgaṇa*

The courtyard around which the individual wings of an *eka-, dvi-, tri-*, or *catuḥśāla* are grouped; in the latter case it can contain a well or pond, which, being covered, is called *garbhagṛha* (18.20). But according to 19.27, the inner courtyard of a *catuḥśāla* is known as *garbhagṛha* irrespective of any well or roofing; it is also referred to as *kakṣā* (cf. note on 18.25 below). The *aṅgaṇa* of a *catuḥśāla* is surrounded by an *alinda* on all sides, which is also called *vitardi* (18.16, see below). The *aṅgaṇa* is an indispensible part of *śālā* architecture, and its ritual importance can be inferred from the fact that it covers the central area, the *brahmapada*, of the *vāstupuruṣamaṇḍala*; cf. also the following observations made in 20th century Nepal by GABORIEAU (1991:36):

> The courtyard, 'agan' [i.e. *ā̃gan*], is the heart of the residential complex. [...]There is a barrier at the entrance and if a connecting passage links the neighbouring house, two barriers are built. [...] It marks an important limit; physically, it keeps in the cattle [...] . Socially, it is the beginning of the private space of the family; being admitted into the courtyard means that one has been received by the family [...] . Finally, it is a religious limit: the first rites of protection against evil spirits, witches in particular, are performed at the barrier. [...] The courtyard is also a religious and social space. Some of the ceremonies relating to the life cycle are performed here, the rest taking place in the interior of the house: presentation of the child and dances on the sixth day after birth; sacrifices on an altar specially made for initiation and marriage rituals; ceremonies to make [sic!] the various stages of mourning.

The etymology of *aṅgaṇa* is not undisputed (EWA q.v.); DET (s.v. 37) groups it with Tamil *aṅkāṭi*, Kannaḍa *aṅaḍi* 'bazaar, bazaar street', Parji *aṅgoḍ* 'courtyard, compound'.[102] RHYS DAVIDS (1898), on thc other hand, referring to Pāli literature, denies that *aṅgaṇa*/*aṅgana* could have the meaning of 'courtyard' at all, giving 'clearing' or 'open space' as its basic meaning instead, from which the secondary meaning 'untilled open space in front of a hut' can be derived;[103] he quotes BÜHLER as calling his attention to Molesworth's Marāṭhi Dictionary in a private communication,

> where the old meaning 'house-yard' is given; but also, as an alternative, 'the cleared and dung-smeared level in front of the doorway,' and Hofrath Bühler suggests that the word may be derived from *añj*, 'to smear.' (1898:194)

That *aṅgaṇa* can indeed refer to a clearing in the forest is suggested by the context of SAS 18.29, where *ajira* is used as a synonym for *aṅgaṇa*.[104] In a reply to RHYS DAVIDS, SINCLAIR (1898) quotes, among others, the following uses of *aṅgaṇa* (or rather, its NIA equivalents) current in Western India at the time:

> (a) The square courtyard surrounded by buildings, mentioned by Mr. Beames.[105]
> (b) Court with buildings on two or three sides, and a screen wall or walls completing the enclosure [...].[106]
> (c) Space in front of a house, fenced off more or less lightly [...].
> (d) Space in front of or around a house or hut, or even cattle-shed, with no screen or fence, but having boundaries recognizable in some way, generally by the ground being gravelled, paved, or rammed hard and plastered with cow-dung mud.

Although the last item seems to support Bühler's etymological note, it is hard to see how *aṅgaṇa*/*aṅgana* could be derived from *añj*; the suffix *-ana* is usually employed to form *nomina actionis* or *agentis* (*añjana* 'the act of smearing,' or 'smearing'), the object of the action being rather expressed by the past passive participle (*akta* 'smeared'). In any event, the change *n* > *n*/*ṇ* would be quite irregular.

Cf. also the discussion of *aṅgaṇa* as part of the title under 1.3 above.

1.5.2 *Alinda*

A sort of verandah; it can be situated either outside the *śālā* as a sort of front porch (20.10-13, 19-20), or on the inside of a *catuḥśāla*, facing the courtyard in either instance (19.22, 27).[107] In the former case, it is also referred to as *alindā* (18.23), but cf. 1.3.1.1.1 above. A house with an *alinda* on its outside is known as *saprabha* (20.10), while a house with a continuous *alinda* around the interior courtyard is called *saparikrama* (20.09). The *alinda* surrounding the interior courtyard of a *catuḥśāla* is also referred to as *vitardi* (18.16); its timber framing is said to be connected with the lower end of the roof (*chadamūlaga-*), which suggests that the *alinda* of the groundfloor is repeated on each consecutive storey as a kind of gallery which is also known as *alinda* (see COOMARASWAMY quoted below).

That *alinda* may also translate as 'corridor' is suggested by Utpala; in his commentary on BṛS 52.17, he writes:

> The word *alinda* refers to a small passage (? *gamanikā*) that is built on the outside of the *śālā*-wall, covered with lattice-windows, and facing the courtyard.[108]

Although it is situated outside the *śālā* proper, the *alinda* is still considered part of the living area; this can be seen from the fact that the *pada*s of the *vāstupuruṣamaṇḍala* that are said to constitute the *veśman* or *bhavana* within the *vāstu* include the area of the *alinda* (figg. 1, 2). Cf. also the following observation from GABORIEAU (1991:48):

> The verandah [...] is the first part of the house which is the most accessible; no one is denied entrance, not even the untouchables [...] ; the more respectable guests are welcomed here and according to their status and proximity to the family, they settle themselves permanently in this verandah to rest, eat and sleep [...] ; or one waits temporarily in the verandah before being invited to the ground floor for ceremonies, meals and to sleep. [...] The verandah is also a place of work [...] .

The original meaning of *alinda* (P. *ālinda*/*āḷinda*) seems to have been 'verandah in front of the main entrance, front porch;' this can be inferred from the following passages in the Pāli canon:

> MV 6.36.4 – *es' āvuso Roja vihāro saṃvutadvāro, tena appasaddo upasaṃkamitvā ataramāno* ***ālindaṃ*** *pavisitvā ukkāsitvā aggaḷaṃ ākoṭehi, vivarissati te bhagavā dvāran ti*

'This, friend Roja, is his dwelling-place, the door is closed; having approached quietly, having entered the verandah (but) without crossing it, having coughed, tap on the door-bolt. The lord will open the door to you.' [Tr. HORNER]

> CV 6.3.5 – *tena kho pana samayena vihārā an****ālinda****kā honti apaṭissaraṇā. bhagavato etam atthaṃ ārocesuṃ. anujānāmi bhikkhave* ***ālindaṃ*** *paghanaṃ pakuṭaṃ osarakan ti.* ***ālindā*** *pākaṭā honti, bhikkhū hirīyanti nipajjituṃ. anujānāmi bhikkhave saṃsaraṇakiṭikaṃ ugghāṭanakiṭikan ti*

'Now at that time dwelling-places had no verandahs and were without shelter. They told this matter to the Lord. He said: 'I allow, monks, a verandah, a covered terrace, an inner court, a verandah roofing.' The verandahs were public. Monks were (too) modest to lie down. 'I allow, monks, a moveable screen, a screen that can be drawn." [Tr. HORNER]

But MhV 35.3 clearly shows that an 'inner *ālinda*' can also be situated around the inner courtyard:

> *tatheva Lohapāsāde Thūpārāmūposathavhaye*
> *kucchiājiraṃ kāresi kucchi****ālindam*** *eva ca.*

'And in like manner he made an inner courtyard and an inner verandah to the Lohapāsāda and to the (building) called the Uposatha (house) of the Thūpārāma.' [Tr. GEIGER]

COOMARASWAMY (1928:252) takes exception with GEIGER's rendering of *ālinda* as 'terrace in front of a house door' (1964:246 fn.2), arguing that it refers to a balcony or gallery instead;[109] the arguments he produces in support of this hypothesis (1928:258sq.) are rather contrived, as they depend on the interpretation of *hasti-*

nakha (cf. KA 2.3.29) as 'pillar having an elephant capital', which is altogether unlikely. Nevertheless, Mṛcch. 2.20+ shows that an *alinda* could very well be situated on the upper floor: *hañje uvari-daṇaṃ* ***aliṇdaaṃ*** *āruhia ajjacārudattaṃ pekkhemha* – 'Wench, we shall ascend the upper terrace and have a look at the noble Charudatta' [Tr. KANE]; there is thus no need to assume that the alternative renderings of *alinda* as 'verandah' or 'gallery' are mutually exclusive.

1.5.3 *Utsaṅga, pūrṇabāhu, hīnabāhu, pratyakṣāya*[110]

These terms are defined in 39.11-17 as well as 48.25-31; they describe the relative position of the main living area – here referred to as *veśman* or *gṛha* – with reference to the main entrance of the *vāstu*, which here translates as 'compound.' What matters seems to be the direction in which entry into the dwelling takes place: if the person entering the compound can walk in a straight line from the gate to the door of the *veśman*, the house is said to be *utsaṅga*, and to cause a variety of dangers for the owner (39.12, 48.28); if they have to perform a right turn, the house is of the auspicious *pūrṇa-bāhu*-type (39.14, 48.26, 29); if on entering the compound one has to make a turn to the left, or even turn around because the gate is situated on the back of the *veśman*, the house is *hīnabāhu* (39.13, 48.27, 30) or *pratyakṣāya* (39.17, 48.27, 31), neither of which is said to be conducive to the welfare of the inmates.

Although the terminology introduced here is absent from BṛS, it is obvious that the underlying principle was accepted by Varāhamihira as well; cf. BṛS 52.68:

> *vāsagṛhāṇi ca vindyād viprādīnām udagdigādyāni |*
> *viśatāṃ ca yathā bhavanaṃ bhavanti tāny eva dakṣiṇataḥ ||*

'The dwelling-houses of brahmans etc. shall be situated on the northern side etc.; for those entering, the dwelling shall be on the right-hand side.'

Although this is further elucidated by Utpala,[111] KERN (1872:291) did not understand this stanza correctly, and translated:

> The dwelling-houses of the Brahmans are situated to the north, of the Kshatriyas to the east, and so on with the rest. They are, moreover, made in such a way that on entering the door you have (the greater part of) the space of the house to your right.[112]

From the footnote on the same page, it becomes apparent what he meant, viz. that the door should be situated on the right hand side of the façade (as implicitly forbidden in BṛS 69-73,[113] cf. fig. 3); quoting Utpala's commentary (but omitting the first sentence), KERN goes on to say: 'How a house can be said to face the east, without having its door facing the same quarter, is beyond our comprehension.' The key lies in the differentiation between *gṛha* and *vāsagṛha/bhavana* (BṛS) or *vāstu* and *veśman/gṛha/bhavana* (SAS, see 1.5.5 below) that KERN seems not to have been aware of: by the principle of *pūrṇabāhu*, it automatically follows that if the door of the former faces one quarter, the door of the latter will face the quarter adjoining it in clockwise direction.

1.5.4 *Upasthāna, apavaraka, koṣṭhaka*

These three terms occur only in two places in the 18th *adhyāya*; from 18.26, it can be inferred that the generic term for 'room' is *koṣṭhaka* (> Nepālī *koṭhā*). According to its function as either a reception room or private chamber, a room can be either *upasthāna/-ka* (18.21) or *apavaraka* (18.24), which latter term seems to include the female apartments, *śuddhānta* (*gṛhe* [...] *abhyantarasthānam*, 'the innermost place in a house'), as well. Whereas an *upasthāna* is supposed to be three-walled (*trikuḍya*),[114] *apavaraka* is described as 'very small' (*alpālpa*)[115] and four-walled (*catuṣkuḍya*).

What is interesting to note is that SAS contains no further functional differentiation of the living quarters, which is a common feature of BṛS, MP, MM, and MS;[116] as the names *apavaraka* (< *apa-vṛ* 'to cover, conceal') and *śuddhānta* (lit. 'the pure end' or 'the end, i.e. highest degree of what is pure') imply, these chambers seem to be considered more private than the *upasthāna* (cf. 18.21, *gṛhe mahājanasthānaṃ*, 'a place for a multitude of people in a house').

1.5.5 *Gṛha, bhavana, vāstu, veśman, śālā*

The meaning of *gṛha* differs: usually it refers to the edifice in its entirety, in which case it is virtually synonymous with *vāstu*, and clearly distinguished from *śālā*, the main body of the edifice (e.g. 24.35-42); but in some instances (39.06, 09, 15, 17), it refers to the dwelling in the narrowest sense, i.e. the main living area within the edifice. It that case, it refers only to a single *śālā* within the compound, and alternates with *bhavana* and *veśman*, both meaning 'abode.' These latter terms, it seems, are widely synonymous with *gṛha*, and are used according to the exigencies of metre.

The term *vāstu* is perhaps best translated as 'compound, ground plan, property;' unlike *gṛha*, it never refers to individual parts of the edifice, but always to the entire plot including both covered and open spaces. The *vāstu* is two-dimensional: it never implies height. When the number of storeys or the height of the building are given (39.20-34), *gṛha* or one of its synonyms are used.

The opposition between *vāstu* 'plot' and *śālā* 'main body' is strictly observed in every instance; the latter never refers to the entire dwelling, which it constitutes together with the courtyard, *aṅgaṇa* (see above). Thus, it is usally distinguished from *gṛha* as well, with the exception noted above. This is in contrast to the usage of MS, where *gṛha, maṇḍapa,* and *śālā* are often freely interchangeable.[117]

That *vāstu* originally referred to the building grounds exclusively can be inferred from the oldest references to *vāstuvidyā* that I have been able to find;[118] cf. Jāt. 257:

> *Tassa nisinnakāle amaccā ekaṃ dvipādehi vicaraṇamakkataṃ vatthuvijjācariyavesaṃ gāhāpetvā vinicchayaṭṭhānaṃ netvā 'deva ayaṃ puriso pitu mahārājassa kāle vatthuvijjācariyo paguṇavijjo, antobhūmiyaṃ sattaratanaṭṭhāne dosaṃ passati, eten' eva gahitaṃ rājakulānaṃ gehaṭṭhānaṃ hoti, imaṃ devo saṃgaṇhitvā ṭhānantare ṭhāpetu' 'ti āhaṃsu.*

'Now at the time when the king sat down for judgement, the courtiers had dressed up a monkey, in the garb of a man who is skilled in the lore which tells what are good sites for a building. They made him go upon two feet, and brought him into the judgement hall.
"My lord," said they, "in the time of the king your father this man was one who divined by magic as to desirable sites, and well did he know his art. Down in the earth as deep as seven cubits he can see a fault. By his help there was a place chosen for the-kings house; let the king provide for him, and give him a post."' [Tr. ROUSE]

The term *vatthuvijjā* is defined accordingly in DNA 01.01.21:

> *Vatthuvijjā ti, gharavatthuārāmavatthādīnaṃ guṇadosasallakkhaṇavijjā. Mattikâdivisesaṃ disvā pi hi vijjaṃ parijapitvā heṭṭhā paṭhaviyaṃ tiṅsaratanamatte ākāse ca asītiratanamatte padese guṇadosaṃ passanti.*

'*Vatthuvijjā* [is] the science of ascertaining the merits and faults of the grounds of a house, the grounds of a park, etc.; having divined [their] knowledge merely from having seen the characteristics of the soil etc., [the *vatthuvijjācariya*s] see the merits and faults underneath the ground in a space measuring thirty cubits, and in an area measuring eighty cubits.'

Likewise, the *vāstuka* in KA never seems to be concerned with the process of construction; his job is merely to determine the suitable site. Cf. KA 01.20.01:

> *vāstukapraśaste deśe saprākāraparikhādvāram anekakakṣyāparigatam antaḥpuraṃ kārayet* |

'On a site recommended by experts in building, he should cause the royal residence to be built, with a rampart, a moat and gates and provided with many halls.'

KA 02.03.03:

> *janapadamadhye samudayasthānaṃ sthānīyaṃ niveśayet, vāstukapraśaste deśe nadīsaṅgame hradasyāviśoṣasyāṅke sarasastaṭākasya vā, vṛttaṃ dīrghaṃ caturaśraṃ vā vāstuvaśena vā pradakṣiṇodakaṃ paṇyapuṭabhedanam aṃsapathavāripathābhyām upetam |*

'In the centre of the country, he should lay out a *sthānīya*, the headquarters for revenue, on a site recommended by experts in the science of building, at the confluence of rivers or on the bank of a lake that never dries up, either a (natural) lake or a (man-made) tank, round, rectangular or square or in accordance with the nature of the building site, with water flowing from left to right, a market town, served by a land-route and a water-route.'

KA 10.01.01:

> *vāstukapraśaste vāstuni nāyakavardhakimauhūrtikāḥ skandhāvāraṃ, vṛttaṃ dīrghaṃ caturaśraṃ vā bhūmivaśena vā, caturdvāraṃ ṣaṭpathaṃ navasaṃsthānaṃ māpayeyuḥ khātavaprasāladvārāṭṭālakasampannaṃ bhaye sthāne ca |*

'On a site, approved by experts in the science of building, the commandant, carpenters and astrologers should cause the camp to be set up, circular, rectangular or square or in conformity with the nature of the ground, with four gates, six roads and nine divisions, endowed with a moat, a rampart, a parapet, gates and towers, when there is danger and when the army has to halt.' [All tr. KANGLE]

Like the *vatthuvijjācariya* of the Pāli texts, the *vāstuka* seems to be a geomancer rather than an 'expert in the science of building.' Neither is he an astrologer, who is expressly mentioned in KA 10.01.01.[119]

1.5.6 *Catuḥśāla, hīnavāstu*

The well-known basic model of the urban dwelling, of which *eka-, dvi-*, and *triśāla* are merely gradations collectively known as *hīnavāstu* (24.25b; 24.45d): the idca is that of four *śālā*s grouped around an open courtyard (*aṅgaṇa*). Although I have not come across the expression *hīnavāstu* elsewhere, the concept under discussion here is widely accepted by *vāstu* texts both of the 'southern' and 'northern schools,'[120] and it is a regular feature of the secondary literature as well.[121]

The assumption that *catuḥśāla* is to be considered the basic type is warranted on account of the simple fact that it is the only one mentioned in other branches of Sanskrit literature as well.[122]

1.5.7 *Prastāra*[123]

This term is derived from metrics, where it is the first of the six *pratyayas*;[124] originally, it refers to a method by which all mathematically possible combinations of 'heavy' and 'light' syllables in a stanza can be ascertained. Applied to *vāstuvidyā*, it serves a similar purpose, viz. to ascertain all mathematically possible arrangements of certain architectural objects in a building; the presence or absence of the object under discussion corresponds to and is indicated by *laghu* and *guru* respectively.[125] This principle is best illustrated with an example:

In a *catuḥśāla*, the walls of the individual *śālā*s facing the courtyard are divided by *mūṣā*s, i.e. they are divided into eight sections (corresponding to the *paṅkti*s, cf. ALSDORF 1933:105) which can be distinguished by the presence or absence of an opening.[126] This allows for $2^8 = 256$ different varieties of the basic *catuḥśāla*, which are classified as *eka-* through *aṣṭamūṣa* or *-bhadra* depending on the number of *mūṣā*s (cf. 1.5.8 below). Each of these varieties, which are distinguished only by the number and distribution of their *mūṣā*s, is then given a name, which is usually indicative of the dwelling's auspicious or inauspicious character.[127]

In SAS, *prastāra* is sometimes referred to as *chandas* (24.05b), a reference to its origin in metrics; it does not indicate the 'rhythmical disposition' (SHUKLA 1958:217) of the building. Rather prosaically, *prastāra* as applicable to *vāstuvidyā* seems to be a purely mental exercise serving the purpose of making the academic treatment of residential buildings in a given *śāstra* as comprehensive as possible.

While SAS makes excessive use of this device, it is by no means the first treatise to apply the method of *prastāra* to an architectural context: VP 02.101-102 gives the rule mentioned in SAS 19.35cd-36 and 23.02-03, and goes on to present in 103-107 a *prastāra*-table for the sixteen basic varieties of *ekaśāla* virtually identical with that contained in SAS 23.06-12ab (cf. note on 20.11-12 below). None of this occurs in BṛS or MP;[128] it is interesting to note that the author of VP should have contented himself with applying this device to the *ekaśāla* exclusively.

1.5.8 *Mūṣā*

This technical term is rather elusive; SHUKLA (1958:318) has attempted the following explanation:

> Mūṣā originally denoted a crucible for melting gold or silver. It was cylindrical in shape with a round bottom and open at the other end. The hole in the wall to admit light and air resembling exactly the shape of such a crucible or Mūṣā, used to be laid horizontally into the wall. From the original connotation of an aperture in the wall to admit light and air was developed the meaning of Mūṣā, as a fullfledged ventilator or window.

But a few pages later (1958:341), it is said to refer to a portico, 'the intermediatory porch between a Śālā and Alinda.' The second half of the stanza given as the source, viz. SAS 19.29, runs as follows:

> *alindaśālayor madhye yā syān mūṣeti sā smṛtā* ||

> 'That which is [situated] in between the *śālā* and the *alinda* – that is known as *mūṣā*.'

ŚKD (q.v.) glosses it as *gavākṣa* (hence the asterisked entry in pd), citing the *Śreṭīvyavahāra* of Bhāskara's *Līlāvatī* as reference;

however, I have not been able to locate the quotation given there in the printed edition of Bhāskara's work:

> *ekadvitryādimūṣāvahanam iti maho brūmi me bhūmibhartur harmye ramye 'ṣṭamūṣe caturaviracite ślakṣṇaśālāviśāle* |

PSM (q.v.) classes *mūsā* as *deśi* and gives 'a small door (*laghu dvār, choṭā darvājā*)' as its meaning, quoting DNM 6.137 as source:

> *mūsāmūsāāiṃ lahuaduvārammi* [...]

'[The words] *mūsā* [and] *mūsāa* [have the meaning] 'a small door' [...].'

That *mūṣā* in SAS indeed refers to some kind of door rather than a window, or in any event an opening from the ground up, is suggested by SAS 48.34:

> *mūṣāgatān bhramān kuryān na śālāṃ pratibhedayet* |
> *bhramabhagnāsu śālāsu vipadyante kuṭumbinaḥ* ||

'One should make the drains in the *mūṣās*, one should not pierce the [wall of the] *śālā* [for this purpose]; the householders perish in *śālās* [whose walls are] pierced.'

The truth, then, seems to be somewhere halfway between SHUKLA's two contradictory statements: a *mūṣā* is an opening in the wall that is larger than a window, but it is not a portico; whether or not the *mūṣā* is supposed to serve as a passage is not entirely clear. In any event, and as indicated by its inclusion in DNM, the word is clearly not derived from Skr *mūṣā* 'crucible' (which is likewise of unclear origin – cf. EWA q.v.), and apparently not round in shape either.

1.6 The dwelling according to SAS

The following section contains a brief description of the basic setup of the human dwelling as described in SAS. For the sake of brevity, the houses of *karmopajīvins* will not be considered here; as we shall see (under 1.7.2 below), the treatment accorded these dwellings in SAS is rather inconsistent: the only *karmopajīvins* for whose houses the basic dimensions are given are the king, the *senāpati*, and the *purodhasa* (cf. tab. 3). Consequently, we shall restrict our discussion to the dwellings of the *varṇins* as described in *adhyāyas* 19, 20, 24, 28, and 39.

The ground plan of each dwelling is rectangular approximating a square; depending on the owner's *varṇa*, one-tenth, one-eighth, one-sixth, or one-fourth of the width is added to the length (19.19; fig. 11).[129]

Each dwelling consists of a courtyard and one to four *śālās* (originally 'cottages'), which are grouped around it. A dwelling with one *śālā* is called *ekaśāla*, one with two *dviśāla*, a house consisting of three *śālās* is known as *triśāla*, and a house whose courtyard is surrounded by an uninterrupted chain of four *śālās* is called *catuḥśāla* (18.18-19; fig. 5). This latter edifice can be considered the basic model of the urban dwelling – cf. 1.5.6 above. The centre of the plot is never covered by a *śālā*; it is either left open to the sky, or covered by a *vāpī* 'well' which may or may not have some kind of roofing (18.20; cf. also 1.5.1 above).

The width of the indivudual *śālās* of a *catuḥśāla* is said to be one-fourth of the width of the *vāstu* (19.22);[130] they are linked by square *karṇaśālās* or *avakosimās* situated in the corners of the *vāstu*, whose width and length are equal to the width of the *śālās* (19.28). Along the side of each *śālā* facing the courtyard, there is an *alinda* 'verandah' (cf. 1.5.2 above). This *alinda* is approximately half as wide as the *śālā* (19.22, but cf. also 19.23-24).

Although no data are given concerning the width of *śālā* and *alinda* in the *hīnavāstus* (see 1.5.6 above), 28.18 gives the length of the *śala* as 17, 10, and 5 cubits for the largest, middle-sized, and smallest dwelling (~7.65m, ~4.5m, and ~2.25m) respectively; a similar rule is found in 19.25.[131]

The height of the ground floor is ascertained by adding four cubits to one-sixteenth of the width of the *vāstu* (28.16);[132] alternatively, it should be seven cubits (~3.15m) for the largest, six (~2.7m) for the middle-sized, and five cubits (~2.25m) for the smallest dwelling (28.17). In multi-storeyed buildings, the height of each consecutive storey should be dimished by one-twelfth of the preceding storey (28.47).

The height of the door is arrived at by adding seventy to the width of the *vāstu* and dividing that figure by 24; the width of the door is said to be half its height (24.26-27; 28.02).[133] The door is described as having five *śākhā*s;[134] it is to be assumed that these are supposed to be arranged in pairs, giving the impression of a trabeated door frame, or rather a set of five concentric frames. This kind of arrangement is not only well-known from temple doors, but also from Newārī residential architecture – characteristically with the same number of door posts (cf. GUTSCHOW, KÖLVER and SHRESTHACHARYA 1987:225 sqq.).

The thickness of the wall is arrived at by dividing the width of the *śālā* by four (24.22); the walls of the five *vāstu*s should thus be 2, 1 3/4, 1 1/2, 1 1/4, and one cubit (~.9m, ~.8m, ~.7m, ~.6m, and ~.45m) respectively.[135]

The height of the building and the total number of storeys are also subject to reglementation, again with reference to the owner's *varṇa*: The house of a *śūdra* should have at least one and not more than three and a half storeys, that of a *vaiśya* between one and a half and four and a half, that of a *kṣatriya* between two and five and a half, and a brahman should reside in a dwelling with at least two and a half, at most six and a half storeys (39.21-24, 32cd-34(1)).[136] This is in contradiction to 39.29-30, where the overall height of the dwellings are given in cubits (cf. Note on 39.29-30 below).

Are these dimensions, apart from the contradiction just noted, at all plausible, that is to say: does the text of SAS describe buildings that could actually have been built? In order to answer that question, it may be helpful first to compare the specifications of SAS with those given in the anterior *śāstra*s, and to note the differences. For the sake of convenience, we shall restrict our investigation to the regulations given in BṛS, and quote from MP and VP only where these texts differ markedly.

As we shall see, all four texts agree on the permissible size of the plot where the king, the *senāpati*, and the *varṇin*s are concerned; the height of the ground floor is also generally accepted, and so is the thickness of the walls.[137] None of these measurements is particularly suspicious. There is, however, some disagreement regarding the width of the *śālā*: according to SAS 19.22, it is said to be one quarter of the width of the *vāstu* in all instances; for the houses of *karmopajīvin*s, BṛS 52.18 has a much more flexible (and thus more plausible) rule, which can be stated as follows:

(width of *vāstu* + 70)/14 = width of *śālā*.[138]

Applied to the largest house for the king (108 cubits) and the smallest dwelling for the minister (44 cubits), this yields a *śālā*-width of 12 10/14 cubits (~5.7m) and 8 1/7 cubits (~3.65m) respectively. For the houses of the *varṇin*s, there is no formula; instead, the *śālā* of a *vāstu* 32 cubits wide is said to be 4 17/24 cubits (~2.1m) in width, and the *śālā*s of the remaining four should be 4 1/8 cubits (~1.85m), 3 5/8 cubits (~1.625m), 3 13/24 cubits (~1.6m), and 3 1/6 cubits (~1.425m) respectively (fig. 12ab). Obviously, these figures give the width of the *śālā* from wall to wall, i.e. the dimensions of the room rather than the 'cottage;' otherwise, the rooms would get much too narrow. This is precisely the problem with the dimensions of the *śālā* given in SAS: if the thickness of the walls is added to the width of the *śālā* and the *alinda*, there is no space left for the courtyard. On the other hand, if we assume that SAS 19.22 gives the width of the *śālā* on the outside, then the rooms of the smaller *vāstu*s get exceedingly narrow – as little as two cubits or roughly .9m, whereas the smallest room according to BṛS 52.18 is still over 1.4m wide; the difference is that BṛS employs a kind of sliding scale: the ratio *śālā* : *vāstu* increases with decreasing size of the *vāstu*, resulting in more plausible dimensions (cf. tab. 2).[139]

Tab. 2 – Ratio *śālā* : *vāstu* in SAS and BṛS

size of *vāstu*	SAS		BṛS	
	outside	inside	outside	inside
32 c	.25	.125	.272	.147
28 c	.25	.125	.272	.147
24 c	.25	.125	.276	.151
20 c	.25	.125	.302	.177
16 c	.25	.125	.322	.198

There is a similar problem with reference to the *alinda*, which is said to be half the width of the *śālā* in SAS 19.22, while BṛS 52.18 gives a different rule for the houses of *karmopajīvins*,[140] and fixed measurements for *varṇins*.[141]

Another point on which BṛS and SAS disagree is the relative size of the door: the formula given in SAS 24.26-27 and 28.02 roughly corresponds to the formula given in BṛS 52.24, which is said to apply to the houses of *karmopajīvins* exclusively (cf. note on 24.26-27 below); the formulae for the dimensions of the door in a *varṇin*'s dwelling as stated in BṛS 52.25 are:

[[(width of *vāstu*/5) + 18] + {[(width of *vāstu*/5) + 18]/8}] /24 = width of door;
width of door * 3 = height of door.[142]

According to Utpala, this yields a size of the front door of 1 1/8 x 3 3/8 cubits (~.5m x ~1.52m) for the largest dwelling of the *varṇins*;[143] the remaining four should be 1 1/8 x 3 3/8 cubits (~.5m x ~1.52m), 1 1/12 x 3 1/4 cubits (~.48m x ~1.46m), 1 1/24 x 3 1/8 (~.47m x ~1.41m) and 1 x 3 cubits (~.45m x ~1.35m) respectively.

In this instance, it is impossible to decide which of these specifications is more plausible; although the ratio width : height of the door of 1 : 3 or 1 : 2 in particular has been the subject of some discussion,[144] I would argue that both are equally credible, since for either of them instances from the archaeological record or extant buildings can be cited as supporting evidence.[145]

Although the rules and regulations of SAS governing the construction of a residential building are thus by and large plausible (with the exceptions noted above), it is highly unlikely that any house was ever modelled on them – and it seems that that was not their purpose to begin with. As indicated above, I believe that in order to do justice to our text, we need to follow its author, or rather: authors in distinguishing carefully between sacred and residential architecture; the focus of the work is clearly on the latter, while the former seems to have been incorporated chiefly in imitation of previous authorities, and because a *vāstuśāstra* without any treatment of residential architecture would have been considered incomplete. More generally, we will do well to call to mind the statement of MAXWELL (1991:11 sqq.) on the relationship of śāstric tradition and artistic practice (which, I believe, holds good for the construction of human dwellings as much as for the sculpting of images):

> Very often the instructions dictated by a putative *ārṣeya* or even *daiva* authority are seen to be wildly inaccurate or inadequate when applied to the mass of ancient sculptural material. The fact is that on the whole they simply were not used by the sculptors. This does not mean that art historians should abandon such literature, but rather that it

> should be treated as a distinct literary category to a certain extent divorced from the realities of image-making, the creative act, and reflecting the suppositions of a priestly class concerning the correct way of conceiving a deity according to local perceptions. [...] The brahman class, or its writers at least, did not concern itself directly with the practical business of hewing and carving stone, but rather with the broader inherited task of perpetuating the essential outlines of cultural tradition. They asserted the necessity of making images but it was not their job to make them. In this sense, the shastric injunctions have the effect of authorizing (but not authoring) the work of the *śilpin*. Working within the scope of another's authority – and authorizing without trespassing – was and remains a primary cohesive social understanding [...]

Applied to house construction, this means that the *śāstra* sanctions the activities of the builder (without actually describing or governing them), incorporating them as an integral part into the brahmanical tradition[146] by putting them into a wider religious and doctrinal context: the *śāstrin* 'asserts the necessitiy of making' dwellings – and of making them in accordance with certain ritual and cosmological rules – but it is not his job to build them.

If we accept MAXWELL's arguments, we should consider the injunctions of SAS as basically part of a śāstric tradition distinct from the building practice in 11th century Mālava – though probably not entirely uninfluenced by it. As we have seen, the basic dimensions of the dwelling have been copied more or less faithfully from older texts, and can thus be regarded as part of the śāstric tradition; at the same time, there are certain descriptive passages relating to the door frame, the pillars, and the woodwork in the 24th and 28th *adhyāya*s that cannot be traced back to BṛS, MP, or VP, and that are of a much greater practical applicability than the bone-dry *prastāra*s of the 19th and 21st to 23rd *adhyāya*s. That these passages, especially 28.09-15, are part of the core of SAS is indicated by the fact that almost all of the technical terms occuring there are also used in the context of the temple door as described in the 53rd and 54th *adhyāyas*; my assumption is that in these instances, the śāstric tradition (exemplified by the older treatises and those portions of SAS that have their origin in them) responded to developments within the contemporaneous artistic tradition by incorporating new concepts and vocabulary items. It is only reasonable to assume that this must have happened from time to time; else the gap between the śāstric tradition and the building practice it was supposed to sanction would have become too wide, and the system would have run the risk of becoming dysfunctional.

But in order to maintain its legitimising function, the *śāstra* must not be seen to abandon the older, traditional tenets of its predecessors – hence the at times rather half-hearted incorporation of rules and regulations inherited from BṛS, MP, or VP, which in their turn seem to have their origin in the building practice of their own times.[147]

1.7 SAS and other sources

The following is a brief description of the sources other than the text of SAS which have been made use of in the course of this study.

1.7.1 *Aparājitapṛcchā* (AP)

This *vāstuśāstra* was edited from two mss. by P. A. MANKAD as GOS No. 115 in 1950; it consists of 239 chapters called *sūtras*. The colophons mention Bhuvanadeva as author. According to MANKAD (1950:xii), the work was probably composed between the 12th and the first half of the 13th century, and has borrowed freely from SAS;[148] it is even modelled on the same frame story of Viśvakarman's *purāṇa*-style dialogue with his four sons. The frequent repetitions, especially in the first quarter or so of the text, seem to be due to interpolations.[149]

It has not been deemed necessary to compare the rules given in SAS with those of AP at every step; the relationship between the two texts is generally established, and a comparison of that kind would have altered the character of this study completely. Instead, some passages from AP have been quoted in the notes on my translation wherever it was found helpful.

1.7.2 *Bṛhatsaṃhitā* (BṛS), *Matsyapurāṇa* (MP), and *Viśvakarmaprakāśa* (VP)

Varāhamihira's BṛS is generally believed to have been composed in the second half of the 6th century;[150] the commentary on the entire text by the Kashmiri author Utpala was completed in 967 AD. The edition used here is TRIPĀṬHI's re-edition of the text as published by DVIVEDIN in 1895-97.[151] Kern's translation in JRAS VI (New Series) was also consulted, as well as BHAT's translation of the text which was published together with an edition of the stanzas and a summary of Utpala's commentary. With the exception of the chapter on *vāstuvidyā* contained in the (as yet unpublished) *Gargasaṃhitā*, which is believed to have been composed in the first century BC or AD,[152] the chapter in question contained in BṛS – the 52nd – can be considered the oldest datable work on *vāstuvidyā*;[153] and a comparison of its contents with those stanzas from the *Gargasaṃhitā* quoted by Utpala shows that Varāhamihira has relied rather heavily on this source, which only adds to the importance of the text.

Fixing a date for the composition or compilation of MP is a much trickier business; it has been variously assumed to have developed between the 4th century BC and the 3rd century AD; the 4th century BC and AD 1250; and AD 200 and 400.[154] No critical edition is available to date.

The same is unfortunately true of VP as well; the only edition available for this study was the 2002 reprint from Shri Venkateshwar Press. The text is in a pitiable condition; it abounds in grotesque printing errors, and it is quite obvious that the text of the ms from which it was published was in rather bad shape as well, exhibiting a mass of bad or uncertain readings and some considerable lacunae. This is all the more regrettable as VP is one of the few *vāstu* texts for which a reliable *terminus ante quem* is available on account of the quotations from it in Utpala's commentary on BṛS 52.

A comparison of BṛS 52, MP 254-255, and VP 02, 07 reveals a remarkable degree of congruence, not just in contents, but also in the order in which the topics at hand are discussed (cf. Appendix): it will be found that BṛS 52.04-30 corresponds more or less directly to MP 254.14cd-255.06 and VP 02.135-169, even though the order of the topics discussed is far from self-evident. The degree of congruence, especially between BṛS and VP, becomes even more obvious when one considers the treatment of the houses of *karmopajīvins*, which strongly suggests that all three texts have a common origin (cf. tab. 3). At the same time, the difference between them and SAS becomes apparent.

Given the absence of a critical edition of either MP or VP, it is probably idle to try to establish a relative chronology of the three texts under discussion; BHATTACHARYYA (^{2}1963:103-107) has made a valiant attempt, concluding that VP was older than MP, which in turn precedes BṛS. But this seems rather unlikely given the fact that VP contains some material that is clearly a development on the precepts of the other two – e.g. the introduction of *prastāra* and its application to the single *śālā* resulting in the sixteen basic varieties also encountered in later works, including SAS.[155] Be that as it may, what matters in our present context is not so much the chronology of BṛS, MP, and VP, but the indebtedness of SAS to these texts. In this context, the question arises whether any one of them can be taken to be the source on which SAS has drawn, or whether its author has relied more generally on the tradition constituted by these texts and probably a number of others which are now lost.

Tab. 3 – Concordance of *karmopajīvins* in Br̥S, MP, VP, and SAS

Br̥S 52.04-10	MP 254.14-27	VP 02-135-145	SAS 19.15-18
nr̥pa	*pr̥thivīpati*	*nr̥pa*	*rājan*
senāpati	*senāpati*	<*senāpati*>[156]	*senāpati*
saciva	*mantrin*	*saciva*	—
rājamahiṣī	—	*rājamahiṣī*	—
yuvarāja	*yuvarāja*	*yuvarāja*	—
sāmantapra-varārājapuruṣa	*sāmantāmātya-loka*	*sāmantarāja-putrapravara*	*rājapuruṣa*
kañcuki, veśyā, kalājña	*śilpin, kañcuki, veśyā*	*kañcuki, veśyā, kalājña*	—
adhyakṣādhikr̥ta	—	*adhyakṣādhikr̥ta*	—
karmāntā-dhyakṣa, dūta	*dūtī, karmā-ntika, etc.*	*adhyakṣa, dūta*	—
daivajña, purodhasa, bhiṣaj	*daivajña, guru, vaidya, sabhā-stara, purodhasa*	*daivajña, bhiṣaj, purohita*	*purodhasa*

As we shall see below (note on 20.11-12), SAS contains some material also found in VP, but not in Br̥S or MP, viz. the sixteen types of *ekaśāla* alluded to above. At the same time, the treatment of the six basic types of *dviśāla* as given in SAS 20.28-32 differs considerably from that contained in VP, while at the same time being virtually identical with that given in Br̥S and, to a lesser extent, MP.[157] The positions of the front door given in SAS 39.02-10 can be harmonized with the injunctions of BṛS 52.70-73 and VP 07.56-65ab, but are partly in contradiction to MP 254.08-09 (cf. note on 39.01); the constellation of front door and living area according to *varṇa* in the same passage in SAS agrees with BṛS 52.68 and MP 254.07ab, but is incompatible with VP 07.12; and the contents of SAS 39.35-67 is by and large congruent with BṛS 52.74-80, MP 254.10-18, and VP 07.71-106.

We are thus left with two alternatives regarding the relationship between SAS and the three older treatises under discussion: Either the author(s) of SAS used the texts available to them eclectically, following BṛS at times, and MP or VP in other instances; or SAS was modelled on a different text that has not come down to us, but which was composed in a similarly eclectic fashion. The relatively high degree of independence displayed by SAS, not just in the arrangement of contents but also in the contents proper, makes it impossible to decide this matter conclusively. That some influence has taken place is undeniable; but it is also obvious that this influence was rather inconsistent, as borne out by the seemingly half-remembered, half-forgotten rules regarding the dwellings of the *karmopajīvin*s in SAS 19.15-18, and by the fact that those stanzas which can be shown to have their origin in either of the older texts are not found all in one place, but are scattered all over the chapters dealing with residential architecture.

1.8 The text passages selected for translation

This section contains a brief description of those passages of SAS that have been selected for translation and analysis in this study. As has already been indicated, there are far more text passages in SAS relating to residential architecture, even if by that term we understand the individual dwelling excluding the settlement (SAS 10); given the relative wealth of source material to be taken into consideration, it was thought desirable to limit the scope of this study to 200 - 250 stanzas. Hence, it was necessary to decide on certain basic criteria which could be applied to the text in order to make a selection:

As in any *vāstuśāstra*, the treatment of residential architecture contained in SAS can be broadly divided into three more or less distinct aspects: (1) astrology – rules governing the building process as well as the shape of the structure according to astral constellations and the horoscope of the owner; (2) ritual – rites that have to be performed at certain times during the constructional process, and rules determining the physical structure of the dwelling according to the owner's *varṇa* and/or profession; and (3) building technology – the basic dimensions and structural properties of the dwelling. It is open to debate whether this (admittedly arbitrary) division is really helpful, especially as the three categories postulated here are interrelated to a high degree; they presuppose and condition each other. Further, it is a moot point whether the merits and defects of buildings and their results for the inmates should come under (1) or (2) – or indeed (3).

I have felt justified in maintaining this distinction simply because to a certain degree, it is reflected in the text itself: astrological rules in the more restricted sense (including the *vāstupuruṣa-maṇḍala*) are given in *adhyāya*s 11-14 and 26; and rituals to be performed by the *sthapati* are the subject of *adhyāya*s 17, 35-37, 42, and 46.[158] The rules regarding the esoterically good or bad properties of buildings and the regulations regarding the owner's *varṇa*, on the other hand, are inextricably entwined with and seem to constitute an integral part of building technology.

It was decided that the technological aspect of the human dwelling as described in SAS should be the focus of this study; accordingly, the chapters on ritual and astrology were ruled out.[159] At the same time, it was felt desirable to translate entire chapters rather than isolated passages in order to present the text as faithfully as possible, yet without getting bogged down by lengthy discussions that had little bearing on the basic setup of the dwelling, e.g. the *prastāras* contained in the 19th and 21st to 23rd *adhyāyas*. It will be seen that this principle seems to have been violated in two instances, viz. where *adhyāyas* 19 and 39 are translated only in part, and not in their entirety; for the reasons, see 1.8.2 and 1.8.5 below.

Before introducing the contents and structure of the selected *adhyāyas*, a word of apology is probably in order regarding the exclusion of the 28th *adhyāya* (*gṛhadravyapramāṇāni*); it cannot be denied that there is no other single chapter containing a similar wealth of terminology relating to the the individual building elements of the dwelling. Unfortunately, it is almost impossible to write a meaningful translation of this chapter due to the obscurity of its technical terms, most of which are not found elsewhere in the text (or, for that matter, in any other available *śilpaśāstra*) with reference to residential buildings, though not a few of them are encountered again in chapters relating to temples. There is some reason to believe that the undertaking of translating the 28th *adhyāya* and of analysing its technical vocabulary will have much brighter prospects of success once the text of SAS has been subjected to a detailed comparison with the temples constructed under the Paramāra dynasty.

1.8.1 *Adhyāya* 18

This *adhyaya* is among the most remarkable passages of SAS; it does not contain any rules regarding the setup of the dwelling, but consists of a series of definitions in the style of a traditional lexicon. As I have argued above (1.3.5), it is quite likely that it was composed by a different author than the remaining chapters on residential architecture; it has no parallel in the sphere of *vāstuvidyā* that I am aware of,[160] which raises the question of its parallels and/or sources in the sphere of lexicography.

There are a number of *kośa*s which contain a section on towns and buildings, most notably AK 2.2, which consists of 20 stanzas; ACM 971cd-1015ab; ARM 02.130-150. As none of these is too far removed from SAS in date,[161] it has been though worthwhile to subject their technical vocabulary to a brief comparison with that of SAS 18;[162] the results are to be found in the notes on that chapter. It does not seem that either AK or ARM were the chief source of SAS 18, nor does ACM seem to have been influenced at all by the latter, as there is a considerable number of technical terms peculiar to SAS 18 that are not found in any of the other three *kośa*s – e.g. *harmya* 'rooftop terrace,' *abhigupti* 'temporary structure on the rooftop terrace,' **ulloka* 'open space above the central courtyard.'[163] A familiarity of the author of SAS 18 with AK and/or ARM can be inferred from a small but significant number of instances where two or more words occur in the same context as in said texts.[164] Yet in the majority of instances, AK, ACM, and ARM read against SAS; the following example may suffice to illustrate this point:

SAS 19.18-19 contains a definition of the terms *catuḥśāla*, *triśāla*, *dviśāla*, *ekaśāla*, and *śāla*. As against this, AK 02.02.06, ACM 992, and 02.137 only explain *catuḥśāla*, which is glossed as *saṃjavanam* in all three instances – a term that is absent from SAS.

1.8.2 *Adhyāya* 19.15-29

The colophon gives *catuḥśālavidhāna* as the title of this *adhyāya*; 19.02-12 give the total numbers of *eka*- to *daśaśālā*s, including the 15 *halaka*s (19.12) described in 24.01-18ab; 19.13-14 seem to discuss different varieties of houses – cf. note on 20.35.; 19.15-22 seem to represent a rather corrupt version of the description of the houses of *karmopajīvin*s and *varṇin*s given in BṛS 52.04-19, MP 254.14cd-36, and VP 02.135-153 (cf. Appendix); 19.22d-26 give the different sizes of *śālā* and *alinda*; 19.27-29 concerns itself with the *karṇaśālā*. The remaining portion (19.30-224) is devoted to an enumeration of 256 different types of *catuḥśāla* distinguished by the number and position of their *mūṣā*s – in effect, an exercise in *prastāra*.

The selection made for this study may seem arbitrary – which it certainly is, to an extent, at least as far as the preceding two and the following three or four stanzas are concerned. The main criteria were (1) the relevance of the stanzas for the basic setup of the dwelling – the dimensions of *śālā*, *alinda*, and *karṇaśālā* given in 19.22d-29 come under this heading; and (2) the connection that could be established with other, preferably older texts – hence 19.15-22 were included, which bear a striking though indistinct resemblance to BṛS 52.04-19, MP 254.14cd-36, and VP 02.135-153 – cf. 1.7.2 above.

1.8.3 *Adhyāya* 20

Above (1.3.5), this chapter has been referred to as a 'motley collection of miscellanea;' a brief survey of its contents will go some way to justify this designation: 20.01 gives a definition of the expressions *agrataḥ* and *pṛṣṭhataḥ* with reference to the door of the edifice, which is used throughout 20.02-20; 20.02-03 give the negative results of excessive dimensions of the house, while 20.04-07 dicuss the positive or negative *phala*s of any proclivities or declivities of the building grounds; 20.08-10 offer a fourfold distinction of the house, apparently depending on the presence or absence of an interior courtyard and the position of the *alinda*(s); 20.11-20 give the positive and negative results of all mathematically possible positions of one and two *alinda*s respectively – 20.19-20 are a repetition of the contents of 20.11-12; 20.21-23 contain a brief but euphoric praise of the house that is built according to the regulations of the *śāstra*; 20.24-27ab describe the four basic types of *triśāla*, and 20.27cd-32 give the six basic types of *dviśāla*; 20.33-34 give the names of four different constellations of a *catuḥ*- and a *triśāla* resulting in a *saptaśāla*; 20.35 contains a definition of *gṛha-saṅghaṭṭa*; the concluding stanza 20.36 indicates most of these topics – as many, presumably, as fit into a *vasantatilakā*. The colophon also shows that the 20th *adhyāya* must have had its present extent already at the time the colophons were introduced.

As indicated above, there are only four stanzas (20.01; 20.08-10) – not counting the concluding stanza – that do not treat of subject matter also discussed elsewhere in the text.

1.8.4 *Adhyāya* 24

The contents of this chapter is as follows: 24.01-18ab give the shapes, names, and *phala*s of the buildings referred to as *halaka*s; 24.18cd-20 indicate the subjects discussed in the remaining stanzas of this *adhyāya*, with some discrepancies indicating that a stanza or half-stanza might have been lost later in the text – cf. note below; 24.21-22 give the widths of the five different *vāstu*s fit for *varṇin*s, as well as a rule regarding the thickness of the wall; 24.23-24 contain a general rule for avoiding injury to the *marman*s or vulnerable spots of the *vāstupuruṣa*; 24.25-28ab give the rules regarding the size and position of the *alinda* in a *hīnavāstu*, the height of the *pīṭha*, and the basic dimensions of the door; 24.28cd-34 contain a description of the woodcarving, presumably in connection with the door frame; 24.35-43 give the names and orientation of four types of *vāstu* and *śālā* respectively, as well as the position of their doors with reference to the *vāstupuruṣamaṇḍala*; 24.44 seems to be a stray reference to the five types of *catuḥśāla* as described in BṛS 52.31-35; the concluding stanza (24.45) indicates the measurements of door, *pīṭha*, and walls, as well as the woodwork and the kinds of *hīnavāstu* described in 24.35-42 as the topics of this *adhyāya*. Nothing is said there about the fifteen types of *halaka*, and they are not mentioned in the colophon either (*dvārapīṭha-bhittimānadārukalāhīnavāstulakṣaṇam*). It is possible that they were inserted at a later date and by a different author, probably in continuation of the discussion of *catuḥ-*, *tri-*, *dvi-*, and *ekaśāla*s in SAS 19 and 21-23; it should be noted that they are expressly mentioned in the enumeration of the various types of dwelling given in 19.01-12.

1.8.5 *Adhyāya* 39.01-34

Of this *adhyāya*, only the first 34 1/2 stanzas have been selected for translation, for reasons already explained (1.2.1). The contents of this passage can be summarized as follows: 39.01 is a typical introductory stanza broadly indicating the subject matter of the passage; 39.02-10 give the cardinal directions suitable for the main living area depending on the owner's *varṇa*, as well as the precise position of the front door, which is the same as the one given in 24.35-42; 39.11-17 describe the four mathematically possible constellations of the front door and the door of the main living area within the *vāstu* (cf. 1.5.3); 39.18-19 take up the subject of the part of the *vāstu* suitable for the main living area as treated in 39.02-10, adding the area suitable for sleeping;[165] 39.20-28 give the maximum height of the dwellings of *varṇin*s and kings in storeys, and 39.29-30 in cubits (for the discrepancy between these two passages, cf. note on 39.29-30); 39.31-34(1) contain a rule about the relative height of the abodes of men and of heavenly beings, and go on to state the minimum height of the dwellings of *varṇin*s and kings in storeys; the concluding stanza contains a warning against violating these rules.

Notes

1. Bhoja's dates are given variously as ca. 1000 - 1055 (GANGULY [3]1979:66sq.; SIRCAR, 1958:10; JAIN 1973:345-352; AGRAWALA 1966:xi), ca. 1010 - 1055 (GRAY 1950:2; MISHRA 1973:9), 1018 - 1060 (SHUKLA 1958:25; PAREEK 2002:16), 1018 - 1063 (KRISHNAMACHARIAR 1937:500); BÜHLER (1892a:233) offered the opinion that 'the death of Bhoja must fall some time after the year A.D. 1062'.

2. This statement perhaps requires some clarification: After all, the entire œuvre of D.N. Shukla is based on his reading of SAS. But despite Shukla's efforts, most important points regarding the history and function of the text still remain unclear, and it would appear that despite its acknowledged importance, SAS has never been at the centre of any scholarly debate. For instance, the only relevant review article that I have been able to find is a brief notice by F. WILHELM, which appeared in ZDMG 122 (1972), p. 431.

3. These are: Ka – Baroda 3606. 136ff. (19ff. missing), copied in Saṃ. 1594 = AD 1537, incomplete (ends in *adhyāya* 82); Kha – Baroda 6858. 136ff., incomplete (ends in *adhyāya* 55); Ga – Pattan (10ff. missing), incomplete (ends in *adhyāya* 49); for his revised edition, AGRAWALA also made use of Da – Baroda -, incomplete (ends at 82,237); cf. PINGREE (1981a:339), who lists two more mss, viz.: AS Bombay 413, ff. 2-120, incomplete (1, 11-48, 116); BORI 356 of 1880/81, ff. 1-61 and 70; incomplete.

4. AGRAWALA (1966:v), Foreword by B.J. SANDESARA, Director of the Oriental Institute, Baroda.

5. Both KERN's translation and BHAT's edition-cum-translation include one additional *adhyāya* not contained in TRIPATHI's edition; hence, the *vāstuvidyā* is counted as the 53rd *adhyāya* in these publications.

6. I have seen fit to adopt BṛS 52 as my primary source for comparison; of the three available *vāstuśāstra*s anterior to SAS, it is the most reliably edited, and has the added advantage of Utpala's commentary. On the relationship of BṛS, MP, and VP cf. 1.7.4 below.

7. One cubit (*hasta, kara*) consisting of 24 digits (*aṅgula*) roughly corresponds to .45m – cf. PARAMAHANS (1984).

8. Cf. also note on 19.16.

9. BṛSṬ 52.04: *rājaveśmottamaṃ pradhānam* ***aṣṭābhyadhikam*** *aṣṭottaraṃ hastaśataṃ* ***pṛthutvena*** *vistāreṇa kāryam | anyāni catvāri gṛhāṇy* ***aṣṭāṣṭonāni****, aṣṭabhir aṣṭabhir hastair ūnāni kāryāṇi | etad uktaṃ bhavati – prathamaṃ nṛpagṛham aṣṭādhikaṃ hastaśataṃ vistīrṇam, dvitīyaṃ śatam, tṛtīyaṃ dvinavatiḥ, caturthaṃ caturaśītiḥ, pañcamaṃ ṣaṭsaptatir iti* | [...] . The difference between SAS 19.16 and BṛS 52.04 is, of course, that the former does not contain any prescription regarding the length of the ground plan and that the diminution of its width does not take place evenly in steps of eight cubits, but rather gradually in increasing steps of four, six, eight, and – presumably – ten cubits. The principle introduced here – a set of five different-sized ground plans for each householder, depending on his social and ritual status – will be discussed under 1.6 and in the note on 19.16.

10. Residential architecture is mainly treated of in the 26th and 27th *adhyāya*s, which contain a total of 356 stanzas. Of course, it should be noted that these buildings are expressly stated to be fit for abodes of the gods as well. Vice versa, most of the building elements described in the other *adhyāya*s can be applied to residential buildings as well, since the distinction between sacred and residential architecture is generally much less strictly observed than is the case in BṛS, MP, VP, or SAS.

11. Written in Keralā between the 15th and the 17th century AD by Nīlakaṇṭhan Mūsat, MĀC can boast more than a dozen commentaries in Malayāḷam testifying to its immense popularity even in modern times (ACHYUTHAN and PRABHU 1998:x-xiii).

12. Cf. 1.3.3 and 1.3.4 below.

13. The only two occurences of the term *prāsāda* in the chapters of SAS dealing with residential buildings, viz. 18.22a and 28.13c rather suggest that it refers to a kind of raised platform in this context. (Cf. also 48.10d, where *prāsāda* obviously refers to a temple.) The term for 'royal palace' generally used in SAS is *rājagṛha*, to which no more than three individual *adhyāya*s, the 15th, 30th, and the 51st, have been devoted. I do not think that *prāsāda* in *adhyāya*s 49 and 50 can refer to a palace as well

as a temple (cf. AGRAWALA 1966:xviii); the kings and *varṇins* mentioned in 49.01 are probably the patrons of the *prāsāda*s described in that chapter, rather than their residents.

14. SHUKLA 1958:307: 'A perusal of the extant Śilpa works like Mānasāra, and Mayamata, will convince the reader that buildings in general are described in one category alone. If there are some additional delineations, they are just like appendices to them differing only in degree and not in kind. Let us take for instance either Mānasāra or Mayamata (as the arrangement of the chapters and the subjects treated therein are more or less similar); we find that in Mānasāra all the 98 types of mansions, either may be taken as the residences of gods (the Mānasāra temples) or of men or the gorgeous mansions or princely palaces. [...] In my opinion there is a complete absence of fundamental distinction to be made in the two realms of architectural planning belonging to two different and divergent sets of buildings – Mānava-Vāsa and Deva-Vāsa.'

15. Cf. also the following statement by DAGENS (1970:3) with reference to the vocabulary of the texts belonging to the 'southern school,' to which MS belongs: '[*C*]*omme dans les* āgama, *un certain nombre de termes ou d'expressions ne peuvent se comprendre que dans un contexte tamoul ou parfois malayalam. Et le vocabulaire employé s'oppose, en particulier dans les descriptions architecturales, à celui de textes du Nord tels que le* Prāsādamaṇḍana. *Cette opposition s'explique parfaitement par l'opposition qui existe entre les monuments que décrivent ces différents textes.*'

16. '[W]e shall perhaps be justified in placing the *Mānasāra* before the *Bṛhat-Saṃhitā* and somewhere close to the *Matsyapurāṇa*. In any event, we venture to hold that the evidences submitted above would warrant the extension of the period of the *Mānasāra* from A.D. 500 to 700, if not from the time of Vitruvius or earlier.' (1946bb:282)

17. Cf. BHATTACHARYA ([2]1963:190-195): 'Acharya [...] says that the book was written under the patronage of Vaiṣṇava kings, and at a time when Vaiṣṇavism was the predominant religion. This [...] connects the Mānasāra with a period after the rise of Ramanuja (11th century) and with the Cholas and the late Paṇḍyas rather than the Guptas [...] taking into consideration the elaborate treatment of architecture in the Mānasāra, it is [...] very difficult to place the book in the Gupta period. The work

deals with the Dravidian style which could not have originated much earlier than the 6th century A.D. [...] Dr. Acharya's contention that all available works on Vāstuvidyā are indebted to the Mānasāra cannot be upheld. The available published Mānasāra is undoubtedly a later 'recension of recensions."

18. In the printed edition, the 57th *adhyāya* contains about 966 *ślokas* about 756 of which are unnumbered, due to two missing folios in the ms; from this it can be inferred that the *ślokas* are not numbered in the mss. According to the editors, about 50 *ślokas* may be missing after 57.211a ([...] *upapañcāśāḥ ślokā naṣṭāḥ saṃbhāvyante*, SAS p. 369).

19. This is in clear contrast to AP, whose *sūtras* usually lack a concluding stanza, and are composed in the *anuṣṭubh* metre throughout. Of the *adhyāya*s of SAS, only the 17th lacks a concluding stanza in a longer metre, which is obviously due to the fact that it is incomplete.

20. One important exception to this rule is the 31st *adhyāya* (*yantravidhāna*), which is mostly composed in *āryā* stanzas, but also *anuṣṭubh* and longer metres more usually encountered in *kāvya* texts than in technical treatises. There is good reason to believe that most of this *adhyāya* is a relatively late addition, the passages in the longer metres having been inserted between the *anuṣṭubh* stanzas. The fact that no part of this *adhyāya* is missing in any of the known mss. provides us with a safe *terminus ante quem*. Cf. also 1.3.5 below.

21. DAGENS 1994:xli, fn. 7.

22. RAGHAVAN 1963:5 fn.2: 'According to Ājaḍa who commented on Bhoja's *Sarasvatīkaṇṭhābharaṇa*, Bhoja wrote 84 works and all these were given names which were Bhoja's own titles, Birudas. 'Sarasvatīkaṇṭhābharaṇa' and Śṛṅgāraprakāśa' were also Bhoja's titles like 'Rājamṛgāṅka', 'Samarāṅgaṇasūtradhāra' etc.' Whether or not these *biruda*s were current in Bhoja's own days is not clear; only one of those mentioned by RAGHAVAN occurs frequently in the Bhojabhīmaprabandha of PCM, viz. *sarasvatīkaṇṭhābharaṇa*.

23. The problem of Indian literati kings has been briefly discussed in NARIMAN, WILLIAMS JACKSON and OGDEN (1923:35-39). I have not deemed it necessary to rehearse the arguments put forward there, as they have little bearing on the problem of Bhoja's authorship in the particular case of SAS.

24. GRAY (1950:4). It is perhaps no coincidence that there are two separate treatises ascribed to Bhoja called Sarasvatīkaṇṭhābharaṇa, one on poetics, the other on Pāninian grammar; and SHUKLA's (1958:25 sq.) list of 34 works allegedly composed by the king contains no less than four titles made up of or containing the word *rājamārtaṇḍa*, viz. (1) Rājamārtaṇḍa (astronomy), (2) Rājamārtaṇḍayogasūtravṛtti (Yoga), (3) Rājamārtaṇḍasārasaṃgraha (medicine), and (4) Rājamārtaṇḍa (Vedānta). This seems to suggest that the word *rājamārtaṇḍa* 'sun of kings' had some currency as *biruda* of the Paramāra king, and was indeed applied freely to texts ascribed to him. We will have to pick up this thread again under 1.4.4 below.

25. Cf. SASTRI's preface to the first edition (AGRAWALA 1966:viii).

26. (1892b:377); cf. also ACHARYA 1934:ix. It must be pointed out, however, that BÜHLER's drastic statement certainly does not apply to all *vāstuśāstra*s – consider for instance MM and MĀC, which latter treatise is composed in rather elaborate metres.

27. The exclusive use of the *anuṣṭubh* (excepting of course the concluding stanzas of the individual *adhyāya*s) is quite reminiscent of the purāṇic style, and may not seem to befit a *kavirāja*. But we should not forget that the dual character of SAS as a purāṇic imitation (with its fictitious dialogue of Viśvakarman and his sons) and a technical treatise precludes the use of more elaborate and fanciful metres in the first place. Also, it should be borne in mind that SKĀ (Bhoja's authorship of which is generally accepted) uses the *anuṣṭubh* metre in the *kārikā*s more or less throughout all five *paricchedas*.

28. There are, however, a number of instances where the second half of a stanza forms a syntactic unit with the first half of the following stanza; also, consider the case of 19.21cd-22ab under 2.2 below.

29. 21.58 contains six *pāda*s in the printed edition; there are several other instances of two *pāda*s in the *anuṣṭubh* metre occurring directly before the concluding stanza (01.24; 03.60; 04.38; 07.34; 09.54; 12.37; 13.24; 15.50; 16.51; 19.224; 21.58; 22.52; 23.41; 29.51; 30.140; 33.79; 34.46; 36.28; 37.81; 39.34; 40.14; 45.48; 50.18; 51.23; 52.27; 53.12; the concluding stanza of SAS 57; 60.99; 66.64; 67.114; 68.55; 70.157; 72.43; 73;22; 74.19; 75.38; 76.56; 80.42). In the printed edition, the 'additional' stanza is alternately counted as the last line of the penulti-

mate and the first line of the concluding stanza; in this study, they are constistently quoted as separate stanzas (e.g., 21.58(1) and 21.58(2)). The prevalence of this feature – half an *anuṣṭubh* before the concluding stanza, which occurs in nearly half of SAS' *adhyāya*s – indicates that it is due neither to accident nor to inaptitude, but rather a stylistic idiosyncrasy of the author of these chapters, which may have some implications for the question under discussion. Alternatively, this peculiarity may be indicative of the fact that the chapters of SAS (with the exception of the concluding stanzas) originally did not consist of stanzas, but rather of lines made up of half-verses. The fact that the stanzas are not always congruent with the syntactic units seems to support this assumption.

30. For a discussion of the term *mūṣā* cf. 1.5.8 below.

31. This also raises the question whether indeed the caesuras within the half stanzas are as important in, say, the 19th *adhyāya* as they are in the 18th, where they usually fulfil a structural role by separating the term defined from the definition.

32. In the instance of 39.03ab, though, the elided *sandhi* could be easily restored by emending **vāpy*.

33. For a detailed discussion of the term *alinda*, see 1.5.2 below.

34. *sa ca prākāra ity uktaḥ kaṇṭhaḥ syād aṅgaṇasya yaḥ* – 'And that is called *prākāra* which may be the *kaṇṭha* of the courtyard.'

35. Cf. ACHARYA 1946a:97: 'This is a quadrangular moulding, sometimes square and sometimes rectangular.'

36. *harmyaprākārakaḥ sa syāt kaṇṭhā harmyatalasya yā* – 'That which is the *kaṇṭhā* of the *harmya*-level – that shall be the *harmyaprākāraḥ*;' [...] *yā tu kaṇṭhā kuḍyaṃ bhittiś cayaś ca sā* – '[...] that which is the *kaṇṭhā* is *kuḍya*, *bhitti*, and *caya*.'

37. Cf. APTE s.v. *kalpaḥ*: '**9** A termination added to nouns and adjectives in the sense of 'a little less than,' almost like,' 'nearly equal to,'(denoting similarity with a degree of inferiority.)'

38. RHYS DAVIDS (1903:45): 'We nowhere hear of isolated houses. The houses were all together, in a group, separated only by narrow lanes.'

39. The only exception to this rule that has come to my notice is the 40th *adhyāya*, which describes the *pīṭha*s of gods and men alike.

40. AP, for instance, has made the *sūtradhāreṇa jñātavyā viṣayāḥ* the subject of its second *sūtra*; due to the compilatory character of the text, the topic is taken up again in *sūtra*s 49-50 (*sūtradhāraparīkṣā* and *sūtra-dhāralakṣaṇam*). MS likewise discusses the qualifications of the *śilpin* in its second *adhyāya* (*mānopakaraṇavidhāna*).

41. See SHUKLA 1958:98sqq.

42. Leaving aside the most obvious objection – viz. that the theory of an accidental disturbance of an originally logical sequence of *adhyāya*s is rather unlikely, for which reason there is no point in restoring an order that probably never existed –, it is highly doubtful that *adhyāya*s 17 and 35 (*indradhvajanirūpaṇa* and *śilānyāsavidhi*) are really part of the pre-liminaries of building a residential house, and the contents of the 18th *adhyāya* is very inadequately described as 'towns and their categories,' and certainly does not belong under the heading 'Town-Planning' (loc. cit.).

43. It should of course not be forgotten that the division of the text into four sections offered here is introduced only for expository reasons, and does not constitute a hypothesis on the genesis and history of the text of SAS.

44. SHUKLA (1958:29) is probably right in assuming that *gajaśālā* and *aśvaśālā* belong to the 'accessory buildings and establishments of the royal palace.'

45. This also accounts for the fact that PINGREE (1981a:339) quotes two of the Baroda mss – mss Ka and Da of the edition – as breaking off in the 82nd *adhyāya*, when in fact they break off in the 83rd.

46. *pūrvāmukhaṃ gr̥haṃ yat tu dvāraṃ māhendrasaṃyutam | hastinī ca bhavec chālā tad gr̥haṃ bhadrasaṃjñitam || 35 || bhadraṃ bhadra-karaṃ bhartur yaśobalavivardhanam | sidhyanti cāsya kāryāṇi bhadrā-khye vasato gr̥he || 36 || dakṣiṇābhimukhaṃ veśma dvāraṃ cāsya gr̥ha-kṣatam | mahiṣī ca bhavec chālā tad gr̥haṃ nandapīṭhakam || 37 || nandapīṭhagr̥haṃ puṃsā nityānandakaraṃ smr̥tam | sarvasaṃpadguṇo-petaṃ dhanadhānyavivardhanam || 38 || vāruṇyabhimukhaṃ sadma dvāraṃ ca kusumāhvayam | gāvī caiva bhavec chālā saurabhaṃ tad*

vidur budhāḥ || 39 || *saurabhe nityahṛṣṭatvaṃ vasatāṃ gṛhamedhinām* | *saphalaṃ kṛṣivāṇijyaṃ putrāṃś ca vaśavartinaḥ* || 40 || *uttarābhimukhaṃ dhiṣṇyaṃ dvāraṃ bhallāṭasaṃyutam* | *chagalī ca bhavec chālā puṣkarākhyaṃ tad ucyate* || 41 || *śīlavān nityasaṃtuṣṭaḥ suhṛtsujanavatsalaḥ* | *subhagaḥ puṣkarākhye ca bahuputradhanānvitaḥ* || 42 ||

47. *bhallāṭe dhanade yad vā carake pṛthivīdhare* | *brāhmaṇasya bhaved veśma māhendradvāram uttamam* || 02 || *māhendre 'rke 'tha satye vā* [!] *āryake vā niketanam* | *kāryaṃ gṛhakṣatadvāraṃ kṣatriyasya śubhāvaham* || 03 || *yāmye vaivasvate vāpi gāndharve 'tha gṛhakṣate* | *vaiśyasya bhavanaṃ kāryaṃ dvāraṃ puṣpāhvahe śubham* || 04 || *vāruṇe pauṣpadante vā yad vā maitre 'thavāsure* | *śūdrasya sadanaṃ kāryaṃ bhallāṭadvāram uttamam* || 05 || *viprāṇāṃ prāṅmukhaṃ vāstu gṛhaṃ syād dakṣiṇāmukham* | *vardhate dhanadhānyena putrapautraiś ca nityaśaḥ* || 06 || *dakṣiṇābhimukhaṃ vāstu bhavanaṃ paścimāmukham* | *kṣatriyasya dhanaṃ dhānyaṃ vikramaś ceha vardhate* || 07 || *vāstunaḥ paścimaṃ dvāraṃ bhavanasyottarāmukham* | *tatraidhate dhanair dhānyaiḥ putrapaśvādibhiś ca viṭ* || 08 || *vāstu syād uttaradvāraṃ gṛhaṃ pūrvāmukhaṃ tathā* | *śūdrasya karmavṛttis tu dhanadhānyair vivardhate* || 09 ||

48. *kathitaṃ tac ca saṃsthānair nāmabhiś ca yathākramam* | *hastinī mahiṣī gāvī chāgalī ca yathākramam* ||

49. *utsaṅgo hīnabāhuś ca pūrṇabāhus tathāparaḥ* | *pratyakṣāyaś caturthaś ca niveśaḥ parikīrtitaḥ* || 11 || *utsaṅga ekadikkābhyāṃ dvārābhyāṃ vāstuveśmanoḥ* | *sa saubhāgyaprajāvṛddhidhanadhānya*-**kṣaya*pradaḥ* || 12 || *yatra praveśato vāstugṛhaṃ bhavati vāmataḥ* | *tad dhīnabāhukaṃ vāstu ninditaṃ vāstucintakaiḥ* || 13 || *tasmin vasann alpavittaḥ svalpamitro 'lpabāndhavaḥ* | *strījitaś ca bhaven nityaṃ vividhavyādhipīḍitaḥ* || 14 || *vāstupraveśato yat tu gṛhaṃ dakṣiṇato bhavet* | *pradakṣiṇapraveśatvāt tad vidyāt pūrṇabāhukam* || 15 || *tatra putrāṃś ca pautrāṃś ca dhanadhānyasukhāni ca* | *prāpnuvanti narā nityaṃ vasanto vāstuni dhruvam* || 16 || *gṛhapṛṣṭhaṃ samāśritya vāstudvāraṃ yadā bhavet* | *pratyakṣāyas tv asau nindyo vāmāvartapraveśavat* || 17 ||

50. *utsaṅgaḥ pūrṇabāhuś ca hīnabāhus tathāparaḥ* | *pratyakṣāya iti proktaṃ praveśanaṃ catuṣṭayam* || 25 || *gṛhasya saṃmukhaṃ yatra dvāraṃ bhavati vāstunaḥ* | *utsaṅga iti sa proktaḥ pūrṇabāhuḥ pradakṣiṇaḥ* || 26 || *vāmato hīnabāhuḥ syāt *pratyakṣāyas* tu pṛṣṭhataḥ* |

caturtho 'yaṃ samuddiṣṭaḥ praveśo vāstuno budhaiḥ || 27 || *utsaṅgākhye praveśe syāt prajāhāniḥ kuṭumbinaḥ* | *dhanadhānyakṣayo vāsya maraṇaṃ vā dhruvaṃ bhavet* || 28 || *pūrṇabāhau putrapautrā dhanadhānyasukhāni ca* | *bhavanti vasato nityaṃ gṛhiṇas tatra vāstuni* || 29 || *alpamitro gṛhī hīnabāhāv atyalpabāndhavaḥ* | *syād alpavitto jīyeta strībhiḥ pīḍyeta vāmayaiḥ* || 30 || *pratyakṣāyapraveśas tu vihito yatra veśmani* | *tasmin nivasatāṃ puṃsāṃ niścitaḥ syād dhanakṣayaḥ* || 31 ||

51. *eko 'lindas tu kartavyo mukhato dakṣiṇena vā* | *mukhe rājaprasādāya dakṣiṇe 'rthavivardhanaḥ* || 11 || *vāmatas tu na kartavya eko 'lindo na pṛṣṭhataḥ* | *vāmato 'rthavināśāya pṛṣṭhato mriyate gṛhī* || 12 ||

52. *pṛṣṭhato vāmataś caiva purato dakṣiṇena vā* | *alindasya kṛtasyātha vakṣyāmo 'nukramāt phalam* || 19 || *pṛṣṭhato dāranāśāya dhanalābhāya dakṣiṇe* | *agre rājaprasādāya vāmato 'rthavināśanaḥ* || 20 ||

53. *mukhyāni teṣu catvāri kathyante tāni nāmataḥ* | *hiraṇyanābhaṃ sukṣetraṃ cullī pakṣaghnam eva ca* || 02 || *hiraṇyanābham utkṛṣṭaṃ hīnam uttaraśālayā* | *tat syād dhanapradaṃ bhartuḥ sukṣetraṃ pūrvayā vinā* || 03 || *sukṣetraṃ lakṣaṇopetam ṛddhivṛddhipradaṃ vibhoḥ* | *cullī dakṣiṇayā hīnā śālayā vittanāśinī* || 04 || *pakṣaghnaṃ paścimāhīnaṃ vairakṛt kulanāśanam* | [...] || 05 ||

54. *tatra naikaprakārāṇi triśālāny upalakṣayet* | *prakāreṣu ca sarveṣu nindyau yāmyāparojjhitau* || 24 || *ekasmin svāmino mṛtyur aparasmin dhanakṣayaḥ* | *pūrvottarojjhitau dhanyau saṃjñāś caiṣāṃ prakārataḥ* || 25 || *syur udakpūrvayāmy*ādya*śālāhīnāny anukramāt* | *hiraṇyanābhasukṣetracullīpakṣaghnanāmabhiḥ* || 26 ||

55. *hastinī mahiṣī ceti dve śāle yatra veśmani* | *tat siddhārtham iti jñeyaṃ vittasampattikārakam* || 07 || *mṛtyudaṃ mahiṣīgāvībhyāṃ bhaved yamasūryakam* | *daṇḍaṃ syāc chagalīgāvīśālābhyāṃ daṇḍabhītidam* || 08 || *vātaṃ kareṇucchagalīyuktam udvegakārakam* | *mahiṣyajābhyām udvegakarī cullī dhanāpahā* || 09 || *kācaṃ kareṇugāvībhyāṃ suhṛtprītivināśanam* | [...] || 10 ||

56. *dikkarṇeṣu dviśālāni tatkarṇānyeṣu nirdiśet* | *saṃmukhe dve sametāni ṣaḍ etāny upalakṣayet* || 28 || *siddhārthaṃ dakṣiṇāpratyag bhavanty atrārthasiddhayaḥ* | *yamasūryam udakpratyak tatra mṛtyubhayaṃ sadā* || 29 || *prāgudīcyos tu daṇḍaḥ syād daṇḍas tatra sadā bhavet* | *prāgyāmyayos tu vātākhyaṃ vāstu tat kalahottaram* || 30 ||

udagdakṣiṇasāṃmukhye dviśālaṃ kācavāstv iti | tatra jñātivirodhaḥ syān na tat kuryāt kadācana || 31 || prākpratīcyos tu sāṃmukhye cullīvāstu vinirdiśet | tatra vittakṣayo ghoraḥ kadāpy etan na kārayet || 32 ||

57. For a more detailed discussion of the term *prastāra*, see 1.5.7 below.

58. *aṣṭāv ādau gurūn nyasyet tataś cādyaguror adhaḥ || 35 || laghuṃ nyasyet tataḥ śeṣān vidadhīta yathopari | gurubhiḥ pūrayet ādiṃ yāvat syur laghavo 'khilāḥ || 36 || ādyapaṅktau guruś caikau laghuś caikau yathākramam | ataḥ paraṃ tu dviguṇāḥ pratipaṅkti bhavanty amī || 37 ||*

59. *vinyasyec caturaḥ pūrvaṃ gurūn varṇān yathāvidhi | ebhya eva prasūyante bhedāḥ ṣoḍaśa veśmanām || 02 || guror adho laghuṃ nyasyet pūrvaṃ śeṣaṃ yathopari | gurubhiḥ pūrayet paścād yāvat syur laghavo 'khilāḥ || 03 ||*

60. *dravyāyāmodayavyāsaiḥ śālā yatrādhikā bhavet | vāmā vā dakṣiṇā vāpi agrataḥ pṛṣṭhato 'pi vā || 2 || hanti dravyādhikā dravyam āyāmābhyadhikā kulam | ucchrāyābhyadhikā pūjāṃ saṃtatiṃ vistarādhikā || 3 ||*

61. *dravyaṃ dravyādhikaṃ hanti kulam āyāmato 'dhikam | ucchrayābhyadhikaṃ pūjāṃ santatiṃ vistarādhikam ||*

62. *yasya nimnā bhaved bhūmir vāmā dakṣiṇakā sthalā | bahudoṣaṃ hi tad vāstu putrapautravināśakam || 04 || yasya dakṣiṇakā nimnā bhūmir vāmā sthalā bhavet | yatnenāpi kṛtaṃ tat syād bhartur alpaphalodayam || 05 || paścimena bhaven nimnā bhūmiḥ sthūlatarāgrataḥ | yatra tat sarvavarṇeṣu sarvakāmapradaṃ gṛham || 06 || agrataś ca yadā hīnaṃ pṛṣṭhataś cocchritaṃ bhavet | bhavanaṃ svāmino hy āśu virāgavyasanāya tat || 07 ||*

63. *rakṣombunāthakīnāśamaruddahanadikplavā | madhyaplavā ca bhūr vyādhidāridryamarakavahā || 02 || vahniplavā vahnibhiye* [?] *mṛtaye dakṣiṇaplavā | ruje rakṣaḥplavā pratyakplavā dhānyadhanacchide || 03 || kalahāya pravāsāya rogāya ca marutplavā | madhyaplavā tu bhūmir yā sarvanāśāya sā bhavet || 04 ||*

64. *anūṣarā bahutṛṇā śastā snigdhottaraplavā || prāgīśānaplavā sarvaplavā vā darpaṇōdarā |*

65. For *kapotāli* and *marālapallī*, cf. *marālapālī* in the note on 18.41.

66. *siṃhakarṇakapotālīghaṇṭākarṇārdhapakṣagāḥ* | *dhvajacchatrakumārāṃś ca gṛheṣu parivarjayet* || 55 || *na pakṣarājidhvajasiṃhakarṇakumāraghaṇṭāḥ samarālapallīḥ* | *na praskhalārdhāni na caiva patrāny āyojayed veśmasu maṅgalārthī* || 56 ||

67. *karṇāvāt*[?]*pakṣirāṅghaṇṭādhvajacchatrakumārakān* I *siṃhakarṇakapotāliṃ gṛheṣu parivarjayet* ||

68. For trees marking boundaries, cf. KA 02.01.03.

69. *puraśmaśānagrāmādhva*hrada*caityāśramodbhavān* | *kṣetropavanasīmāntarviṣamasthalanimnajān* || 05 || *kaṭvamlatiktalavaṇāsv avanīṣu tathodgatān* | *śvabhrāvṛtān sthirorvīṣu saṃbhūtāṃś ca tyajed drumān* || 06 || *samyak saṃlakṣya vṛkṣāṇāṃ varṇasnehatvagādikam* | *vijānīyād vayas teṣāṃ bālān vṛddhāṃś ca saṃtyajet* || 07 || *śatāni trīṇi varṣāṇāṃ sāradrumavayaḥ smṛtam* | *gṛhṇīyāt ṣoḍaśād ūrdhvaṃ sārdhavarṣaśatāv adheḥ* || 08 || *vayasaḥ pariṇāmena nirvīryatvaṃ yathā nṛṇām* | *proktaṃ tadvad drumāṇāṃ ca syāt tathā chidrapatratā* || 09 || *bhaṅgurāḥ suṣirās te syuḥ sakolākṣāḥ kharatvacaḥ* | *tasmād imāṃs tyajed vṛkṣāṃs tathā caivordhvaśoṣiṇaḥ* || 10 || *vakrān rūkṣān avapluṣṭān duḥsthitān api ca drumān* | *varjayed bhagnaśākhāṃś ca dvyekaśākhānvitāṃs tathā* || 11 || *anyair adhiṣṭhitān vidyutpātavātasaritkṣatān* | *granthiniryuktadānāṃś ca bhramarāhikṛtāśrayān* || 12 || *saṃsṛṣṭān ekato bhraṣṭān madhubhir balibhir vṛtān* | *māṃsāmedhyāśanais tadvad dūṣitān api pakṣibhiḥ* || 13 || *lūtātantvāvṛtān vanyasattvodghṛṣṭān gajakṣatān* | *budhnato 'tibṛhatskandhāṃś cihnabhūtāṃs tathādhvanaḥ* || 14 || *akāle puṣpaphalino rogair api ca pīḍitān* | *vāsabhūtān ulūkānāṃ tyajed anyān apīdṛśān* || 15 || [...] *karṇikāradhavaplakṣakapitthaviṣamacchadāḥ* | *śirīṣodumbarāśvatthaśelunyagrodhacampakāḥ* || 19 || *nimbāmrakovidārākṣavyādhighātāś ca garhitāḥ* | *gṛhakarmaṇi neṣṭās te yatas te 'neṣṭadāyinaḥ* || 20 || *neṣṭāḥ kaṇṭakinaḥ svāduphalāḥ kṣīradrumāś ca ye* | *sugandhayaś ca ye tadvad dhruvaṃ teṣu paśukṣayaḥ* || 21 ||

70. *pātitān varjayed vṛkṣān dvipāśvāgnijalānilaiḥ* | *prabhūtapakṣinilayān kākakauśikasevitān* || 112 || *madhugrahapiśācāhiduṣṭāṃś caityaśmaśānajān* | *catuṣpathatrikamahānadīsaṅgamamārgajān* || 113 || *devatāyatane jātān ūrdhvaśuṣkān kṣatacchadān* | *vallīpinaddhān suṣirakoṭaragranthisaṃkulān* || 114 || *yāmyāparāśāpatitāṃs tyajet kaṇṭakino 'pi ca* | *kapitthodumbarāśvatthaśirīṣavaṭacampakān* || 115 || *kovidāradhavāriṣṭaśleṣmātakavibhītakān* | *kiṃca saptacchadakṣīriphaladāṃś ca drumāṃs tyajet* || 116 ||

71. The portents of the direction in which the tree falls has also been mentioned in SAS 16, but in a different context; cf. 16.35: *prācyāṃ śubhas taroḥ pāta udīcyāṃ karmasādhakaḥ | yāmyapratyaṅnipāte tu śāntiṃ kr̥tvā drumaṃ tyajet* || – It is auspicious if the tree falls towards the east, [if it falls] towards the north, it fulfils one's works; but if it falls towards the south or the west, one shall perform a rite of pacification and leave the tree.

72. The relationship between the 39th and 48th *adhyāya*s is a different matter; I am not sure whether the repetition of 39.11-17 in 48.25-31 can be considered sufficient proof that either passage is an interpolation; it is also conceivable that the same matter was treated under two different but equally appropriate headings by the same author. The same might be true of the numerous other repetitions contained in the 48th *adhyāya*. It should be noted that, although AP has borrowed three of the four technical terms introduced in 39.11-17, their use in that treatise differs markedly from that in SAS; it can thus be said with some justification that the concept of *utsaṅga – pūrṇabāhu – hīnabāhu – pratyakṣāya* is peculiar to SAS (cf. 1.7.1 below). But cf. also 1.5.3 below.

73. *nagarasya vibhāgo 'yaṃ yathāvat samudīritaḥ | kheṭaṃ tadardhaviṣkambham āhur grāmaṃ tadardhataḥ || 79 || yojanena purāt kheṭaṃ kheṭād grāmaṃ pracakṣate | gavyūtiparimāṇena grāmād grāmaṃ pracakṣate || 80 || dvikrośād viṣaye sīmā tadardhena purasya sā | kheṭake purasīmārdhaṃ grāme kheṭārdhataḥ smr̥tā || 81 || triṃśad dhanūṃṣi viṣkambhaḥ pure digvartmasu smr̥taḥ | viṃśatiḥ kheṭake mārgo grāme daśa ca darśitaḥ* || 82 || – '79. This is the division of the city, as declared; a *kheṭa* is of half that width, a village they say to be half of that. 80. One knows the *kheṭa* to be one *yojana* away from the city, [and] the village from the *kheṭa*; one knows one village to be a *gavyūti* away from the [neighbouring] village. 81. Two *krośa*s away is the border in the case of a realm, that of a city – half of that; in the case of a *kheṭa*, half of the city's border, in a village, half of that of a *kheta*. 82. The width of the main roads in [the case of] a city is known to be thirty *dhanus*', twenty in a *kheṭa*, and the road of a village has been shown to be ten [*dhanus*' in width].'

74. *yat prākārāśritaṃ dvāraṃ pure tad gopuraṃ viduḥ* – that door in a city which is linked to the wall – that they call *gopura*.

75. *pratolīṃ tāṃ vidur lokaḥ suraṅgām iva yāṃ vaset* – that they call *pratolī* which people may inhabit as a *suraṅgā*. Cf. note on 18.25.

76. The question arises as to what extent the 10th *adhyāya* can be considered original at all; it seems to have undergone various changes and additions at the hands of several authors. To note just a few points: (1) with the exception of a few stanzas (26-37, 54), the words used for 'width' are *vyāsa* and *viskambha*, rather than *vistara*, *vistāra*, and *vistṛti* (rarely *vyāsa*) usually encountered in SAS wherever residential architecture is discussed; (2) some stanzas, e.g. 10.77, are strangely unconnected to either the preceding or the following stanza; (3) the same stanza refers to *sthāpatya* as having four divisions (*catuḥprakāra°*), rather than eight – cf. the 45th *adhyāya* (*aṣṭāṅgalakṣaṇam*); (4) in 10.47, it is said that great gates should be built for the sake of the city's prosperity, beauty, and safety (*vṛddhiśobhābhiguptyarthaṃ purasya*); but 18.13 has *abhigupti* (which is not recorded elsewhere) as a kind of structure on the rooftop terrace; (5) in 10.28, it is said that the parapet should not be an even number of cubits in height (*nāpi yugmakaronmitam*); but while the opposition 'odd-even number of cubits' is a regular feature of 'southern' treatises (e.g. MM), it is not found elsewhere in the residential section of SAS.

77. Viz., 02-03, 04-07, 11-20, 24-27ab, 27cd-32. 33-34, which briefly discuss different *chandas* of *saptaśālas*, would have fit into the context of the 25th *adhyāya* equally well – cf. note on 20.33-34 below.

78. On the other hand, it should be noted that the 20th *adhyāya*, although giving the 'correct' definition of the six basic types of *dviśālas*, exhibits some stylistic weaknesses not generally encountered in SAS; mention has already been made of the elision of *sandhi* in 20.02cd, to which may perhaps be added the construction of *niyata-* with the instrumental case in 20.01, as well as the rather monotonous style. By no stretch of the imagination could it be the work of the same author as ŚP or SKĀ. If my assumptions regarding the relative age of this chapter are correct, that would mean that the author of SAS (whether or not identical with the Paramāra king) incorporated older material into his work.

79. *hastinī cendrasaṃsthāne mahiṣī ca yamasthale | gāvī ca varuṇasthāne saumyasthāne tu chāgalī* – '*hastinī* [is situated] in the place of Indra [E], and *mahiṣī* in the place of Yama [S]; and *gāvī* in the place of

Varuṇa [W], but *chāgalī* in the place of Soma [N].' What is puzzling about the contents of this stanza is that the *padas* of the *vāstupuruṣa-maṇḍala* referred to here are too small for an entire *śālā*, assuming that the *maṇḍala* is to be applied to the plot of a house rather than to an entire city; and in contrast to the other three deities mentioned here, Indra does not occupy a *pada* in a cardinal direction, but rather the northeastern *pada* in the eastern section of the *vāstupuruṣamaṇḍala* – which suggests that the names of the deities are not simply used as a code for the cardinal directions in general, but actually as a reference to *padas* of the *vāstupuruṣamaṇḍala*.

80. That is not to say that 23.38 and 24.35-42 are necessarily the work of one and the same author; it is just as likely that it is the 22nd and 23rd *adhyāyas* that come from the same pen.

81. There is another criterion which may be helpful in considering the problem of authorship of which no mention has been made so far: that of plausibility. The measurements of the ground plan, doors, height of storeys etc. given in SAS 24 and 28, while generally in agreement with the canonical measurements supplied in BṛS 52, MP 254, and VP 02, will mostly be found to be plausible in the sense that they seem to describe a habitable building that could actually have been built – cf. 1.6 below. This is in stark contrast with the dimensions of the three types of cities given in 10.02: the smallest city with a width of 1,000 *dhanus*' (1,800 metres) would have an area of 3.24 km^2, and thus outsize Kauśāmbī, with an area of 2.29 km^2 the most extensive ancient Indian city excavated *in toto* so far (SCHLINGLOFF 1969:12sq.); and the largest city of SAS, 4,000 *dhanus*' wide, would have an area of 51.84 km^2, more than three times larger than imperial Rome within the Aurelian wall (op. cit.:29). In this context, cf. also SARMA (1986:50).

82. AGRAWALA 1966:vii.

83. Op. cit.:xii.

84. 'The architect of those (that is to say, dwellings) that have *aṅgaṇas* (that is to say, dwellings [or] *śālā*-dwellings of that kind) [which are] *sam + ara* [?] *samara* (i.e. beings), or *aṅgaṇas* [which are] *samara* [and] *saṃyukta*.' There are a number of problems with this analysis: it is a complete mystery what *saṃyañci arāṇi* is supposed to be, as nouns derived from prefixed verbal roots usually take the finite verb as their basis

(**samyag ṛṇvanti yāni**); *tathā bhūtāni* is either supposed to mean 'i.e., beings,' or a misspelt *tathābhūta-*, a regular technical term in Sanskrit commentaries roughly meaning 'of such qualities (as);' and the gloss *saṃyuktāni* for *samarāṇi* is hard to make any sense of. And what is meant by *sam-ara* as referring to human beings? 'The grand and eloquent title of the book – "Samarāṅgaṇa Sūtradhāra", literally means an "archi tect of human dwellings"' [loc.cit].

85. The remaining four are: (1) *Samaramanoharī*, (2) *Samaravijaya*, (3) *Samarasāra*, (4) *Samarasārasaṅgraha* (CC s.vv.).

86. Cf. also the quote from GABORIEAU 1991 under 1.5.1.

87. PD quotes *Veṇīsaṃhāra* 29.20 and *Kathāsaritsāgara* 47.91, 54.211 as sources.

88. E.g., 10.74, 37.16, 42.05; the 44th *adhyāya* is entitled *sthapati-lakṣaṇam*; the art of building, *vāstuvidyā*, is also referred to as *sthāpatya*, cf. 44.22, 45.01. In some instances, *śilpin* is used instead of *sthapati*, apparently *metri causa* – 44.22, 39.34(2).

89. DHAVALIKAR (1971:215sq.) is mistaken when he avows that '[i]n the Mānasāra, artists are first divided into four categories. [...] They consist of the chief architect (*sthapati*), the draughtsman or the chief designer (*sūtragrāhin*), the painter (*vardhaki*) and the joiner (*sūtra-dhāra*).' The source he quotes (correctly) is ACHARYA (1928:137), which proves to be in open contradiction both to the testimony of the text and to ACHARYA's other writings; cf. ACHARYA (1946a: 578), where the correct hierarchy *sthapati – sūtragrāhin – vardhaki – takṣaka* is given. It seems that DHAVALIKAR's attention was called to the faulty source by Stella KRAMRISCH, who mentions it an editor's note on DHAVALIKAR (1969). – ŚRK has *sthāpaka* and *sthāpakatattva* instead of *sthapati* and *sthāpatya* throughout.

90. E.g. 02.15; it is perhaps no coincidence that AP is divided into *sūtra*s rather than *adhyāya*s.

91. Even though this is hardly the place for a discussion of the term *sūtradhāra* as used in the dramatic tradition, a reference to STEINER (1997:107-117) is probably not uncalled for. As for the dissenting opinion of STRAUCH (2003:179 sqq.), we should call to mind the results of DHAVALIKAR's (loc. cit.) survey, viz. that the word *sūtradhāra* seems not

to have been widely used with reference to the *śilpin*, as it does not occur in inscriptions prior to the 5th century. Its limited applicability in *vāstu* texts has already been pointed out above.

92. The number is arrived at by adding up the stanzas of *adhyāyas* 10, 15, 18-25, 27, 28-30, 32-34, 38, 39, 48, and 51. It will be observed that this list includes not just the chapters dealing directly with the human dwelling, but all of those related to civic, rather than sacred, architecture; absent from the list are also the chapters containing general rules applicable both to sacred and civil architecture, as well as the famous 31st *adhyāya*, *yantravidhāna*. The 40th *adhyāya, pīṭhamāna*, has not been included either as it contains material related both to the *pīṭha*s of (sacred) images, and to the seats of men.

93. The division 'preliminary – residential – *prāsāda*' goes back to SHUKLA (1958:98 sqq.).

94. This number includes the stanzas of *adhyāya*s 15, 18-25, 28, 30, 39, 48, and 51; 15, 30, and 51 deal with the royal palace, *aśvaśālā* and *gajaśālā* not included. For the distinction *karmopajīvin* – *varṇin* cf. 1.7.2 below.

95. Cf. CC p.568; NGMPP Reel Nos. B 378/2, E 425/24, E 1631/14, E 1631/29.

96. Cf. NGMPP Reel Nos. A 1075/3, X 1030/1, X 1113/1, X 1132/1.

97. Thus, AGRAWALA (1966:xii) was not too wide of the mark when he said that 'the title as applicable to Bhoja would signify [...] that he was the architect of the fortunes on the battlefield,' and merely missed the precise meaning of *sūtradhāra* in this context.

98. As mentioned above (note 22), the panegyric name *sarasvatīkaṇṭhābharaṇa* is well attested in the *Bhojabhīmaprabandha* of Merutuṅga's PCM.

99. Further evidence could likely be supplied by a comparison of the temples built under the patronage of the Paramāra kings of the 11th century with the specifications of SAS.

100. Cf. MAXWELL (1991:13): 'Much modern secondary literature claims to impart to the general reader and the unwary student "the canons of Indian sculpture," for example; in fact there exists no single canon,

and certainly no single authoritative text, for any of the Indian arts. There is no Pāṇini at any stage in the development of sculpture [...] .'

101. As a perusal of the notes on the 18th *adhyāya* will demonstrate, not even the *kośa*s agree in every instance when it comes to architectural terminology.

102. There seems to be a little-known variant of *aṅgaṇa*/*aṅgana*, viz. *aṅkana* (eg. MS 34.72, 88), which alternates freely with *aṅgaṇa* throughout the text of MS. A Tamilism?

103. 'There is nothing about a courtyard in any of these passages, and I think that sense may be said to be excluded in each of them. But we can see how the mistake arose, for we have *rājaṅgaṇe* at [Jāt.] 2.290, 316 – where at 290 the horses are tethered, and at 316 the Bodisat is seated, and seen from a window. Here courtyard would fit, and from some such passages, unknown to me, in Sanskrit books, Wilson's authorities may have got that meaning. [...] In Ceylon, at the present day, the peasants' huts, built under the palms, have an open space in front of the hut, sometimes covered with grass, sometimes not, always kept clear of shrubs and bushes, and swept clean so that nothing can grow there. It is there that the people sit; it is their parlour, the hut itself being used as bedroom and as a place to keep things in. This open space is the *midula*. This is what is meant in the passage from the Culla Vagga given above [Vinaya 2.218], and it exactly corresponds to the *aṅgaṇa-bhūmi* in front of the leaf huts (the *uṭaja*'s) of the rishis mentioned in the Raghuvaṃsa [...] .' (192 sq.) The question is whether RHYS DAVID's inference from 19th century Sri Lanka regarding the etymology (!) of *aṅgaṇa*/*aṅgana* carries much weight – especially as the open space referred to seems to go by a very different, and ostensibly unrelated name.

104. *bhavanasyāṅgaṇaṃ yat tu tad āhur bhavanājiram | vanājiraṃ vanamahī tv āśramājiram āśrame* – 'That which is the courtyard of a dwelling – that they call *bhavanājira*; but *vanājira* [they call] the ground of the forest, in the case of a hermitage [it is called] *āśramājira*.'

105. I have not been able to locate this source; BEAMES (1872:II.17) does quote Skr *aṅgana* 'courtyard', but without mentioning any buildings surrounding it.

106. In effect, a *dvi*- or *triśāla*.

107. Since the *śālā* is supposed to be accessed from the courtyard, the front porch of a *hīnavāstu*, i.e. an *eka-*, *dvi-*, or *triśāla*, must face the courtyard as well.

108. *alindaśabdena śālābhitter bāhyā yā gamanikā jālakāvṛtāṅgaṇa-saṃmukhā kriyate sā jñeyeti* | pd (q.v.) only has *gamanikā* as *'Richtschnur, Norm.'* Cf., however, KERN (1871:282, fn. 3): 'The word might as well be rendered by 'balcony,' 'gallery.'

109. Cf. preceding note.

110. Cf. SHUKLA (1958:334).

111. *gṛhe catuḥśāle grāme nagare vā brāhmaṇānām uttarasyāṃ diśi vāsagṛhāṇi kāryāṇi, pūrvasyāṃ kṣatriyāṇām, dakṣiṇasyāṃ vaiśyānām, paścimāyāṃ śūdrāṇām iti | tathā ca kāryāṇi yathā bhavanaṃ gṛhābhyantaram aṅgaṇaṃ viśatāṃ tany eva vāsagṛhāṇi dakṣiṇasyāṃ diśi bhavanti | etad uktaṃ bhavati – prāṅmukhasya gṛhasyāṅgaṇadvāram uttarābhimukhaṃ kāryam, dakṣiṇābhimukhasya prāṅmukham, paścimābhimukhasya dakṣiṇābhimukham, uttarābhimukhasya paścimābhimukham iti* – 'In a house, *catuḥśāla*, village, or town, the dwelling-houses of brahmans shall be made in northerly direction, in the east those of *kṣatriyas*, in the south those of *vaiśyas*, in the west those of *śūdras*. They shall be made so that those entering the dwelling, [i.e.] the courtyard on the inside of the house, have the dwelling-houses on their right-hand side, that is to say: the courtyard-door of a house facing east shall be made facing north, that of a house facing south: facing east, that of a house facing west: facing south, that of a house facing north: facing west.' Obviously, *aṅgaṇadvāra* refers to the door of the *vāsagṛha* (SAS: *gṛha, veśman*) leading onto the courtyard, while *gṛha* is the equivalent of *vāstu* as used in SAS.

112. BHAT ([2]1986:476) translates the second half of the stanza thus: 'The houses are to be constructed in such a way that for the people who enter the courtyard the houses lie to their right.'

113. The *padas* of the *vāstupuruṣamaṇḍala* recommended for the door in BṛS 52.69-73 include the *padas* that are given in SAS 39.02-05 – cf. note on SAS 39.01 below.

114. This seems to imply that the *upasthāna* should be open to the courtyard.

115. If we accept the thickness of the walls given in 24.22, the rooms of the largest type of *catuḥśāla* with a width of 32 cubits (~14.4 m) would be 4 cubits (~1.8m) wide – see below.

116. Cf. BṛS 52.118; MP 256.33cd-35; MM 27.114cd-119ab, 123cd-125ab; MS 36.15-83. The only prescriptions contained in SAS concern the relative position of the main living area with reference to the owner's *varṇa* (39.02-09).

117. Cf. ACHARYA (1946a:484).

118. The reference is given in SHUKLA (1958:73).

119. This yields an important clue for the origin and the further history of *vāstuvidyā*: below (1.6), we will see that the tradition of the *vāstuśāstra*s was by and large divorced from the actual building practice; yet it is obvious that the śāstric tradition cannot have originated out of nothing. While the astrological component cannot be denied (the earliest treatises on *vāstuvidyā* that have come down to us are contained in astrological works, cf. 1.7.2 below), it seems that *vāstuvidyā* in its earliest stage of development as a form of geomancy was quite distinct from both astrology and building technology. Seen in this light, it is perhaps no coincidence that the older treatises are invariably styled *vāstuśāstra*, and that the designation *śilpaśāstra* occurs only in relatively recent texts.

120. Cf. BṛS 52; MP 254; MM 26; VP 02; it appears to be absent from MS.

121. Cf. SHUKLA (1958:316 sqq.); PAREEK (2002:43 sq.).

122. KA 2.5.5 recommends the *catuḥśāla* design for a ware-house or magazine: *pakveṣṭakāstambhaṃ* ***catuḥśālam*** *ekadvāram anekasthānatalaṃ vivṛtastambhāpasāram ubhayataḥ paṇyagṛhaṃ koṣṭhāgāraṃ ca* [...] *kārayet* – 'He should cause to be made a ware-house and a magazine with pillars of baked bricks, with four halls (opening on to a quadrangle), with many, ground and upper floors, (and) with a (secret) passage for escape through hollow pillars on two sides [...]' [Tr. KANGLE]; and Mṛcch. seems to conceive of it as the central unit of Cārudatta's house, cf. 3.6+, 7ab: *vidūṣakaḥ* – [...] *bhovaassa abbhantara**cadussālaaṃ** pavesaāmi ṇam* | *cārudattaḥ* – *alaṃ* ***catuḥśālam*** *imaṃ praveśya prakāśanārīdhṛta eṣa yasmāt* – 'VID. – [...] Friend, I am going to keep it inside, in the interior quadrangle. CHAR. – Do not take it inside the quadrangle; for it has

been worn by a courtesan;' 3.10+: *vṛkṣavāṭikāparisare sandhiṃ kṛtvā praviṣṭo 'smi madhyamakam | tad yāvad idānīṃ* ***catuḥśālakam*** *api dūṣayāmi* – 'Having made a hole in the surrounding wall of the park, I have (now) reached the central building. So now I shall force an entry into the (inner) quadrangle also;' and 6.0+: *vasantasenā* – [...] *hañje kiṃ paviṭṭā ahaṃ iha abbhantara****cadussālaam*** | *ceṭī* – *ṇa kevalaṃ abbhanta-****racadussālaam*** | *savvajaṇassa vi hiaaṃ paviṭṭā* – 'VAS. – [...] Girl, have I here entered the inner quadrangle? THE MAID – Not only the inner quadrangle, but you have entered (*i.e.* captured) the hearts of all persons (here), too' [All tr. KALE].

123. Cf. MANKAD (1950:lxxviii-lxxxvi).

124. Cf. ALSDORF (1933:102-106); HAHN (1982:4, 11 sqq.).

125. MANKAD (1950:lxxviii) is wrong to believe that '[i]n *vāstu*, *guru* means a wall and *laghu* means an *alinda*;' regardless of the object under discussion – *alinda, mūṣā, halal-ka*, etc. –, *laghu* always denotes its presence, and *guru* its absence.

126. 19.27cd: *mūṣāvacchinnam icchanti śālādairghyaṃ vipaścitaḥ* – 'the learned know the length of the *śālā* to be subdivided by *mūṣā*s.' That this applies only to the wall of the *śālā* that faces the courtyard can be seen from 19.29cd, *alindaśālayor madhye yā syān mūṣēti sā smṛtā* – 'that which may be in between the *alinda* and the *śālā* – that is called *mūṣā*.' The starting point – to the north of the eastern door – is fixed in 19.30ab, and the numbers one through eight are assigned in 19.33cd.

127. As the stanzas giving the rules for working out a *prastāra* (19.35cd-37, 23.02-03) have already been quoted under 1.3.3 above, there is no need to repeat them here; suffice it to point out that 19.35cd-36 and 23.02-03 correspond to arrangement A, 19.37 to arrangement B in HAHN (1982:4).

128. One might argue that it is already contained in the earlier treatises *in nucleo* insofar as the presentation of the basic varieties of *dvi-*, *tri-*, and *catuḥśāla*s given there exhibit the same tendency to exhaustiveness, in the sense that it leaves out no possible combination of two, three, or four *śālā*s respectively around a square courtyard.

129. The width of the plot can be 32, 28, 24, 20, or 16 cubits (~14.4m, ~12.6m, ~10.8m, ~9m, or ~7.2 m respectively); for more detail,

cf. note on 19.19 below. The width of the *vāstu* is taken as the basis for calculating most of the remaining measurements, i.e. the width of *śālā* and *alinda*, height of storeys, dimension of the door etc.

130. 8, 7, 6, 5, or 4 cubits (~3.6m, ~3.15m, ~2.7m, ~2.25m, or ~1.8m) respectively.

131. The text of SAS seems to use the threefold distinction 'largest – middle-sized – smallest' as an alternative to the concept of *gṛhapañcaka* (cf. note on 24.21-22 below) throughout – cf. 19.17-18; 19.25; 28.03-04; 28.18. It is not clear whether the former concept is supposed to be applied to the five dwellings of the latter (32 cubits: largest; 28, 24, and 20 cubits: middle-sized; 16 cubits: smallest), or whether the two systems are conceived of as independent of each other. Cf. also note on 19.20 below.

132. For the five ground plans given in 24.21-22, this formula yields a height of 6, 5 3/4, 5 1/2, and 5 1/4 cubits or ~2.7m, ~2.6m, ~2.5m, and ~2.35m respectively; in all probability, this is meant to be the height of the storey including the floor of the upper storey, rather than the height of the ceiling.

133. The doors of the five *vāstus* of 24.21-22 are thus 4 1/4 x 2 1/8 (~1.9 x 0.95m), 4 1/12 x 2 1/14 (~1.85 x 0.925m), 3 11/12 x 1 17/24 (~1.75 x 0.875m), 3 3/4 x 1 7/8 (~1.7 x 0.85m), and 3 7/12 x 1 13/24 (~1.6 x 0.8m) respectively. Alternatively, the height of the door shall be the height of the storey multiplied by 2/3 (28.07); cf. note on 24-26-27 below.

134. SAS 28.11-15; their names are given as (1) *śākhā* or *devī*, (2) *rūpaśākhā* or *nandinī*, (3) *khalvaśākhā* or *sundarī*, (4) *bāhyamaṇḍalā* or *priyānanā*, (5) *bhāraśākhā* or *bhadrā*; SHUKLA (1958:332) has tried to arrange these in such a way as to produce a ventilator above the door, with both *devī* and *nandinī* doing service as lintels, *sundarī* and *priyānana* as jambs, and *bhadrā* as threshold. This is completely impossible – not just because threshold and lintel are mentioned in the preceding and following stanzas (*udumbara*/*pedyā* and *masūraka*), but also because the jambs would be of unequal dimensions.

135. The thickness of the walls as given in SAS may seem rather excessive; but it may be pointed out that load-bearing walls of brick-built residential buildings excavated at Nagarjunakonda varied between .5m and .9m (cf. REDDY 1998:122).

136. SAS 39.26-27, 34(1) also give the number of storeys for the house of a king – at least three, at most seven and a half storeys –, and for a brahman who has performed the *vājapeya* ritual, whose house may have the same number of storeys.

137. If the *śālā* is said to be one quarter of the *vāstu* in width in all instances, it makes no difference whether the wall is said to be one sixteenth of the *vāstu* in width, or one quarter of the *śālā*.

138. For the parallels in MP and VP, cf. note on 19.22 below.

139. This may seem rather narrow; cf. however the rooms of the '*dviśāla*' from the Sātavāhana or Mahārāṭhī period excavated at Adam in Nagpur Dist., which measure roughly 2.4 x 4.5m, 2.7 x 1m, 2.7 x 2m, 2.2 x 1.9m, and 2 x 1.4m, and the rooms of the '*ekaśāla*' of the same period (~2.2 x 1.8m, ~2.2 x 2m, ~2.2 x 2m, and ~2.2 x 1.3m) given in IA 1990-91:47 sqq.; house complex No. 2 (Kuṣāna to Gupta period) at Śrāvastī (4.55 x 2.65m; 2.03 x 2.65m; 2.9 x 2.65m; 2.4 x 2.35m; 2.5 x 2.35m; 5 x 2.12m; 2.65 x 2.55m; 2.65 x 2.55m; and 3.42 x 3.22m – IA 1995-96:96 sq.); and the rooms of the Kuṣāṇa period uncovered at Muhammadnagar, Gurgaon Dist. (IA 1997/98:45), measuring 1.7 x 1.9m, 1.75 x 1.84 m, and 1.27 x 1.22 m respectively.

140. (Width of the *vāstu* + 70)/35 = width of the *alinda*.

141. According to SAS, the width of the *alinda* comes out at 4, 3.5, 3, 2.5, and 2 cubits (~1.8m, ~1.575m, ~1.35m, ~1.125m, and ~.9m) respectively for the houses of *varṇins*, but cf. note on 19.23; BṛS gives its width as 3 19/24, 3 1/3, 2 5/6, 2 3/4, and 2 1/8 cubits (~1.7m, ~1.5m, ~1.275m, ~1.25m, and ~.95m).

142. As we shall see (note on 24.26-27 below), the rules given in MP and VP seem to be incorrect due to errors in the textual transmission.

143. Cf. KERN (1872:284 fn.3): 'A rough measuring only is intended; [...] the first house of a Brahman has a breadth of 32 cubits. We are directed to take one-fifth of it, but the meaning is, we should roughly take 6; adding 18 to it, we get 24; again adding 24/8 = 3, we get 27, being the number of digits for the width of the door; the height comes to 81.'

144. Cf. KERN (1872:284 fn.3): 'Instead of *dviguṇa* read *triguṇa* [...];' SHUKLA (1958:333): 'Regarding the dimensions, the common rule is that

the height of the door should be twice the breadth. But this, I believe, is too low a height. A height twice the width must make the door too low for daily use unless, of course, the width itself is of a large dimension, say not less that four feet.' While KERN is perfectly justified in rejecting the reading *dviguṇa* in BṛS 52.25, where the relatively small width of the door would yield a height between ~.9m and ~1.0m, SHUKLA seems to have had in mind the doors of urban 20th century mansions, rather than those of ancient or medieval houses.

145. For a ratio approximating 1:3, cf. the doors of the individual cells in early Buddhist cave monasteries (pl.45, 46, 99 in MITRA [2]1980; pl. 6 in DHAVALIKAR 2004). The doors of traditional residential buildings in the towns of the Kāṭhmāṇḍu valley are generally half as wide as they are tall – cf. GUTSCHOW, KÖLVER, and SHRESTHACHARYA (1987:225-227).

146. We must beware of generalising this statement; there seem to be a number of instances where the *śāstra* was composed by the builder himself, who in effect sanctioned or, in MAXWELL's words, 'authorized' his own practical work simply by writing about it in Sanskrit – cf. the *Maṇḍapadruma* of Mahādevasūri (SARMA:1958). These texts can usually be distinguished by exhibiting a rather limited knowledge of Sanskrit on the author's side, as well as an occasionally pronounced contempt for the 'theoreticians' – cf. the second stanza of the Maṇḍapadruma, where the author asserts that 'this art is to be performed by the hands, and it is not at all to be performed by speech' (*iyaṃ hastakriyā śailpī na ca vādakriyā khalu*).

147. The practical applicability as well as the relative complexitiy of the rules regarding the size of the doors, the height of storeys, and the size of the *śālā*s as given in BṛS indeed suggest that they are not the result of idle speculation, but rather of the experience of generations of builders. Similar rules and graded sets of basic dimensions are still used by traditional builders in Nepal – cf. JEST (1991:155). Unfortunately, our assumption about the information transfer from craftsmen to *śāstrin*s raises certain (socio-)linguistic issues – concerning, among other things, the languages involved, and the principles according to which technical terms were rendered in Sanskrit – that we will be unable to address within the scope of this study.

148. Cf. MANKAD (1950:xi sq); PAREEK (2003:16). It is interesting to note that of the material related to residential architecture, AP seems to have borrowed only the rather pedantic exercises in *prastāra*. Either they were all that the compilator had access to, or the chapters describing the component parts of the residential building in more detail (e.g., the 24th and 28th *adhyāyas*) were of no interest to him.

149. Cf. for instance *sūtras* 4 and 35.

150. PINGREE (1981b:139); according to DHAVALE (1968), Varāhamihira is believed to have been born either in the year 427 or 509 of the Śaka era (= 504/505 or 586/587 AD).

151. Cf. PINGREE (1981b:72 fn.36).

152. PINGREE (1981b:69 sqq.).

153. In BHAT's edition, the chapter on *vāstuvidyā* is counted as the 53rd – see above, note 5.

154. Cf. ROCHER (1986:199).

155. Of course, it is also conceivable that the rules of VP regarding the *ekaśāla* were considered to be outside the mainstream of *vāstuvidyā* in his own time, and hence not incorporated into BṛS and MP; the same could be true of VP's treatment of the *dviśāla*, which clearly represents a 'minority opinion.' But if that were the case, one wonders why the text was transmitted at all, and the remarkable degree of congruence between BṛS, MP, and VP would also become rather difficult to account for.

156. VP 02.137 gives the same dimensions that are given in BṛS and MP for the house of the *senāpati*; as no owner for this house is mentioned at all in VP, it seems that one stanza was lost.

157. The text of MP 254.08cd-14ab is corrupt; some of the names given in BṛS, VP, and SAS are missing, and others are given in a disfigured way. Cf. note on 20.28-32 below.

158. There are also some scattered remarks on ritual in the 16th and 31st *adhyāyas*.

159. Another reason for excluding astrological and ritualistic matters was supplied by the secondary aim of this study, viz. to present the technical vocabulary pertaining to the building itself, rather than the astronomical and ritual preliminaries of the building process.

160. Although ŚRK, as indicated by its title, is also conceived as a dictionary of sorts, its purpose is radically different from that of SAS 18: it is designed to describe exhaustively the individual components encountered in the temple architecture of Orissa, and consequently restricts itself to technical terms in actual use. SAS 18, on the other hand, seems to be a much more deliberate collection of definitions and synonyms. In the latter context, one might also consider MM 15.02, which gives the synonyms of *stambha* 'pillar:' *sthāṇuḥ sthūṇaś ca pādaś ca jaṅghā ca caraṇo 'ṅghrikaḥ | stambhaś ca talipaḥ kampaḥ paryāyavacanāni hi ||*

161. No date has been determined for Amarasiṃha, cf. VOGEL (1979:309 sq.); as he is supposed to have been an adherent of the Buddhist faith (loc. cit.), it is unlikely that he lived after Bhoja. Bhaṭṭa Halāyudha, author of ARM, is believed to have been born in the first half of the 10th century; it appears that he spent some time at the court of Bhoja's ancestor Vākpati II.; cf. VOGEL (1979:321). Hemacandra's dates are given as 1088 - 1172/73 (VOGEL 1979:335 sq.).

162. Mention should be made in this context of the two *kośa*s ascribed to Bhoja, viz. *Nāmamālikā* and *Śālihotra*, which latter is a technical lexicon related to *aśvacikitsā*. VOGEL (1979:325) does not believe that the Nāmamālikā could really have been written by Bhoja, and a brief survey of the word index contained in the edition by KULKARNI and GOKHALE will reveal that hardly any of the technical terms of SAS 18 are found in the *Nāmamālikā*. As for the *Śālihotra*, Bhoja's authorship has been rejected by SARMA (1986:49), though not by KULKARNI (1953:xvi sqq.).

163. At the same time, it is interesting to note that the earliest commentator on AK, Kṣīrasvāmin, should agree with SAS 18.02 in the interpretation of the word *śākhānagara/-pura*; his commentary contains a number of quotations from 'Bhoja' or 'Śrībhoja,' though none of them are found in the *puravarga*. VOGEL (1979:314) takes this Bhoja to be identical with the Paramāra king. Cf. also AUFRECHT (1874:103 sqq.).

164. E.g. *pattana* and *puṭabhedana* in SAS 18.05, where *pattana* is interpreted differently than seems to be the case in AK 2.2.01; **kṣauma* and *aṭṭālaka* in 18.53.

165. Despite the partial repetition in this place it is unlikely that 39.18-19 are an interpolation, since the latter stanza contains a direct reference to 39.02-10 (*ete vaiśeṣikāḥ sarve varṇānām anupūrvaśaḥ*).

2. Text, Translation, and Notes

2.1 *adhyāya* 18

18.01:

nagaraṃ mandiraṃ durgaṃ puṣkaraṃ sāmparāyikam |
nivāsaḥ sadanaṃ sadma kṣayaḥ kṣitilayas tathā ||

anuṣṭubh (pathyā)

'A city, a building [or: temple], a fort, a reservoir, a warlike structure; an abode (5 synonyms).'

This stanza is reminiscent of a synonymical dictionary in style, especially the second half, which consists of a list of five synonyms for 'dwelling place, abode;' cf. note on 18.08-09 below. *Puṣkara*, really the blue lotus, is also attested as 'pond, lake' in the lexicons (Cf. pd, q.v.). *Sāmparāyika*, a *vṛddhi*-derivation of *saṃparāya*, 'death; battle' here seems to refer to some building related to battle, thus a kind of fortification; it should be noted, however, that this expression does not occur in SAS 10, where the defences of the city are described in some detail; cf. 1.3.4 above.

There is no occurrence of *laya* in the sense of 'dwelling place, abode' on record, the more usual form being *layana*. The compounded form *kṣitilaya* is particularly noteworthy; it cannot be a *dvandva*-compound, since it does not have a dual ending, nor is it neuter.

18.02:

yatrāste nagare rājā rājadhānīṃ tu tāṃ viduḥ |
śākhānagarasaṃjñāni tato 'nyāni pracakṣate ||

anuṣṭubh (pathyā)

'Where the king resides in a city – that they call *rājadhānī* ; as differing from that (*tato 'nyāni*) one knows those called *śākhānagara* [or: next (*tataḥ*), the other names of the *śākhānagara* are explained].'

The term *rājadhānī* requires some specification: pd gives its meaning as *'Residenz eines Fürsten'*; APTE has 'the king's residence, the capital metropolis, the seat of government'. But either interpretation is ambiguous insofar as the German word *Residenz* can refer both to the buildings and institutions of the court, and to the city where the court is situated. This leads to the question whether *rājadhānī* in this context refers to the royal capital, or to the royal court. As we shall see (18.05ab below), the term *pattana* is defined as a city where the royal assembly is situated (*upasthānaṃ bhaved rājñāṃ yatra tat pattanaṃ viduḥ*) – in effect, the capital; since it is unlikely that *pattana* and *rājadhānī* refer to the same thing, the latter must be taken as referring to the royal residence in the more restricted sense.

As indicated in the translation, the second line of 18.02 strictly speaking allows two interpretations: it either defines *śākhānagara* as that which is not a *rājadhānī*, or it indicates the topic of the following stanza or stanzas; the problem hinges on the interpretation of *tatas*. Since *anyat* in the sense of 'different' requires the ablative, *tato 'nyat* should be taken as a syntactic unit, which makes the former interpretation appear more likely. The term *śākhānagara*, literally 'branch city', and usually given as 'suburb', thus refers either to any type of (large) settlement that is not the royal residence in the more restricted sense, or to the settlement surrounding the residence. The evidence of the other *kośa*s mentioned under 1.8.1 above (henceforth simply referred to as 'the *kośa*s') seems to suggest the latter:

SAS 18.02 has a loose parallel in ARM 2.131, where *rājadhānī* is rather ambiguously glossed as *skandhāvāra* 'royal capital or residence', and *śākhānagara* is defined as *upanagara*, which is usually given as 'suburb'; note, however, the fact that the juxtaposition of *rājadhānī* and *śākhānagara* implies a complementary relationship similar to that met with in SAS 18.02:

> *skandhāvāra iti prājñai rājadhānī nigadyate |*
> *śākhānagaram ākhyātaṃ tathopanagaraṃ budhaiḥ ||*

'The capital is called 'royal headquarters' by the learned; and the *upanagara* is called *śākhānagara* by the experts.'

Cf. also the definition of AK 2.2.1-2ab, where *śākhānagara* is glossed as *anyat* [...] *yan mūlanagarāt puram* 'a city that is different from the *mūlanagara*:'

> *pūḥ strī purīnagaryau vā pattanaṃ puṭabhedanam |*
> *sthānīyaṃ nigamo 'nyat tu yan mūlanagarāt puram ||*
> *tac chākhānagaraṃ veśo veśyājanasamāśrayaḥ |*

Cf. Kṣīrasvāmin's commentary (composed in the first half of the 12th century, cf. VOGEL 1979:313 sq.):

> *mūlanagaraṃ rājadhānī tato 'nyat samudāyasthānaṃ (śākhānagaraṃ) śākhety upāṅgopa-lakṣaṇam |*

'*Mūlanagara* [is synonymous with] *rājadhānī*; differing from that is a 'place of a multitude' (*śākhānagara*); *śākhā* indicates a subdivision.'

Cf. also ACM 972cd-972, where *śākhāpura* is glossed as *upapura*:

> *nagarī pūḥ purī draṅgaḥ pattanaṃ puṭabhedanam ||*
> *niveśanam adhiṣṭhānaṃ sthānīyaṃ nigamo 'pi ca |*
> *śākhāpuraṃ tūpapuraṃ kheṭaḥ purārdhavistaraḥ ||*

18.03:

śākhānagaram evāhuḥ karvaṭaṃ nagaropamam |
ūnaṃ karvaṭam eveha guṇair nigama ucyate ||

anuṣṭubh (pathyā)

'*Śākhānagara* they call a *karvaṭa* [that is] similar to a city; a *karvaṭa* lacking [these urban] qualities is here called *nigama*.'

If we take this stanza literally, then the difference between *karvaṭa* and *nigama*, both broadly meaning 'market town,' would lie not so much in their size as in their degree of urbanization; but the intended meaning is probably simply that a *nigama* is smaller than a *karvaṭa*.

In KA 2.1.4 a *kārvaṭika* is defined as the regional headquarters of two hundred villages, and thus smaller than a *droṇamukha*-town (four hundred villages) and a *sthānīya*, which is the centrale for a region with eight hundred villages (*aṣṭaśatagrāmyā madhye sthānīyaṃ, catuḥśātagrāmyā droṇamukhaṃ, dviśatgrāmyāḥ kārvaṭikaṃ* [...]). The author of KSṬ 1.4.3 follows the same classification (***karvaṭaṃ*** *dviśatagrāmīmadhye* | [...] *catuḥśatagrāmīmadhye droṇamukhaṃ nāma karvaṭān mahad bhavati* | Note that *droṇamukha* does not occur in KS 1.4.3, which suggests some familiarity with KA on the commentator's part).

In AK 2.2.1 (quoted in the preceding note) *nigama* is mentioned together with another technical term of KA, viz. *sthānīya*, which is not found in SAS.

Cf. also note on 18.05 below.

18.04:

grāmaḥ syān nigamād ūno grāmakalpo gṛhas tv asau |
gokulāvāsam icchanti goṣṭham alpaṃ tu goṣṭhakam ||

b) *grāmakalpagṛhas* (Kha Da)
anuṣṭubh (pathyā)

'A village shall be [that which is] smaller than a *nigama*, that [which is a] house, though, [shall be] similar to a village [but smaller]; the abode of a cattle-herd [or: the place where the dwellings of cowherders is situated] they call a *goṣṭha*, [if it is] small, though, a *goṣṭhaka*.'

A settlement that is smaller than a small market town is thus a village; the relationship between *grāma* and *gṛha*, however, is not quite clear. As final member of a compound, *kalpa-* usually means 'having the shape or nature of, similar to', according to APTE 'denoting similarity with a degree of inferiority' (s.v. *kalpaḥ*). Accordingly, SHUKLA ([2]2003:99) has translated the first half of this stanza as 'smaller than a *nigama* is a *grāma*, smaller than a *grāma* is a *gr̥ha (**nigama** se kam grāma, **grāma** se kam **gr̥ha** hotā hai)*'.

Note also that this is the only time that *gr̥ha* occurs in the masculine nominative in SAS, all other occurrences being either neuter nominative or inflected cases common to both genders, including eleven occurrences in the 18th *adhyāya*. – Cf. 1.3.1.1.3.

– The second line obviously refers to a herders' camp.

18.05:

upasthānaṃ bhaved rājñāṃ yatra tat pattanaṃ viduḥ |
bahusphītavaṇigyuktaṃ tad uktaṃ puṭabhedanam ||

d) *puṭabhedakam* (Ka)
anuṣṭubh (pathyā)

'Where there may be the assembly of [or: attendance on] kings that they know as *pattana*; [if it is] endowed with many wealthy merchants, it is called *puṭabhedanam.*'

In 18.21, *upasthāna* is defined as a sort of assembly hall (*gr̥he mahājanasthānaṃ* [...] *upasthānaṃ tad atrāhuḥ* [...]); here, it seems to refer to the royal court. This assumption is corroborated by KSṬ 1.4.3: ***pattanaṃ** yatra rājadhānī sthitā:* 'a *pattana* [is a city] where the *rājadhānī* is situated'. Since KSṬ seems to have the same basic concept of *pattana*, *upasthāna* can safely be taken as a synonym for *rājadhānī* in our context. What is puzzling, though, is the plural genitive *rājñāṃ*; an assembly of kings is arguably something different from a royal assembly. Perhaps one should emend *rājñaḥ*?

The accounts of *pattana* contained in KA, however, do not tally with the meaning attributed to that term in SAS and KSṬ; cf. KA 2.6.3:

> *sītā bhāgo baliḥ karo vaṇik nadīpālas taro nāvaḥ **pattanaṃ** vivītaṃ vartanī rajjuś corarajjuś ca rāṣṭram |*

'Agricultural produce, share, tribute, tax, the trader, the river-guard, the ferry, ships, **the port**, pastures, road-cess, land-survey and thief-catching: these constitute 'country' [as a source of revenue, cf. KA 2.6.1];'

KA 2.28.4:

> ***pattanā****nuvṛttaṃ śulbabhāgaṃ vaṇijo dadyuḥ, yātrāvetanaṃ rājanau-bhiḥ saṃpatantaḥ* |

'Traders shall pay a part (of the goods) as duty according as it may be current at **the ports**, those travelling by the king's ships (shall pay) hire for the voyage;'

and KA 2.28.7:

> ***pattanā****dhyakṣanibaddhaṃ paṇya****pattana****cāritraṃ nāvadhya-kṣaḥ pālayet* |

'The Controller of Shipping shall observe the regulations in **a port town** as fixed by the Commissioner **of Ports**.' [All tr. KANGLE, my emphases]

Obviously, the translation 'city of the royal residence' for *pattana* would not fit here.

For the etymology of *puṭabhedana*, which occurs frequently as an attribute to *sthānīya* in KA, cf. KÖLVER (1985): The breaking (*bhedana*) of the seals on the parcels (*puṭa*) was performed by the customs officer, with the goods being put up for sale immediately after and under his supervision. The original meaning seems to have got lost in the course of time and to have been incorporated into the literary cliché of the prosperous city.

It is perhaps not without significance that in the *kośas*, *pattana* and *puṭabhedana* are usually mentioned in the same breath; cf. AK 2.2.1 and ACM 972cd-972 quoted in the note on 18.02 above. Cf. also ARM 2.130:

> *pattanaṃ syād adhiṣṭhānaṃ nigamaḥ puṭabhedanam* |
> *nagaraṃ nagarī draṅgaḥ sthānīyaṃ pūḥ purī puram* ||

Note that here, too, *pattana* is defined as [city of] the royal residence (*adhiṣṭhāna*), as well as market town (*nigama*), and *puṭabhedana*.

18.06:
vidhāya kuṭikā yatra patraśākhātṛṇopalaiḥ |
pulindāḥ kurvate vāsaṃ pallī svalpā tu pallikā ||
anuṣṭubh (pathyā)

'Where the *pulindas* take their abode after having erected huts from leaves, branches, reeds, and stone – [that is called] *pallī*, [if it is] small, though, *pallikā*.'

18.07:
nagaraṃ varjayitvānyat sarvaṃ janapadaḥ smṛtaḥ |
nagareṇa samaṃ kṛtsnaṃ rāṣṭraṃ deśo 'tha maṇḍalam ||
anuṣṭubh (pathyā)

'Leaving aside the city, the whole rest [of the country] is called *janapada*; the entire [country] including the city is called *rāṣṭra*, *deśa*, and *maṇḍala*.'

While *janapada* is a rather ambiguous term in its historical vicissitudes, referring in turn to the tribe (or citizenry) and the tribal (or national) territory (cf. RAU 1957:65f.), the meaning intended here is obviously that of 'countryside' as opposed to 'urban centre' – cf. SCHARFE (1968:142).

As for *rāṣṭra* and *maṇḍala*, it is obvious that they are not used here in the technical meaning that they have in KA (cf. SCHARFE 1968:122-127, 142f.).

18.08-09:
āvāsaḥ sadanaṃ sadma niketo mandiraṃ matam |
saṃsthānaṃ nidhanaṃ dhiṣṇyaṃ bhavanaṃ vasatiḥ kṣayaḥ || 08 ||
anuṣṭubh (pathyā)

agāraṃ saṃśrayo nīḍaṃ gehaṃ śaraṇam ālayaḥ |
nilayo layanaṃ veśma gṛham okaḥ pratiśrayaḥ || 09 ||
anuṣṭubh (pathyā)

08.-09. 'An abode (24 synonyms).'

These stanzas mark a change of subject; stanzas 18.02-07 were mainly concerned with conglomerations of settlements and their classification, whereas 18.08-58 contain descriptions and classifications of individual buildings and their components, as well as the city defences.

SAS 18.01cd, 08-09 have a loose parallel in AK 2.2.04cd-06ab:

> *gṛhaṃ gehodavasitaṃ veśma sadma niketanam* || 04 ||
> *niśāntavastyasadanaṃ bhavanāgāramandiram* |
> *gṛhāḥ puṃsi ca bhūmny eva nikāyyanilayālayāḥ* || 05 ||
> *vāsaḥ kuṭī dvayōḥ śālā sabhā saṃjavanaṃ tv idam* |

Cf. also ACM 989cd-991:

> *gṛhaṃ veśma niketanam* || 989 ||
> *mandiraṃ sadanaṃ sadma nikāyyo bhavanaṃ kuṭaḥ* |
> *ālayo nilayaḥ śālā sabhedavasitaṃ kulam* || 990 ||
> *dhiṣṇyam āvasathaḥ sthānaṃ pastyaṃ saṃstyāya āśrayaḥ* |
> *oko nivāsa āvāso vasatiḥ śaraṇaṃ kṣayaḥ* || 991 ||

Cf. also ARM 2.136:

> *āvāsāvasathaṃ gṛhaṃ ca bhavanaṃ sthānaṃ niśāntaṃ kulaṃ*
> *saṃstyāyo nilayo nikāyyam uṭajaṃ gehaṃ kuṭaṃ mandiram* |
> *dhiṣṇyaṃ dhāma niketanaṃ ca sadanaṃ pastyaṃ ca vāstu kṣayaḥ* |
> *śālā veśma niveśanodavasite prokte ca sadmaukasī* ||

– Note that 18.01, 08-09 do not give a complete list of the synonyms for 'abode' used throughout the text; among the terms missing here are *dhāman* (19.21c) and *niveśa* (19.25c).

18.10:
gṛhasyoparibhūmir yā harmyaṃ tat parikīrtitam |
tasyārohaṇamārgo yaḥ sopānaṃ tat pracakṣate ||
anuṣṭubh (pathyā)

'That which is the upper storey of a house is known as *harmya*; the way leading up to it one knows as *sopāna*.'

There is a considerable degree of confusion concerning the precise meaning of the word *harmya*; according to pd, it is *'ein festes Gebäude: Burg, Schloss, Palast, Herrenhaus, Wohnhaus, Vorrathshaus; Gefängniss'*. The meaning intended here pd assigns to its next entry, *harmyatala*.

The etymology of *harmya* is unclear (cf. MAYRHOFER 1956 s.v. *harmyá*), although ELIZARENKOVA (1992) has shown that its original meaning was probably 'safe place, shelter;' throughout the text of SAS it is only used in the sense of 'upper storey, rooftop terrace'. From a similar meaning, the secondary meaning 'large building' seems to have been derived by synecdoche: '[a building with an] upper storey'. Cf. PED s.v. *hammiya*: 'customarily given as "a long, storied mansion which has an upper chamber placed on the top" [...] *-gabbha* a chamber on the upper storey'; and the top part of a Buddhist *stūpa*, which is usually referred to as *harmikā* (cf. GUPTA 2002:8).

The *kośa*s give *harmya* as 'house of the rich' (AK 2.2.09: *harmyādi dhanināṃ vāsaḥ*; ACM993: *harmyaṃ tu dhaninām gṛham*; ARM 2.138: *dhanavatāṃ harmyam*).

18.11:
kāṣṭhakair yatra racitaṃ sthūṇayor adhirohaṇam |
sā niḥśreṇir iti proktā sopānair vipulaiḥ padaiḥ ||
a) *koṣṭhakair* (Ka)
anuṣṭubh (na-vipulā)

'That ascent which is made of planks and two posts is called *niḥśreṇi*; with stairways [having] broad *padas* [?].'

The kind of ascent described here is obviously a ladder; pd has *niḥśreṇi* as a variant of *niśreṇi*, 'Stiege, Leiter'. The last quarter of this stanza is difficult to construe; it is unlikely that the three instrumentals plural refer to objects that a *niḥśreṇi* is made of, as *sopāna* is a staircase in its own right, and *pada* is not attested as a building element (step?). Perhaps one should emend **sopānaṃ** *vipulaiḥ padaiḥ* 'with broad steps [?] [it is called] *sopāna*.'

18.12:

smr̥taḥ kāṣṭhaviṭaṅko 'sau yat kāṣṭhaiḥ saṃvr̥taṃ gr̥ham |
sudhāliptatalaṃ harmyaṃ saudhaṃ syāt kuṭṭimaṃ ca tat ||
anuṣṭubh (pathyā)

'That house is called *kāṣṭhaviṭaṅka* that is covered with planks; a [house with a] *harmya* whose [upper] floor is coated with lime shall be a *saudha*, and it [shall be] a *kuṭṭima*.'

The literal meaning of *kāṣṭhaviṭaṅka* is '[having a] wooden crown or ridge pole'; in the second half of the stanza it is not entirely clear whether *harmya* refers to the uppermost storey (as in 18.10), or to a building having an upper storey (cf. discussion of the etymology of *harmya* under 18.10). Perhaps the ambiguity is intended, since *harmya* is glossed both as *saudha* and *kuṭṭima*, the former being given in pd as *'ein mit stucco überzogenes Haus, das Haus eines vornehmen Herrn, Palast'*, while the latter usually means 'floor coated with clay or lime'. Both terms occur in ACM 992, where *kuṭṭima* is glossed as 'rammed earth' (*baddhabhūḥ*), and *saudha* as 'royal dwelling' (*nr̥pamandiram* – cf. also AK 2.2.10a *saudho 'strī rājasadanam*); and in ARM 2.139, where *saudha* is given as 'lime-coated [house] (*sudhādhavalitam*), and *kuṭṭima* as 'rammed earth' (*baddhabhūmikam*).

Note the slight difference between the etymology of *saudha*, a *vr̥ddhi*-derivation from *sudhā*, 'lime', suggested in pd (cf. also Kṣīrasvāmin with reference to AK 2.2.10: *sudhāśubhraṃ saudham*) and that apparently underlying 18.12: whereas according to the former it is the entire mansion that is coated with lime (*'stucco'*), in the latter instance it is only the *tala* of the *harmya*, in effect the rooftop terrace, that is said to be coated. The difference between a house of the *kāṣṭhaviṭaṅka*-type and a *saudha*, then, is the fact that the former has a gabled roof, whereas the latter has a level roof used as a terrace.

But this alternative interpretation does not exclude the derived meaning given in pd, and encountered frequently in *kāvya* literature, viz. *'das Haus eines vornehmen Herrn, Palast'*; unless where timber is a rare commodity, a gabled house is arguably cheaper than a house with a rooftop terrace, at least in maintenance if not in construction. Even in a region with comparatively scarce precipitation such as the Manang valley in Northern Nepal, flat roofs may need to be replaced every thirteen years, cf. MARÉCHAUX (1991:211). One can imagine that in Western India, a region with a much fiercer monsoon rainfall, the lifespan of a flat roof would be considerably shorter.

18.13:
***varṣābhayena yā channā tālaśākadalādibhiḥ* |**
***smr̥tābhiguptir antasthā sarvopari gr̥hasya sā* ||**

b) *tālaśāla°* (Ka)

anuṣṭubh (pathyā)

'That [area] at the very top end of the house which is covered with leaves etc. of *Tectona grandis* Linn. and *Borassus flabellifer* Linn. for fear of the rains – that is called *abhigupti*.'

The idea is obviously that of a shed-like structure on the rooftop terrace put up for the rainy season. The leaves of both *Tectona grandis* Linn. and *Borassus flabellifer* Linn. – the teak tree and the palmyra palm respectively – are well suited for the purpose; the broadly elliptical or obvoate leaves of the former are 30-60 cm in length and 20-30 cm wide, and the fan-shaped leaves of the latter are 0.9-1.4 m in diameter (SAHNI 1998:137, 182-183). Alternatively, this stanza might be considered as referring to the kind of rooftop pavillion frequently encountered in the reliefs of Bharhut and Sanchi called *candraśālā* elsewhere in *kāvya* and *vāstu* texts alike (e.g., ŚMK pp. 2ff.; MP 264.38ff; but cf. COOMARASWAMY 1928:253 sq.), if one takes into consideration the fact that the latter term is conspicuously absent from the SAS. In the *kośa*s, it indeed seems to refer to a room on top of the roof, cf. ACM 995d (*candraśālā śirogr̥ham*), ARM 02.149d (*candraśālā śirogr̥ham*); it is missing in AK.

18.14:
vātāyanaṃ tu bhittīnām avalokanam ucyate |
laghur vātayano yaḥ syād avalokanakaṃ hi tat ||

c) *vātāyano* (Śu)
anuṣṭubh (pathyā)

'A *vātāyana* of the walls is called *avalokana*; that which may be a small *vātāyana* – that is an *avalokanaka*.'

The word *vātāyana* is rather vague in meaning; pd gives *'Luftloch, ein rundes Fenster; überh. ein Ort im Hause, an dem man frische Luft geniesst: Balcon, Erker, Söller'*. The fact that its situation with regard to the walls is expressly mentioned here seems to suggest the former. ACHARYA (1946a:453) records the same variance. At first glance, the etymology (and thus the range of meaning) seems clear: *vāta-āyana*, 'the coming of wind, hence: an aperture through which fresh air circulates'. The question is, however, whether the form *vātayana* in 18.14c is merely a printing error – no variant readings other than SHUKLA's tacit correction are recorded – or actually a variant of the more usual *vātāyana*, albeit one for which the etymology proposed above cannot apply, instead of which one might consider *vātayana* to be the *nomen actionis* of the denominative verb *vātayati*, 'to fan'.

A third variant is also on record: *vātayāna*, e.g. in HJM 12.54a (but *vātāyana* in HJM 12.34+, 48c, 53a). This could be explained as an analogous formation of *vātāyana*: *vāta-yāna*, 'the going, or passage, of wind'.

In the *kośa*s, *vātāyana* is glossed as *gavākṣa* 'round window' (or 'lattice window' according to SAS 18.34); cf. AK 2.2.09a; ACM 1012cd and ARM 02.149ab, where *jāla/-ka* 'lattice window' is also mentioned. Cf. also note on 18.34 below.

18.15:

harmyasya madhye yac chidraṃ sa *ulloka iti smṛtaḥ |
harmyaprākārakaḥ sa syāt kaṇṭhā harmyatalasya yā ||

b) *sa u loka* (Śa), *sa uloka* (Śu); c) *harmyaḥ* (Kha Da). d) *kaṇṭho* (Ka); *yaḥ* (Ka)
anuṣṭubh (ma-vipulā)

'The opening in the middle of the *harmya* is known as **ulloka*; that which is the *kaṇṭhā* of the *harmya*-level – that shall be the *harmyaprākāraḥ*.'

While **ulloka* is not recorded in the dictionaries consulted, it is nevertheless easy to construe: a sort of skylight, in the case of a *catuḥśāla* probably simply the opening above the courtyard. The reading in SHASTRI's edition, which seems to represent the reading of the mss, might be due to a lost half-*akṣara* in the archetype, in which case **ulloka* would be the restored original reading. SHUKLA's interpretation (1958:341), '[a] special characteristic of the houses those days was that every roof of every room was provided with a hole (chidra) and it was called Ulūka,' is almost certainly wrong.

Is *kaṇṭhā* feminine singular or masculine plural, with the *visarga* dropped before initial *h*? There seems to have been some confusion even among the mss ; three of them have the feminine sg. relative pronoun *yā*, and the fourth has the masculine sg. *yaḥ*. One should consider the possibility that these readings go back to **yāḥ*. A feminine **kaṇṭhā* is not recorded elsewhere, and according to ACHARYA (1946a:97), a *kaṇṭha* is 'a quadrangular moulding, sometimes square and sometimes rectangular.' On the other hand, 18.26 clearly reads *kaṇṭhā*, in the light of which the reading *yā* has been adopted here. 18.42, however, has the masculine singular, as do 28.26d, 28.39b, and 28.44c, where *kaṇṭha* indeed seems to refer to some kind of moulding.

In 18.15, on the other hand, *kaṇṭhā* obviously refers to some sort of parapet of the rooftop terrace; the literal meaning of *harmyaprākāra(-ka)* is 'wall or parapet of the upper storey or rooftop level'. Cf. discussion under 1.3.1.1.2.

18.16:

vitardikāṣṭhamālā syāt sarvataś chadamūlagā |
tatstambheṣu mr̥gā ye tu te syur īhāmr̥gā iti ||

a) *vitardikāṣṭamālā* (Śu); b) *cheda*° (Kha Da Śu)
anuṣṭubh (pathyā)

'The circle of timbers of the *vitardi* shall be at the base of the ceiling everywhere; the animals on its pillars shall be *īhāmr̥gas*.'

In pd, *vitardi* or *vitardikā* is given as *'eine Terrasse im Hofe eines Hauses zum Aufenthalt und Lustwandeln*;' cf. also SCHLINGLOFF 1969:26 fn.2. In the *kośa*s (AK 02.02.16b; ACM 1004a; ARM 02.144d), *vitardi* is invariably glossed as *vedikā* or, in ACM, as *vedī*; Kṣīrasvāmin describes it as 'a square [piece of] ground for resting, surrounded by timbers; where pain ceases – [that is called] *vitardi* (*dārupariṣkr̥tā caturasrā viśrāntibhūḥ, vigataṃ tardanaṃ* *yatreti vitardiḥ*).' The compound in 18.16a obviously refers to the architrave running around the inner side of the **ulloka* in a *catuḥ-śāla* (cf. 18.15). SHUKLA's tacit emendation yields the following translation ([2]2003:100): 'the *vitardikā* is said to be of eight pillars, and it is *chedamūlagā* [?] on all sides (*āṭh khamboṃ kī* ***vitardikā*** *kahlātī hai, vah sab taraf se chedamūlagā hotī hai*).'

According to a footnote by AGRAWALA, SASTRI had originally adopted the reading of Kha Da *cheda*°; in fact, *chada* and *cheda* alternate rather freely, *chada* occurring in 18.47d (all mss), and *cheda* in 18.17d, 28.29a, and 28.30c (all mss). The problem with the latter variant is that it is not recorded in this sense in any of the dictionaries consulted; it seems to be derived from *chid* 'cut, sever'. It is hard to see how it could refer to the roof or ceiling.

The term *īhāmr̥ga* in this context is remarkable; its primary meaning according to pd is 'wolf', but it can also apply to a sort of hybrid or composite figure; cf. GUPTA (2002:47):

> In Indian art we get *īhāmr̥gas* in the form of winged lions, beaked lions, horned lions, winged bulls, bull with elephant face, crocodile with fish-tail, sea-monsters etc., from the Śuṅga-Sātavāhana-Bactrian Period itself, starting in the second century BC. Such fabulous figures were earlier found in the Greek, Persian and Assyrian art from the seventh-sixth century BC. As the decorative elements of pillars, copings, beams, etc., we find them repeatedly occurring all the time in the Śaiva, Vaiṣṇava, Bauddha and Jain contexts.

PAREEK (2002:11) quotes two Jaina scriptures, viz. *Rāyapa-senīya* and *Bhagavatīsūtra* as containing a refernce to *īhāmr̥ga* as part of a temple structure:

> According to the common usage in canonical works, there is a stereotyped *varṇaka* (description) on the *caitya* [...] . The *varṇaka* contains a number of attributes of the *caityas*, some of which refer to certain component parts of the temple, such as *Chatta, Vedikā, Toraṇa, Stambha, Śālabhanjikā, Ihāmr̥ga, Vyāla, Kalaśa* etc.

While I have not been able to consult the former text, BhS 11.11.138 clearly refers to the ornaments applied to a curtain in the royal palace, rather than a component part of the temple:

> [...] *rayāvettā appaṇo adūrasāmaṃte nāṇāmaṇirayaṇamaṃḍiyaṃ ahiyapecchaṇijjaṃ mahagghavarapaṭṭaṇuggayaṃ saṇhapaṭṭabhattisayacittatāṇaṃ īhāmiyaüsabhaturaganaramagaravihagavālagakiṇṇararurusarabhacamarakuṃjaravaṇalayapaümalayabhatticittaṃ abbhiṃtariyaṃ javaṇiyaṃ aṃchāvei* [...]

'After he had ordered [the eight golden seats] to be prepared he drew an inner curtain in his vicinity, [that was] adorned with manifold gems and dyes, extremely beautiful to observe, costly, produced in the foremost trading centre, [decorated] with hundreds of pictures woven in delicate fabrics, adorned with *īhāmr̥gas*, bulls, horses, men, *makaras*, birds, snakes, *kinnaras*, *rurus*, *śarabhas*, *camaras*, elephants, creepers, and louts-creepers.'

From the context it is impossible to decide whether *īhāmr̥ga* refers to any mythical creatures or simply to wolves; there is no obvious grouping together of the unequivocally mythological beings (*makara, kinnara*, and *śarabha*) and the more 'worldly' creatures within the compound. In any case, it is quite clear that *īhāmr̥ga* refers to a decorative, rather than a structural element.

18.17:
niryūho harmyadeśād yaḥ kāṣṭhānām upanirgamaḥ |
valīkam iti vijñeyaṃ kāṣṭhaṃ chedād vinirgatam ||

ab) °*deśāgrakāṣṭhā*°
anuṣṭubh (pathyā)

'*Niryūha* is the protrusion of the timbers from the area of the upper storey; *valīka* is called the timber protruding from the roof.'

The range of meaning of *niryūha* is rather wide; according to ACHARYA (1946a:283) it can be '[a] kind of turret-like ornament on columns or gates[;] a pinnacle, a turret; a chaplet, a crest, a head ornament, the crest of a helmet; a peg or bracket projecting from a wall to hang or place anything upon [...] ; wood placed in a wall for doves to build their nest upon; a door, a gate'. I would argue that in our text it simply refers to the projection of the joists on the outside of the wall (which can be observed in virtually all buildings depicted in the early Buddhist reliefs).

Valīka, on the other hand, is given in pd as *'ein vorspringendes Stroh- oder Schilfdach'*. The *kośa*s have it as 'eaves' (AK 02.02.14c *valīkanīdhre*; ACM 1011a *nīvraṃ valīkaṃ tatprānta*, with reference to the roof; ARM 02.148 *nīvraṃ valīkaṃ paṭalāntam āhuḥ*). Kṣīrasvāmin explains it in the following manner:

> *chādanānto valīkākhyaḥ, valati saṃvṛṇotīti, kuḍyād bahir vīthī yena cchādyate* |

'The edge of the roof is called *valīka*, it conceals, [i.e.] it covers; [it is that] by which the *vīthī* outside the walls is covered.'

For *vīthī/vīthikā*, cf. notes on 18.40 and 20.08-10 below. – SASTRI gives the variant without reference to a ms.

18.18-19:

channaiś caturbhiḥ pārśvair yat tac catuḥśālam ucyate |
tribhis triśālaṃ tat prāhur dvābhyāṃ tat syād dviśālakam || **18** ||
anuṣṭubh (ma-vipulā)

ekaśālakam ekena cchannena gṛham ucyate |
gṛham ekaṃ tu yac channaṃ sarvaṃ śāleti sā smṛtā || **19** ||
d) *sarvaśāleti* (Ka)
anuṣṭubh (pathyā)

18. 'That [building] which has four covered sides is called *catuḥśāla*; [if it is endowed] with three [covered sides] they call it *triśāla*, [if it is endowed] with two [covered sides] it shall be a *dviśālaka*.

19. A house with one covered [side] is called *ekaśālaka*; one house that is covered entirely is known as *śālā*.'

For a brief discussion of the concept introduced here cf. 1.5.6. *Eka-, dvi-, tri-*, and *catuḥśāla* are always defined with regard to the courtyard around which they are constructed. Seen from this angle, an *ekaśāla* is not so much a house with a courtyard in front, but rather a courtyard which is built up on one side only. That is precisely the difference between *ekaśāla* and *śālā*: the latter is simply a hut without the courtyard, with the *śālā* occupying the entire plot.

Of the five houses described in these stanzas, only one, viz. *catuḥśāla*, is found in the other *kośa*s, where it is invariably glossed as *saṃjavanam* – cf. AK 2.2.06bc; ACM 992c; ARM 02.137d.

18.20:

śālānāṃ yat punar madhyaṃ vāpī puṣkariṇī ca sā |
saṃchannā sāpi yasya syāt tad garbhagṛham ucyate ||

c) *cāpi* (Ka Kha Ga Da)
anuṣṭubh (pathyā)

'That however which is the middle of the *śālā*s – that is [called] *vāpī* and *puṣkariṇī* ; where that is covered [with a roof] – that is called *garbhagṛha*.'

The idea is obviously that of a well in the middle of the central courtyard. The second half, however, is in apparent contradiction to 18.27, where *garbhagṛha* is defined as that part of the plot that is not covered by *śālā* and *alinda*, i.e. the entire inner courtyard; no mention is made of either well or roofing. The *kośa*s seem to take *garbhagṛha*/*garbhāgāra* as 'sleeping chamber' (AK 02.02.08c: *garbhāgāraṃ vāsagṛham*; ACM 995ab: *garbhāgāre 'pavarako vāsaukaḥ śayanāspadam*; ARM 02.137c: *pavarakaṃ garbhagṛham*).

18.21:

gṛhe mahājanasthānaṃ trikuḍyaṃ yat prakalpitam |
upasthānaṃ tad atrāhuḥ syāc copasthānakaṃ laghu ||
anuṣṭubh (pathyā)

'A place for a multitude of people in a house, that is made with three walls – that they call here *upasthāna*, and [if it is] small, it shall be an *upasthānaka*.'

Trikuḍya seems to indicate that this assembly or reception room (cf. 18.05) is supposed to be open on one side; nothing is said about its exact position within the dwelling; it is not mentioned in MS or MM either. In 18.26, however, the *koṣṭhaka*s 'rooms' are said to be the aggregate of the *upasthānaka* and the *apavaraka*s 'inner apartments or sleeping chambers' (cf. note on 18.26 below); *upasthāna/-ka* thus seems to be a functional rather than a structural designation for those rooms that are not sleeping, i.e. private, apartments. For *apavaraka* in the *kośa*s, cf. preceding note.

18.22-23:

prāsādas tu sa eva syād alpā prāsādikā smṛtā |
dīrghaprāsādikā yāsau valabhīty abhidhīyate || 22 ||
anuṣṭubh (pathyā)

śālāgre valabhī yā syād alindeti vadanti tām |
śālāṃ vinā tu valabhī valabheti nigadyate || 23 ||
d) *valabhyeti vidhīyate* (Kha Da)
anuṣṭubh (na-vipulā)

22. 'That, however, shall be a *prāsāda*, [if it is] small, [it is] known as *prāsādikā*; that which is a long *prāsāda* – that is called *valabhī*.

23. The *valabhī* that may be situated in front of the house – that they call *alindā*; but without a *śālā* a *valabhī* is called *valabhā*.'

From the context it is clear that *prāsāda* here cannot refer to a temple, much less to a palace, since *prāsāda* is never used in this sense in SAS (cf. p.65, note 13 above). But what precisely is the context? It is difficult to connect this stanza with the preceding one, but the particle *tu* indicates some sort of opposition to a previous statement – unless, of course, it were used simply as a *pāda-pūraṇa*; in that case, *prāsāda* would refer to *upasthāna* in the preceding stanza.

In order to determine the precise meaning of *prāsāda*, it may be helpful to quote the entry in pd *in extenso*: '*1) ein erhöhter Platz zum Sitzen oder Zuschauen* [...] ; *Thurm, der oberste Stock eines hohen Gebäudes* [...] – *2) ein auf hohem Fundamente ruhendes Gebäude, Palast, Tempel* [...] .' As indicated by his etymological note on *prāsāda* '*Palast,Tempel*,' BÖHTLINGK seems to have supposed *prāsāda* to be derived from *sad* with the prefix *pra-* (with *vr̥ddhi*) or **prā* 'to raise, elevate'. As against this, SHUKLA quotes the popular etymology *prāsāda* < *prasāda* (1958:400); this would hardly fit the basic meaning given in pd, nor the meaning obviously intended in the stanza under discussion. Note also that *prāsāda* is frequently compounded with °*tala*, °*prastara*, and °*pr̥ṣṭha* to yield the meaning 'surface or flat roof of a palace', 'flat roof of a house', and 'balcony on the top of a palace' (APTE s.v. *prāsāda*); since there is no record of **gr̥hatala*, **gr̥haprastara*, or **gr̥ha-pr̥ṣṭha*, it seems that *prāsāda* actually carries the connotation 'high, elevated' suggested by BÖHTLINGK.

Note that the *kośa*s gloss *prāsāda* as 'house of a deity or king' (AK 02.02.09d: *prāsādo devabhūbhujām*; ACM 993c: *prāsādo devabhūpānām*); ARM 2.138ab is more specific with regard to the building material:

gr̥ham iṣṭakādiracitaṃ prāsādo devatānarendrāṇām |

'A house made of bricks etc. [is called] *prāsāda*, [it is] for deities and kings.'

For *valabhī*, pd has '*First, Söller, Zinne eines Hauses*;' the same basic meaning is given by APTE (s.v. *valabhī*) and TURNER (s.v. *vaḍabhi-*). The latter, however, also gives the meaning of Pkt *vadahī*/*valahi* as 'roof-ridge, thatch, veranda.'

The *kośa*s consider *valabhī* to be a type of roof consisting of *gopānasī*s, 'bent timbers' – apparently the rafters of a compass roof, which latter term seems to be the proper meaning of *valabhī* (AK 02.02.15ab *gopānasī tu valabhīchādane vakradāruṇi*; ACM 1009ab *gopānasī tu valabhīchādane vakradāruṇi*; ARM 02.148ab *āchādanaṃ syād valabhī gr̥hāṇāṃ gopānasī dāru ca vakrasaṃstham*).

If we accept the meaning of *valabhī* given in the *kośa*s, then the gloss *dīrghaprāsādikā* becomes rather difficult to understand, as it rather seems to suggest a kind of platform on the rooftop, i.e. a balcony. Either way, the second half of this stanza is rather puzzling; *valabhā* is a *hapax legomenon*. Also, both a verandah and a roof without a building require a certain stretch of the imagination; perhaps the ambiguity of *valabhī* 'rooftop/verandah' is intended rather than accidental, in which case *valabhā* could refer to some kind of open pavilion-like structure – with a roof, as it were, but no walls.

18.24:

alpālpās tu catuṣkuḍyā ye te 'pavarakā matāḥ |
gr̥he cābhyantarasthānaṃ śuddhānta iti kīrtyate ||

c) °*antare* (Ka)

anuṣṭubh (pathyā)

'Those which are very very small [and are made with] four walls – those are known as *apavaraka*; the innermost place in a house is known as *śuddhānta*.'

APTE gives the meaning 'inner apartment' for *apavaraka*, pd has 'Schlafgemach'; the special mention of the fact that an *apava-*

raka is supposed to have four walls suggests an opposition to *upasthāna* from 18.21, as is also the case in 18.26 below. For *apavaraka* in the *kośa*s, cf. note on 18.20 above.

The conventional meaning assigned to *śuddhānta* is 'female apartments'; as the innermost place in a *catuḥśāla* would strictly speaking be the courtyard, *abhyantara-* seems to be used in a figurative sense: the innermost, i.e. most private, best concealed part of the house.

18.25:

pratolīṃ tāṃ vidur lokaḥ suraṅgām iva yāṃ vaset |
sā kakṣety uditā tajjñair yad avasthāntaraṃ gṛhe ||

ab) *pratolīnāṃ vidur loke suraṅgam* (Da)
anuṣṭubh (pathyā)

'That they call *pratolī* which people may inhabit like a *suraṅgā*; that is called *kakṣā* by the experts which has its place on the inside in a house.'

This stanza contains two of the most disputed technical terms occurring in KA; the latter, *suraṅgā* or *suruṅgā*, has been at the heart of an ongoing controversy ever since STEIN ([2]1985:1-40) took a hypothetical etymology *suruṅgā* < Gr. *syrinx* as evidence for the lower age of KA (cf. also WINTERNITZ [2]1991:472-475; KANGLE 1965:76; SCHARFE 1968: 316sq.; TRAUTMANN 1971:6). MISHRA (1992) has interpreted certain underground passages excavated at Kauśāmbī and Pāṭaliputra as *suruṅgā*, quoting KUIPER's proposed etymology from Khmer *ruṅ* 'hole', Santali *suruṅ* 'hole' (Acta Orientalia XVII, Leiden, 1939).

The term *pratolī* is equally obscure; pd gives it as 'breiter Weg, Hauptstrasse'; VOGEL (1903:235-237) has rectified this error by pointing out that *pratolī* (> H. *pol, paulī*) refers to some structure in connection with the city gate. ACHARYA (1946a:321) accordingly gives *pratolī* as 'gate-way, sometimes provided with a flight of steps, a small turret, the main road of a town'; SCHLINGLOFF (1967:62), discussing the city fortifications as described in KA, feels that *pratolī* cannot refer to the main gateway: '*Man wird an Fußgängerpassagen zu denken haben, die zu ihrer Verteidigung einen Oberbau (*harmya*) besassen.*' SHUKLA (1958: 291) equates *pratolī* with *gopura*; this hypothesis is rejected by VAJPEYI (1972), who tries to reconcile the accounts of KA and SAS without reaching any conclusion.

In the *kośas*, *pratolī* invariably refers to some kind of road (AK 02.02.03a: *rathyā pratolī viśikhā*; ACM 981cd: *pūrdvāre gopuraṃ rathyāpratolīviśikhāḥ samāḥ*; ARM 02.134a: *pratolī viśikhā rathyā*), but cf. Kṣīrasvāmin's definition of *gopura* as *pratolī* quoted in the note on SAS 18.52 below. Kṣīrasvāmin explains *suraṅga* (AK03.05.08) as 'an oblong hole in the ground' (*suraṅgā tiryagbhūkhātaḥ*); ACM 985cd has it as 'a secret underground passage' (*suraṅgā tu saṃdhilā syād gūḍhamārgo bhuvo 'ntare*).

– *Kakṣā* is a synonym for *aṅgaṇa*, cf. 1.5.2 above.

18.26:

yad upasthānakaṃ nāma ye cāpavarakās tathā |
te koṣṭhakā yā tu kaṇṭhā kuḍyaṃ bhittiś cayaś ca sā ||

d) *kuḍyamittiś* (Da)

anuṣṭubh (ra-vipulā)

'That which is an *upasthānaka* by name, and those which are [called] *apavaraka* – these are *koṣṭhakas*; that which is the *kaṇṭhā* is *kuḍya*, *bhitti*, and *caya*.'

Koṣṭhaka seems to be the hyponym of *apavaraka* and *upasthāna/-ka*, meaning 'room in general' (cf. Nepālī *koṭhā* 'room, chamber'). No comparable classification is found in the *kośas*; For *upasthāna/-ka* and *apavaraka* cf. 18.21 and 18.24, and also 1.5.4 above. *Kaṇṭhā* f. is only attested in SAS 18.15, cf.1.3.1.1.2 above; the other three terms *kuḍya*, *bhitti*, and *caya* are regular terms for 'wall.'

18.27:

bhaktaśālā bhaved yā tu tan mahānasam ucyate |
yac channaṃ dvāradeśe tu tam āhur dvārakoṣṭhakam ||

a) *bhuktiśālā* (Ka)
anuṣṭubh (pathyā)

'That which may be a *bhaktaśālā* – that is called *mahānasa*; that which is covered [with a roof] in the region of the door – that they call *dvārakoṣṭhaka*.'

For *dvārakoṣṭhaka*, cf. SCHLINGLOFF (1969:25 fn.2). Note that this structure is not only not mentioned anywhere else in SAS, but seems to be absent from discussions of residential buildings in 'northern' *vāstuśāstra*s in general. It is not found in the *kośa*s either.

18.28:

praveśanam iti prāhur dvāranirgamanaṃ tathā |
jalanirgamanasthānaṃ vijñeyam udakabhramaḥ ||

anuṣṭubh (pathyā)

'And the exit that is the door they call *praveśana*; the place where water goes out is to be known as *udakabhrama*.'

18.29:

bhavanasyāṅgaṇaṃ yat tu tad āhur bhavanājiram |
vanājiraṃ vanamahī tv āśramājiram āśrame ||

anuṣṭubh (na-vipulā)

'That which is the courtyard of a dwelling – that they call *bhavanājira*; but *vanājira* [they call] the ground of the forest, in the case of a hermitage [it is called] *āśramājira*.'

For a discussion of the term *aṅgaṇa* see 1.5.1 above.

18.30-31:
uttarodumbarasyādhaḥ śliṣṭāṃ madhye ca kuḍyayoḥ |
tajjñās tāṃ dehalīty āhuḥ kapāṭāśrayam eva ca || 30 ||

b) *piṇḍayoḥ* (Ka)
anuṣṭubh (pathyā)

kapāṭaṃ dvārapakṣaḥ syāt kapāṭapuṭam eva ca |
pakṣaḥ pidhānāvaraṇo dvārasaṃvaraṇaṃ tathā || 31 ||

anuṣṭubh (bha-vipulā)

30. 'And that which is joined in the middle of the two walls, below the *uttarodumbara* – that the experts call *dehalī*, and also *kapāṭāśraya*.

31. The *kapāṭa* shall be [called] *dvārapakṣa*, and also *kapāṭa-puṭa*; *pakṣa, pidhānāvaraṇa*, and *dvārasaṃvaraṇa*.'

Uttarodumbara is the lintel, cf. SAS 28.10 and Utpala on BṛS 53. *Kapāṭāśraya*, literally 'support of the door-leaf,' seems to be a poetic rather than a technical expression; just as *dehalī*, it refers to the threshold. In continuation of the last quarter of the preceding stanza, 18.31 is primarily an exercise in poetic circum-scription; only the more conventional terms occurring in these two stanzas are also found in the *kośa*s, viz. *udumbara* (ACM 1009d), *kapāṭa* (AK 02.02.17c; ACM 1007a; ARM02.133d), and *dehalī* (AK 02.02.13a; ACM 1009c; ARM 02.147b).

18.32:
kapāṭaṃ saṃpuṭas te dve kapāṭayugalaṃ ca tat |
kalikā dvārabandhārthā yā syāt tām argalāṃ viduḥ ||

anuṣṭubh (pathyā)

'*Kapāṭa* [and] *saṃpuṭa* – these two are the pair of door-leaves; the 'bud' that may have the purpose of closing the door – that they call *argalā*.'

As we have seen in the preceding stanza, *kapāṭa* is the generic term for 'door-leaf;' *saṃpuṭa*, on the other hand, usually means 'cavity' or 'casket,' being derived from *saṃ-puṭ*, which root has the primary meaning 'to clasp, bind together, fasten.' As the two leaves of a door are usually symmetrical, one can only assume that the difference between *kapāṭa* and *saṃpuṭa* is that the latter has the baffle plate joined to it. The term *kalikā* is rather mysterious; how can a bolt (*argalā*) be referred to as 'bud'? Perhaps one should think of it as a sort of door-knob, with *argalā* being the generic term for any contrivance by which the door is shut.

18.33:
sā syād argalasūcīti yadi dīrghā pramāṇataḥ |
purāṇāṃ sā tu parighaḥ phaliho gajavāraṇam ||
anuṣṭubh (na-vipulā)

'It shall be an *argalasūcī* if it is long with reference to its size; in the case of cities, it is [called] *parigha, phaliha*, [or] *gaja-vāraṇa.*'

Phaliha seems to be a prakritic variant of *parigha*; cf. PISCHEL § 208. ACM 1004d has *parigha* and *argalā*, likewise ARM 02.145b; according to 1005a, a small door bolt is called *argalikā* or *sūci* (*sālpā tv argalikā sūciḥ*).

18.34:
chidrair gavākṣapratimaiś chidritaṃ sarvatas tu yat |
phalakaṃ tad gavākṣaḥ syāj jālam ity api kathyate ||
anuṣṭubh (na-vipulā)

'That board which is riddled all over with holes that resemble cows' eyes shall be [called] *gavākṣa*, and [it is] also called *jāla.*'

I do not think that COOMARASWAMY (1928:254) is right in equating *gavākṣa* = *candraśālā* = Tamil *kūḍu*; his quotations from

Raghuvaṃśa, at any rate, fit the meaning '(round) window' just as well, if not better – cf. ACHARYA (1946a:148) '[w]indows resembling the cow's eye, a latticed window.' Our stanza seems to attempt to combine both of these meanings: a latticed window (*jāla*) whose openings have the shape of cow's eyes. For *gavākṣa* etc. in the *kośa*s, cf. note on 18.14 above.

18.35:
harmyadvāre gr̥hadvāre tathā harmyāvalokane |
prākārāntarapr̥ṣṭhe tu yā ca prāsādikā bhavet ||
anuṣṭubh (pathyā)

'In the door of the upper storey and the front door, [and] in the *avalokana* of the upper storey: and on the inner side of the wall there shall be that which [is called] *prāsādikā*.'

In 18.22, we have seen that a *prāsādikā* is supposed to be a small platform; I am not sure what precisely it is supposed to refer to in the vicinity of doors and windows. In the latter case, a kind of window seat seems to be implied. Also, it is not entirely clear whether *prākārāntarapr̥ṣṭhe* refers to (1) the inside of the wall, or (2) the inside of the jamb.

18.36-39:
pārśvayor ubhayor eṣāṃ phalakadvayam ucchritam |
uparyupari saṃkṣiptam ardhacandradvayākr̥ti || 36 ||
anuṣṭubh (pathyā)

ānane dve yathā cāsmin śliṣṭair agryair mahādharaiḥ |
tayor upari sandhau ca tārakākr̥ti maṇḍalam || 37 ||
b) *ihādharaiḥ* (Da)
anuṣṭubh (pathyā)

tat toraṇam iti proktaṃ yac ca tena pariṣkr̥tam |
suvarṇatoraṇaṃ ca syān maṇitoraṇam eva ca || 38 ||
anuṣṭubh (pathyā)

puṣpatoraṇam apy etat kriyate puṣpakādibhiḥ |
***toraṇāgre ṭhakāro yaḥ siṃhakarṇaḥ sa ucyate* || 39 ||**

d) *kathyate* (Da)

anuṣṭubh (pathyā)

36. 'On either side of them [there shall be] a pair of vertical boards; above [that there shall be] the small shape of two crescents.

37. And on this [there shall be] two faces; above that, at the connection [or: joint] with the conjoined topmost *mahādhara*s [there shall be] a *maṇḍala* in tha shape of a star.

38. That is called *toraṇa*, and that [*toraṇa*] which is decorated with this [respective material or ornament] shall be a *suvarṇa-toraṇa*, and also a *maṇitoraṇa*;

39. also *puṣpatoraṇa*, this is made with blossoms etc.; the [shape of the] character *ṭha* which is situated on top of the *tora-ṇa* – that is called *siṃhakarṇa*.'

These stanzas furnish a description of the *toraṇa*, which is not so much an independent structure as rather thc aggregate of the decorative elements around the door frame. (Note that in the Newārī architectural tradition, the word *toraṇa*, Newārī *tvalã*, usually only refers to the tympanon, which is a decorative rather than constructive element; cf. GUTSCHOW, KÖLVER, and SHRE-STHACHARYA 1987 s.v. *tvalã*) That thc *toraṇa* does not bear any load is indicated by the use of *phalaka* 'board, plank' instead of, say, *stambha* 'post' in 18.36b. AK 02.02.16c, where *toraṇa* is glossed as 'outer door' (*bahirdvāram*), can be interpreted along similar lines; Kṣīrasvāmin explains it as follows:

> *maṅgalārthaṃ turanty atra toraṇaṃ dvārāgre stambhopari racitaṃ siṃhadvārākhyam* | *maṅgalasraktoraṇordhve bhaved vandanamālikā* |

'They run [?] for the sake of propitiousness, hence [it is called] *toraṇa*; on top of the pillars in front of the door, that which is called *siṃhadvāra* (tympanon?) is made. The garland of auspiciousness above the *toraṇa* shall be [called] *vandanamālikā*.'

Cf. ACM 1007d (*bahirdvāraṃ tu toraṇam*, erroneously interpreted as '*Arcade*' by BÖHTLINGK), and ARM 02.146ab (*budhair vandanamālā tu toraṇaṃ parikīrtyate*, which AUFRECHT takes to refer to 'a festoon suspended across gateways on festive occasions').

In 18.36a, *eṣāṃ* obviously refers to *harmyadvāre, gṛhadvāre*, and *avalokane* in the preceding stanza, implying that the window frames are no less elaborate in execution than the door frame. For *siṃhakarṇa*, cf. 28.55 and 48.106-107, where it is stated that this ornament, among others, should not be used in residential buildings.

18.40:

nāmnā saṃyamanānīti gṛhasaṃcarabhūmayaḥ |
gṛhasya pārśve yady asmiṃs tat tatsaṃyamanaṃ viduḥ ||

b) *gṛhasaṃcārabhūmayaḥ* (Kha Da). d) *saṃyāvanaṃ* (Kha Da?)
anuṣṭubh (ma-vipulā)

'The grounds surrounding the house are *saṃyamana* by name; if it is situated on the side of the house, they call it *tatsaṃyamana*.'

The compound *gṛhasaṃcarabhūmi* is perhaps best analyzed as 'the ground which is a passage of the house,' i.e. the footpath surrounding the house referred to as *vīthikā* in BṛS, MP, and VP (cf. note on SAS 20.08-10 below), and *antarikā* in KA 3.8.13: *sarvavāstukayoḥ prākṣiptayor vā śālayoḥ kiṣkur antarikā tripadī vā* – '[b]etween all two structures or two projecting rooms, (there is to be) an open lane one *kikṣu* (wide) or three *padas*' [Tr. KANGLE]. But what is the special distinction of the footpaths on either side of the house (*gr̥hasya pārśve*)? The expression *tatsaṃyamana* seems to imply a closer association with the edifice than is the case with respect to the path in front of or behind it.

18.41:
bhitter yad vātha dārūṇāṃ taraṅgāgravad ānatam |
marālapālī sā harmyā(t) praṇālī nirgamo 'mbhasaḥ ||

b) *ānavam* (Da). cd) *marālyā bhittisāmānyaṃ bāhyaṃ parisaro mataḥ | vistīrṇam ucchritāṃyalī sā harmyā |* (Kha Da)
anuṣṭubh (ma-vipulā)

'That [one] among the planks of the wall [which is] bent like the crest of a wave – that [is called] *marālapālī*, [it is] a *praṇālī*, [and] the exit of the water from the upper storey.'

It is quite likely that *marālapālī* is related to *kapotapālī* (cf. ACHARYA 1946a:100), and thus refers either to '[a] water-spout used at the roof to drain off water having the shape of pigeon's head or beak,' (KERN 1872:320 fn.2) or to 'a section of moulding made in the form of a pigeon's head' (RAM RAZ, Essay on the Architecture of the Hindus, quoted in ACHARYA 1946a:99); the expression *taraṅgāgravad ānata°* 'bent like the crest of a wave' further corroborates that. The fact that in cd, *marālapālī* is glossed as *praṇālī* lends credence to KERN's interpretation; but cf. Utpala on Br̥S 55.30:

> *kapotapāligrahaṇena bahirnirgatāni siṃhamukhāni kāṣṭhāny ucyante | tathā coktam – kapotapāliṃ bruvate viṭaṅkaṃ ca bahuśrutāḥ |*

'By the term *kapotapāli* are meant the lion-faced timbers protruding on the outside; and it is also said: the *viṭaṅka* is also called *kapotapāli* by the experts.'

Apparently, *kapotapāli* (short *i*!) refers to two completely different objects in Utpala's definition and the half-stanza from an unidentified source quoted by him, viz. a kind of beam head (which we have come to accept as the meaning of *niryūha*, cf. note on 18.17 above), and the ridge pole; neither of these tally with our stanza. AK 02.02.15cd also glosses *kapotapālikā* as *viṭaṅka* (as do ACM 1010a and ARM 02.148d), but Kṣīrasvāmin explains the latter term as follows:

> *viśiṣṭaṃ ṭaṅkyate viṭaṅkaḥ, pakṣiviśrāmārthe bahirnirgamitaṃ dāru, vakradārvādhāraḥ, pakṣipaṅktir hi tatrotkīryate* |

> 'It is covered particularly [i.e. it is adorned], [hence it is called] *viṭaṅka*; [it is] a timber protruding on the outside in order to [provide] a resting-place for birds; it has a bent timber for its support, nothing but [the image of] a flock of birds is engraved there.'

In light of this not inconsiderable dissent regarding the precise nature of *kapotapāli*/-*ī* (the meaning 'dove-cot' still found in the dictionaries has already been rejected by KERN, loc. cit.), one gets to wonder about the original meaning of the word; the most obvious explanation is that it refers to a kind of moulding, and that the name is derived from the fact that doves gather on it (*kapota* 'pigeon' + *pāli* 'line;' SAS 28.55a and 48.106c have *kapotālī*, which can be analyzed in the same way). But this cannot not apply to *marālapālī*, *marāla* being a kind of water bird (pd q.v.). Rather, the author of SAS 18 seems to have had in mind an etymology similar to the one suggested by RAM RAZ (see above). Note that 28.56 has *marālapallī*.

18.42:
***sa ca prākāra ity uktaḥ kaṇṭhaḥ syād aṅgaṇasya yaḥ* |**
***dvārasya tu samīpaṃ yat pradvāraṃ tad ihocyate* ||**

c) *dvārasya ca samīpe* (Ka)

anuṣṭubh (pathyā)

'And that is called *prākāra* which may be the *kaṇṭha* of the courtyard; but that which is close to the door, that here they call *pradvāra*.'

Both *prākāra* and *kaṇṭha*/*-ā* (cf. 1.3.1.1.2) seem to refer generally to an outwall, rather than a wall within the main body (in 18.35, *prākāra* is probably used *metri causa* for *bhitti*); this also seems to be its meaning according to AK 02.02.03cd (*prākāro varaṇaḥ sālaḥ prācīnaṃ prāntato vr̥tiḥ*), ACM 980cd more specifically considers it to be the parapet on top of an earth wall (*prākāro varaṇaḥ sāle cayo vapro 'sya pīṭhabhūḥ*; BÖHTLINGK is not quite right in translating the former three and the latter two terms as '*Wall von aufgeworfener Erde*' and '[*d*]*ie Erde, welche dem Wall als Grundlage dient*'); cf. also ARM 02.133c (*vapraṃ śālaṃ prākāram*).

Pradvāra is usually rendered as 'place before a door or gate' (cf. APTE q.v.).

18.43:

yad iṣṭakacitaṃ mūle dvārasya bhavati sthalam |
dīrghaṃ vā hrāsvam athavā tad āsthalakam iṣyate ||

anuṣṭubh (na-vipulā)

'That which is paved with bricks [and situated] at the foor of the door – that is a *sthala*; if it is wide or low, it is called *āsthalaka*.'

18.44:

mūtrabhūmir amedhyeti varcasko 'vaskaras tathā |
gr̥hāc ca bhittisāmānyaṃ bāhyaṃ parisaro mataḥ ||

anuṣṭubh (pathyā)

'*Mūtrabhūmi*, *amedhyā*, *varcaska*, and *avaskara*; and [if] it has the same wall as the house [but is situated] outside, [it is] called *parisara*.'

The two halves of this stanza are to be taken seperately: *parisara* is another synonym of *mūtrabhūmi*; rather, it seems to refer to a kind of lean-to, or to the grounds adjacent to the building. The *kośa*s treat it as 'country surrounding a village' (AK 02.01.14a: *paryantabhūḥ parisaraḥ*; ACM 963c: *paryantabhūḥ parisaraḥ*; ARM 02.104ab: *grāmāntikam upaśalyaṃ paryantaḥ parisaraḥ kaṭaḥ proktaḥ*).

18.45-46:
vistīrṇam ucchritaṃ yat syād veśma so 'ṭṭa udāhṛtaḥ |
saṃkṣiptam etad evoktaṃ tajjñair aṭṭālakākhyayā || 45 ||
anuṣṭubh (pathyā)

tad evātyantasaṃkṣiptam aṭṭālīti nigadyate |
aṭṭālī yā tu nātyuccā tām atrāṭṭālikāṃ viduḥ || 46 ||
anuṣṭubh (pathyā)

45. 'That abode which may be wide and tall – that is called *aṭṭa*; [if] it is short, the experts call it by the name *aṭṭālaka*.

46. [If] it is very short, it is called *aṭṭālī*; that *aṭṭālī*, though, which is not very tall – that here they call *aṭṭālikā*.'

Both *aṭṭa* and *aṭṭāla/-ka* occur frequently in the context of fortress construction, the latter being more widely used, cf. KA 2.3.10-12; cf. also SCHLINGLOFF (1967:59 fn.48). The other two diminutives seem to be peculiar to SAS, the *kośa*s only have *aṭṭa* (AK 02.02.12b), or *aṭṭa* and *aṭṭālaka* (ACM 981b; ARM 139b, glossed by AUFRECHT as 'a room at the top of a house'). For the etymology of *aṭṭa*, cf. DET (s.v. 83).

See also note on 18.53 below.

18.47:
ekanāḍīgatacchidraiḥ kāṣṭhanālaiḥ pariśritam |
yatra kāṣṭhapraṇālīti chadapṛṣṭhe 'mbu dhāvati ||
c) *praṇālībhiḥ* (Ka)
anuṣṭubh (pathyā)

'Where [the roof is] surrounded by wooden pipes, with a hole situated in one pipe; [that is called] *kāṣṭhapraṇālī*, [and] water showers down on the back of the roof.'

The construction of this stanza is rather awkward; *yatra* in c) obviously refers to *pariśrita* in b), and *chadapr̥ṣṭhe 'mbu dhāvati* in d) should perhaps be grouped with *ekanāḍīgatacchidraiḥ* in a). One might be tempted to group it with 18.48-50, as has indeed been done by SHUKLA ([2]2003:101). But that rather increases the difficulties, especially if one does not emend **kāṣṭhapraṇālībhiś* (guided by the reading of Ka °*praṇālībhiḥ*), which would then have to be grouped with the instrumentals in 18.48d, 49b, 50a (cf. following note). I have chosen not to do so for the simple reason that our stanza taken by itself can be satisfactorily explained as describing a gutter together with the rainpipe: a set of wooden pipes around the roof, with a hole in one of them (*ekanāḍīgata-cchidra*), serving the purpose of draining off the water.

I am not certain whether *kāṣṭhanāla* and *kāṣṭhapraṇālī* should really be rendered with 'wooden pipe;' it is not unlikely that *kāṣṭha* refers not so much to their material, but rather to their situation at the architrave or the roof truss – cf. *kāṣṭhamūlāśrita* (18.48b), and the even more specific *vitardikāṣṭhamālā syāt sarvataś chada-mūlagā* (18.16ab). In that case, one would have to translate 'pipe on [the side of] the roof.'

18.48-50:

stambhaśīrṣakarūpāṇi kāṣṭhamūlāśritāni ca |
***suṣirāṇi prayatnena kāṣṭhanāḍīmukhāntaraiḥ* || 48 ||**

anuṣṭubh (pathyā)

rūpāṇām atha teṣāṃ tu stananāsāmukhākṣibhiḥ |
***nānāsthānasthitānāṃ ca vr̥ṣavānaradaṃṣṭriṇām* || 49 ||**

anuṣṭubh (pathyā)

kṛtasūkṣmāntaracchidraiḥ pravarṣati samantataḥ |
***tad dhārāgṛham ity uktaṃ dhārāgārādināmabhṛt* || 50 ||**
anuṣṭubh (pathyā)

48. 'And [where there are] *śīrṣakarūpa*s on the posts, connected with the lower side of the timber framing, carefully hollowed out;

49. by the [apertures of] the breasts, noses, mouths, [and] eyes [which are] inside the mouths of the wooden pipes, of the [*śīrṣakarūpa*s'] shapes [which are those of] men [or: bulls], monkeys, [and] beasts of prey;

50. [where] it showers down on all sides through the holes [which are] made smooth on the inside [of breasts, noses, etc.] – that is called *dhārāgṛha*, [and] it bears the names of *dhārāgāra* etc.'

There can be no doubt that these stanzas have to be read as one unit; yet they are rather difficult to translate, as the construction is not without ambiguity owing to the rather awkward word order which requires some regrouping in the analysis: *kāṣṭhanāḍīmukhāntaraiḥ* (18.48) probably needs to be construed with *stananāsāmukhākṣibhiḥ* (18.49) and *kṛtasūkṣmāntaracchidraiḥ* (18.50a); likewise *rūpāṇāṃ* [...] *teṣāṃ* (18.49a) with *nānāsthānasthitānāṃ* [...] *vṛṣavānaradaṃṣṭriṇām* (18.49cd). We thus arrive at the following translation:

> 'And [there are] the shapes of "post-heads" [i.e., capitals] connected with the lower end of the timber framing, hollowed [out] carefully; water showers down on all sides through the [apertures of] breasts, noses, mouths, and eyes which have been made smooth on the inside [and are situated] on the inside of the openings of wooden pipes, belonging to the shapes of bulls, monkeys, and beasts of prey standing in various positions – that is called *dhārāgṛha*, [and also] goes by the name of *dhārāgāra*.'

The topic of water coming out of the eyes, breasts etc. of (female) images also occurs in the long and rather poetic description of a *dhārāgṛha* in 31.120-141, which is one of the five types of *vāriyantra* described in 31.109-172; cf. 31.136-137:

> *stanayor yugena sṛjatī jaladhāre tatra kāpi kāryā strī |*
> *ānandāśrulavān iva salilakanān pakṣmabhiḥ kācit || 136 ||*
> *nābhihradanadikām iva vinirgatāṃ kāpi bibhratī dhārām |*
> *kāpy aṅgulīnakhāṃśubhir iva yoṣit siñcatī kāryā || 137 ||*

136. '[The shape of] a woman shall be made there, pouring forth streams of water from the pair of her breasts, another [woman shedding] drops of water from her eyes, like tears of joy.
137. Another one producing streams of water, like a river rising from the lake of her navel; another woman shall be made, sprinkling, as it were, rays [of light] from her fingernails.'

The pipes inside the posts are also mentioned, with a strange repetition, in the description of the device called *pātasamocchraya*, one of the four *vāriyantras*, in 31.112-113:

> *yatra pātasamucchrāyaṃ patitvocchrāyato jalam |*
> *tiryag gatvā prayāty ūrdhvaṃ sacchidrastambhayogataḥ || 112 ||*
> *patitvocchrāyatas toyaṃ tiryag ūrdhvordhvam ety atha |*
> *sacchidrastambhayogena tat syāt pātasamocchrayam || 113 ||*

112. 'Where there is a drop [?], [and] water falls down from a height; moves [along] horizontally; moves upwards by means of a pillar with a hole [in its centre];
113. [where] water falls down, [is led] horizontally, and goes all the way up by means of a pillar with a hole – that shall be [called] *pātasamocchrayam*.'

As mentioned above [18.47], SHUKLA ([2]2003:101) has treated 18.47-50 as a unit; his translation runs as follows:

> ***dhārā-gṛha*** *– eka-nāḍīgata-chidroṃ vāle kāṣṭha-nālōṃ se pariśrit chada-pṛṣṭha par jahāṃ jal dhāvan kartā hai, vah* ***kāṣṭha-praṇālī*** *kahlātī hai tathā kāṣṭha-mūla par āśrit stambha-śīrṣaka-rūpoṃ ko khokhlā banā kar unmeṃ kāṣṭha-nālī ke mukhāntaroṃ se jo puruṣākṛti athavā paśvākṛti rūp jaise vṛṣa,*

vānara gaja rūp (sampann hote haiṃ) unke stana, nāsā, mukha, aur āṃkhoṃ se jab cārōṃ taraf pānī nikaltā hai usko ***dhārā-gṛha*** *athavā* ***dhārāgāra*** *ādi nām se pukārā jātā hai* ||

'Where water runs down on the *chada-pṛṣṭha* which is surrounded by *kāṣṭha-nāla*s which have *eka-nāḍīgata-chidra*s, that is called *kāṣṭha-praṇālī*, and where water comes out on all sides from the breasts, nose, mouths, and eyes of the human shapes or animal shapes like the shapes of bull, monkey, elephant (which have been produced) from the openings of the *kāṣṭha-nālī* inside the hollowed-out *stambha-śīrṣaka-rūpa*s fixed to the *kāṣṭha-mūla*, that they refer to as *dhārā-gṛha* or names like *dhārāgāra*.'

18.51:

***kāṃsyair lohais tathā paṭṭair nirmṛṣṭādarśanirmalaiḥ* |**
***nicitā yasya bhittiḥ syāt tad darpaṇagṛhaṃ viduḥ* ||**

d) *jaguḥ* (Kha Da)

anuṣṭubh (pathyā)

'[A hall] whose walls are covered with plates of brass and copper which are spotless like polished mirrors – that is called *darpaṇagṛha*.'

18.52:

***pakṣadvāraṃ tad atrāhur yan mahādvārato 'param* |**
***yat prākārāśritaṃ dvāraṃ pure tad gopuraṃ viduḥ* ||**

anuṣṭubh (pathyā)

'*Pakṣadvāra* here they call that which is different from the main door; that door in a city which is linked to the wall – that they call *gopura*.'

The term *gopura* has already been under discussion under 1.3.4 above; it occurs only in this stanza, the city gate usually being referred to as *pratolī* in SAS 10. AK 02.02.16 does not mention *pratolī* in its definition of *gopura* (*puradvāraṃ tu gopuram*), but Kṣīrasvāmin does (*gopyate gopuraṃ pratolī*). Cf. also the definition in ACM 981c (*pūrdvāre gopuram*) and ARM 02.133b (*gopuraṃ puradvāram*).

18.53:

nirgatāś cocchritāś caiva prākārasyāntarāntarā |
upakāryā iti proktāḥ kṣemāś cāṭṭālakā matāḥ ||

c) *upakāmyā* (Ka), *upakālyā* (Kha Da)
anuṣṭubh (pathyā)

'[Those which are] both protruding [from the city wall] and elevated [above it] in such a manner as to be inside the [city] wall – those are called *upakāryā*s, and [those which are] safe [or: inhabitable] are known as *aṭṭālakā*s.'

SASTRI had made the emendation **kṣaumā* for *kṣemā*, which was not adopted by AGRAWALA. One might assume that the difference between an *upakārya* and an *aṭṭālaka* is the fact that, while the former is a kind of solid bastion, the latter is an actual tower with a chamber inside; but *kṣauma* is given in ACM 981b as a synonym of *aṭṭālaka* (*kṣaumāṭṭāṭṭālakāḥ samāḥ*). AK 02.02.12 has *kṣoma* instead of *kṣauma*, Kṣīrasvāmin has *kṣauma* (*kṣaumaḥ prākāradhāraṇārtho 'bhyantaraḥ kṣomākhya ity eke* – 'a *kṣauma* [is situated] on the inside [of the wall], it has the purpose of supporting the wall; some call it *kṣoma*;' the term is not found in this meaning in ARM). The word *upakārya* seems to have been of little currency; the mss give two variant readings, viz. *upakāmya* and *upakālya*. APTE has *upakāryā*, 'royal house, palace.'

18.54:

cayaprākāra*sālāḥ* syuḥ purīsaṃvaraṇābhidhāḥ |
prākārād anupālās tu prākāra upaniṣkalāḥ ||

a) °*prakāra*° (Śa); °*śālāḥ* (Ka Kha Ga Da Śa Śu)
anuṣṭubh (pathyā)

'*Caya*, *prākāra*, and *sālā* shall be called *purīsaṃvaraṇa*; the *anupāla*s, though, are outside the wall, the *upaniṣkala*s are inside the wall.'

Prākāra in d) is of course the *sandhi* of loc. *prākāre* + vowel. While *anupāla* is not found in the dictionaries, there is a word *upaniṣkara* which, according to ACM 987 is one of several synonyms of 'main road:'

> *ghaṇṭāpathaḥ saṃsaraṇaṃ śrīpatho rājavartma ca |*
> *upaniṣkramaṇaṃ copaniṣkaraṃ ca mahāpathaḥ ||*

The first of the synonyms given in this stanza is of particular interest in our context, because SAS 10.14 has *ghaṇṭāmārga* as a road encircling the city on the inside of the wall; *anupāla* would then be a kind of road leading away from the fortifications, and *upaniṣkala* synonymous with *ghaṇṭāmārga*. Cf. also AK 02.01.18cd (*ghaṇṭāpathaḥ saṃsaraṇaṃ tat purasyopaniṣkaram*).

18.55:
krīḍāgṛhaṃ yad ārāme tad udyānaṃ pracakṣate |
tīre 'mbhaso jalodyānaṃ jalaveśmāmbumadhyagam ||
anuṣṭubh (pathyā)

'That pleasure house which is [situated] in a park – that is called *udyāna*; [if it is situated] on the banks of a body of water [it is called] *jalodyāna*, *jalaveśman*, [if it is] situated in the middle of a body of water.'

Udyāna usually refers to a park, not to a building inside a park. AK 02.04.03c glosses it as 'sporting [ground] of humans' (*pumān ākrīḍa udyānam*), cf. ACM 1112c (*ākrīḍaḥ punarudyānam*, which BÖHTLINGK explains as '[*k*]*öniglicher Park, zu dem auch die Unterthanen Zutritt haben*').

18.56:
krīḍāgṛhaṃ yad atroktaṃ krīḍāgāraṃ tad ucyate |
vihārabhūmir ākrīḍabhūmir ity abhidhīyate ||
anuṣṭubh (pathyā)

'That which here is called *krīḍāgṛha*, that is called *krīḍāgāra*; the sporting grounds are called *ākrīḍabhūmi*.'

18.57:
devadhiṣṇyaṃ surasthānaṃ caityam arcāgṛhaṃ ca tat |
devatāyatanaṃ prāhur vibudhāgāram ity api ||
anuṣṭubh (pathyā)

'That is called *devadhiṣṇya*, *surasthāna*, *caitya*, and *arcāgṛha*; a *devatāyatana* they also call *vibudhāgāra*.'

18.58:
channaṃ bhaved yat tu mahājanasya
sthānaṃ sabhā sā kathitā ca śālā |
gavāṃ punar mandiram atra goṣṭham
ācakṣate vāstuniveśavijñāḥ ||
upajāti

'That place for a multitude that is covered is called *sabhā* and *śālā*; and the abode of cows the experts on the layout of *vāstu* here call *goṣṭha*.'

iti mahārājādhirājaśrībhojadevaviracite samarāṅgaṇa-sūtradhārāparanāmni vāstuśāstre nagarakarvaṭagrāma-gṛhāyatanasaṃjñā nāmāṣṭādaśo 'dhyāyaḥ |

'Thus [ends] the eighteenth chapter in the *vāstuśāstra* composed by Mahārājādhirāja Śrībhojadeva also called *Samarāṅgaṇasūtradhāra*, called 'The designations of towns, market towns, villages, houses, and sacred places."

2.2 *adhyāya* 19.15-28

19.15:
varṇināṃ syāc catuḥśālaṃ mitaṃ dvātriṃśatā karaiḥ |
senāpateś catuḥṣaṣṭis tadvad eva purodhasaḥ ||
anuṣṭubh (pathyā)

'For *varṇins*, the *catuḥśāla* shall measure thirty-two cubits [in width]; for an army chief, [it shall measure] sixty-four, likewise for the king's preceptor.'

The second half of this stanza has a parallel in BṛS 52.05:

ṣaḍbhiḥ ṣaḍbhir hīnā senāpatisadmanāṃ catuḥṣaṣṭiḥ |
evaṃ pañca gṛhāṇi ṣaḍbhāgasamanvitā dairghyaṃ ||

'The residences of army chiefs shall have [a width of] sixty-four, diminished successively by six [cubits] – thus [have been explained] the five houses, [their widths] augmented by one-sixth [yield their] length.'

Cf. also MP 254.19:

catuḥṣaṣṭis tu vistārāt ṣaḍbhiḥ ṣaḍbhis tu hīyate |
pañcasv eteṣu dairghyaṃ ca ṣaḍbhāgenādhikaṃ bhavet ||

'Sixty-four [cubits] in width, [which] shall be dimished successively by six [cubits]; the length of these five [buildings] shall be augmented by one-sixth.'

For the parallel in VP, cf.Appendix. The first obvious difference is that, in the case of BṛS 52.05, the size of the *senāpati*'s house may be diminished in steps of six cubits each. (For this principle, cf. note on 19.16 below). Also, SAS 19.15 makes no mention of the difference in width and length; a similar rule will, however, be found in SAS 19.19 with respect to the four *varṇas*. The other exception is, that the *purodhasa*'s house it not mentioned in BṛS 52.05; BṛS 52.10 assigns to him a house of rather more humble dimensions than that of the *senāpati*:

catvāriṃśad dhīnā catuścaturbhis tu pañca yāvad iti |
ṣaḍbhāgayutā dairghyaṃ daivajñapurodhasor bhiṣajaḥ ||

'40 [cubits] diminished in steps of four – [these] five [dwellings with] their length augmented by one-sixth [are suitable] for the astrologer, the *purodhasa*, and the physician.'

Cf. also MP 254.26-27:

daivajñaguruvaidyānāṃ sabhāstārapurodhasām |
teṣām api pravakṣyāmi tathā bhavanapañcakam || 26 ||
catvāriṃśat tu vistārāc caturbhir hīyate kramāt |
pañcasv eteṣu dairghyaṃ ca ṣaḍbhāgenādhikaṃ bhavet || 27 ||

26. 'I shall now explain the five dwellings of astrologers, teachers, Vedic scholars, members of the *sabhā*, and preceptors.
27. They shall be 40 cubits in width, which shall be diminished by four successively; and the length of these five [buildings] shall be augmented by one-sixth.'

For the parallel in VP, cf. Appendix.

19.16:
śreṣṭham aṣṭaśataṃ rājñām etāni tu yathākramam |
catuḥṣaḍaṣṭahānyā syuḥ pañcamaṃ ca pṛthak pṛthak ||
anuṣṭubh (pathyā)

'The biggest [house] for kings [shall have a width of] one hundred and eight [cubits], also these [following houses] in due order: they shall be diminished in steps of four, six, and eight respectively, and [there shall be] a fifth [house].'

The dwellings fit for a king thus come in five sizes with a length of 108, 104, 98, 90, and – presumably – 80 cubits. The method employed here – a standard width diminished in successive steps to yield a total of five different measurements – will be encountered again frequently in chapters 19 and 24. It is interesting to note that this system of gradation is usually only alluded to in the text of SAS; apparently the author presupposed some knowledge of this system on the reader's side. For the parallel in BṛS 52.04, cf. introduction, pp. 3 sq. Cf. also MP 254.14cd-16:

> *athātaḥ saṃpravakṣāmi bhavanaṃ pṛthivīpateḥ* || 14 ||
> *pañcaprakāraṃ tatproktam uttamādivibhedataḥ* |
> *aṣṭottaraṃ hastaśataṃ vistaraś cottamo mataḥ* || 15 ||
> *caturṣv anyeṣu vistāro hīyate cāṣṭabhiḥ karaiḥ* |
> *caturthāṃśādhikaṃ dairghyaṃ pañcasv api nigadyate* || 16 ||

14. '[...] I shall now explain the dwelling of the king.
15. It is said to be of five kinds, because of the division into the largest etc,; the maximum width is known to be 108 cubits.
16. In the four other [dwellings], the width is dimished by four cubits [successively]; the length is said to be augmented by a quarter in all five [dwellings].'

Cf. also VP 02.135-136:

> *aṣṭottaraśataṃ hastavistārān nṛpamandiram* |
> *kāryaṃ pradhānam anyāni tathāṣṭāṣṭau ca tāni tu* || 135 ||
> *vistāra{ṃ} pādasaṃyuktaṃ teṣāṃ dairghyaṃ prakalpayet* |
> *evaṃ nṛpāṇāṃ pañcaiva gṛhāṇi śubhadāni ca* || 136 ||

135. 'The first dwelling of a king has a width of 108 cubits, and the others by eight successively [?].
136. One shall fix their length as augmented by a quarter of the width; and this way, the five houses of kings are auspicious.'

In 135cd, one should probably emend **anyeṣāṃ* and **hāni* for *anyāni* and *tāni*.

SHUKLA's translation of SAS 19.16 is rather confusing:

> *rājāoṃ ke lie 102 hāth ke pramāṇ kā catuḥśāl bhavan batāyā gayā hai. in āṭhoṃ meṃ cār kā kram to yah huā. pāṃcveṃ viśiṣṭ bhavan ko alag-alag 4, 6, 8 hāth kī hāni se banānā cāhie* [...] |

'For the kings, a *catuḥśāla*-dwelling with a size of 102 [!] cubits has been mentioned. Among these eight, though, the series of four has been this. The fifth particular dwelling shall be made by a decrease of four, six, and eight cubits respectively [...] .'

19.17:
viśodhayet kanīyobhir madhyamāni yathākramam |
narendrapuruṣāṇāṃ syur veśmāny etāni vṛddhaye ||
anuṣṭubh (pathyā)

'By the smaller [buildings], one shall explain the middle-sized ones in due order. These dwellings shall be [conducive to] the welfare of the king's servants.'

This stanza apparently alludes to BṛS 52.08, where the dimensions of dwellings for the king's officers and other *karmopajīvin*s are given:

> *nṛpasacivāntaratulyaṃ sāmantapravararājapuruṣāṇām |*
> *nṛpayuvarājaviśeṣaḥ kañcukiveśyākalājñānām ||*

'Equal [in size] to the difference [between the houses of] king and minister [are the houses] of provincial gouvernors and high-ranking royal officials; the difference between [the houses of] king and crown prince [yields the size of the houses] of courtiers, courtesans, and artisans.'

Again, the precise meaning of our stanza remains obscure, even in the light of this parallel. *Viśodhayet kanīyobhir madhyamāni* seems to correspond, albeit rather loosely, to *nṛpasacivāntaratulyaṃ*, although in SAS 19 no specifications are given regarding the minister's dwelling.

19.18:
gṛhāṇi śodhayet prāgvaj jyāyāṃsy api ca madhyamaiḥ |
bhavanty etāni bhūpānāṃ ratikośapratiśrayāḥ ||
anuṣṭubh (pathyā)

'As before, one shall explain the largest houses by means of the middle-size ones; these shall be abodes of the king's pleasure and treasure.'

For this stanza, as vague in meaning as the preceding one, cf. BṛS 52.9:

> *adhyakṣādhikṛtānāṃ sarveṣāṃ kośaratitulyam |*
> *yuvarājamantrivivaraṃ karmāntādhyakṣadūtānām ||*

'[The dwellings] of the superintendents [shall be] equal to the treasury and the pleasure house in all instances; the difference between [the houses of] the crown prince and the minister [yields the size of the houses] of the overseers of factories and envoys.'

and BṛS 52.14:

> *nṛpasenāpatigṛhayor antaramānena kośaratibhavane |*
> *senāpaticāturvarṇyavivarato rājapuruṣāṇām ||*

'Of equal size to the difference between the houses of king and *senāpati* [are] the building of the treasury and the pleasure-house; the difference between [the dwellings] of the *senāpati* and the members of the four *varṇa*s [yield the size of the houses] of [low-ranking] royal officials.'

In analogy to the preceding stanza, there seems to be a loose correspondence here between *gṛhāni śodhayet* [...] *jyāyāṃsi* [...] *madhyamaiḥ* and *nṛpasenāpatigṛhayor antaramānena.*

19.19:
daśāṃśayukto vistārād āyāmo vipraveśmanām |
aṣṭaṣaṭcaturaṃśāḍhyaḥ kṣatrāditrayaveśmanām ||

ab) *vistāra āyāmo* (Da)
anuṣṭubh (vipulā)

'For the dwellings of brahmans, the length should be augmented against the width by one-tenth; for the dwellings of *kṣatriyas* and so forth, it shall be increased by one-eighth, one-sixth, and one-fourth [respectively].'

Apparently, although this is not stated explicitly, the idea is that due to its religious significance, the use of the square in a ground plan is to be restricted to temples. The sacred nature of the square is also indicated by the fact that the variance from it increases as the social and ritual status of the house owner decreases. Cf. the parallel in BṛS 52.12-13:

cāturvarṇyavyāso dvātriṃśat sā catuścaturhīnā |
ā ṣoḍaśād iti paraṃ nyūnataram atīva hīnānām || 12 ||
sadaśāṃśaṃ viprāṇāṃ kṣatrasyāṣṭāṃśasaṃyutaṃ dairghyam |
ṣaḍbhāgayutaṃ vaiśyasya bhavati śūdrasya pādayutam || 13 ||

12. 'The width [of the dwelling] of the members of the four *varṇa*s is 32 [cubits] that [shall be] diminished in steps of four, all the way down to 16 [cubits]; smaller [houses] are for the very low [people]. 13. The length [of the building] is augmented by one-tenth [of the width] for brahmans, by one-eighth for a *kṣatriya*; by one-sixth for a *vaiśya*, for a *śūdra*, it is augmented by a quarter.'

According to Utpala, this group of five graded measurements is to be applied to the four *varṇa*s in the following manner:

[...] *brāhmaṇasya prathamagṛhavyāso dvātriṃśad dhastāḥ | anyāni catvāri caturbhiś caturbhir hīnāni | kṣatriyasya prathamagṛhavyāso hastā aṣṭāviṃśatiḥ | anyāni trīṇi caturbhiś caturbhir hīnāni | vaiśyasya prathamagṛhaṃ caturviṃśatiḥ | anye dve caturbhiś caturbhir hīne | śūdrasya pradhānaṃ gṛhaṃ viṃśatir hastāḥ | aparaṃ ṣōḍaśeti | evaṃ brāhmaṇasya pañca gṛhāṇi | kṣatriyasya catvāri | vaiśyasya trīṇi | śūdrasya dve |*

'[...] The width of the first house for a brahman [shall be] thirty-two cubits, the remaining four [shall be] diminished by four [cubits] respectively. The width of the first house for a *kṣatriya* [shall be] twenty-eight in cubits, the remaining four [shall be] diminished by four respectively. The first house for a *vaiśya* shall be twenty-four [cubits in width], the remaining two [shall be] diminished by four respectively. The principal house for a *śūdra* shall be twenty cubits [in width], the other sixteen. Thus there are five [different] houses for a brahman, four for a *kṣatriya*, three for a *vaiśya*, and two for a *śūdra*.'

Since a width of thirty-two cubits is implied by SAS 19.15, and a width of sixteen cubits is mentioned in the 24th *adhyāya*, it is probably safe to assume that the same system of gradation is at the basis of SAS as well; cf. tab. 4.

Tab. 4 – Dimensions of ground plans in cubits			
Brahmaṇa	*Kṣatriya*	*Vaiśya*	*Śūdra*
32 x 35 2/10	—	—	—
28 x 30 8/10	28 x 31 1/2	—	—
24 x 26 4/10	24 x 27	24 x 28	—
20 x 22	20 x 22 1/2	20 x 23 1/3	20 x 25
16 x 17 6/10	16 x 18	16 x 18 2/3	16 x 20

The same numbers are given by Utpala. Cf. also MP 254.28-39 and VP 02.146-153.

19.20:

yo vistāraḥ sa eva syād āyāmo 'smin yathākramam |
viṭśūdrayoḥ syād ādhikyaṃ madhye jyeṣṭhe ca sadmani ||

cd) *ādhikām atha jyeṣṣṭhetha veśmanoḥ* (Da)
anuṣṭubh (vipulā)

'In this case, that which is the width shall also be the length respectively; in the case of *vaiśya* and *śūdra*, there shall be an increase in the case of the middle-sized and large dwelling.'

This stanza is confusing; it seems to override the rule given in the preceding stanza, unless one assumes that the first half of 19.20 simply means that the length follows from the width, a meaning that would fit the preceding stanza rather well but unfortunately cannot be construed from the text as it is. In the absence of any variant readings, I do not feel confident to make any emendations to that effect.

Either way, the second half remains puzzling: precisely which dwellings does *madhye jyeṣṭhe ca sadmani* refer to? In the case of the *vaiśya* the answer is simple (the dwellings with a ground plan of 24 x 28 and 20 x 23 1/3 respectively); the *śūdra*, however, has only two ground plans to choose from, in which case there cannot, strictly speaking, be such a thing as a middle-sized plan. It is quite likely that SAS 19.20cd has its origin in MP 254.24ab:

dviguṇaṃ dairghyam evoktaṃ madhyameṣv evam eva tat |

'Its length is laid down as twice [its width] in the case of the middle-sized [dwellings for *śilpin*s, *kañcukin*s, and *veśyā*s].'

This line does not have a parallel in VP; how precisely the version of SAS came into being is not clear.

19.21:
***karṇasūtrād bahiḥ stambhān nyaset sarvān prayatnataḥ* |**
***dhāmnāṃ ṣoḍaśahastānāṃ pañcānāṃ caturuttarā* ||**
anuṣṭubh (pathyā)

'Outside of the *karṇasūtra*, one shall position all the posts with great care; the five dwellings [with a width of] sixteen cubits [there shall be] an increase in steps of four [cubits].'

The construction of the second half of this stanza is rather awkward; obviously, the initial word of the following stanza (which otherwise would be difficult to construe) needs to be included here as the referent of *caturuttarā*: an increase (*vṛddhiḥ*) proceeding in steps of four (*caturuttarā*). The precise meaning of *karṇasūtra* is unclear to me; since the pillars (of the central courtyard?) are supposed to be erected outside it, it cannot have anything to do with the *karṇakīlāyasa*s of KA 03.08.03. Rather, it seems to mark an area inside the projected building.

19.22:
***vṛddhiḥ śālāstu teṣāṃ syuś caturaṃśena vistṛtāḥ* |**
***śālāvyāsārdhato 'lindaḥ sarveṣām api veśmanām* ||**
anuṣṭubh (pathyā)

'Their *śālās* shall have a width of one-quarter [with reference to the width of the building]; the *alinda* [shall be laid out] on the basis of the width of the *śālā* in all dwellings.'

The first half thus yields a *śālā*-width of eight cubits in the case of a thirty-two-cubit-*vāstu*, seven for a *vāstu* with a width of twenty-eight cubits, six for one of twenty-four, five for one of twenty, and four for a *vāstu* of sixteen cubits. It seems that the width of the *alinda* should approximate half the width of the *śālā* without necessarily reaching it; cf. the following stanza.

The method given here differs somewhat from the one recommended in BṛS 52.17-19:

senāpatinṛpatīnāṃ saptatisahite dvidhākṛte vyāse |
śālā caturdaśahṛte pañcatriṃśaddhṛte 'lindaḥ || 17 ||
hastadvātriṃśādiṣu catuścatustritrikatrikāḥ śālāḥ |
saptadaśatritayatithitrayodaśakṛtāṅgulābhyadhikāḥ || 18 ||
tritridvidvidvisamāḥ kṣayakramād aṅgulāni caiteṣām |
vyekā viṃśatir aṣṭau viṃśatir aṣṭādaśa tritayam || 19 ||

17. 'If one adds 70 to the width [of the house of] the commander, the king, [and all other *karmopajīvin*s] twice – if one divides it [once] by 14, [that yields the width of] the *śālā*, if one divides it [once] by 35, [that yields the width of] the *alinda*.
18. In the houses [of the varṇins] beginning with [the one] 32 cubits [in width], the *śālā* [shall have a width of] 4 cubits and 17 digits, 4 and 3, 3 and 15, 3 and 13, [and] 3 and 4 [respectively].
19. And their [*alinda*] shall be, in descending order, 3 [cubits] and 19 digits, 3 and 8, 2 and 20, 2 and 18, 2 and 3 [respectively].'

Cf. also MP 254.33-36:

senāpater nṛpasyāpi saptatyā sahite 'nvite |
caturdaśahṛte vyāse śālānyāsaḥ prakīrtitaḥ || 33 ||
pañcatriṃśānvite tasminn alindaḥ samudāhṛtaḥ |
tathā ṣaṭtriṃśad hastā tu saptāṅgulasamanvitā || 34 ||
viprasya mahatī śālā na dairghyaṃ parato bhavet |
daśāṅgulādhikā tadvat kṣatriyasya na vidyate || 35 ||
pañcatriṃśatkarā vaiśye hy aṅgulāni trayodaśa |
tāvatkaraiva śūdrasya yutā pañcadaśāṅgulaiḥ || 36 ||

33. 'If 70 is added to the width [of the dwelling of] the commander, the king, [and all other *karmopajīvins*, and if that figure is] divided by 14 – that is recommended as width of the *śālā*.
34. If 35 is added [to the width, and that figure divided by 14] – that is said to be the width of the *alinda*; and 36 cubits plus 7 digits [divided by 14?] –
35. [that] large is the *śālā* of a *brāhmaṇa*, its length shall not be different; accordingly, there is no [?] [*śālā* of 36 cubits?] plus 10 digits for a *kṣatriya*.
36. In the case of a *vaiśya*, [the *śālā* shall be] 35 cubits [and] 13 digits; for a *śūdra*, the same number of cubits augmented by 15 digits.'

The rules for the houses of *varṇin*s in 34cd-36 are rather obscure; VP 02.152cd-153 gives no alternative rule for the houses of *varṇin*s at all:

> [...] *senāpatinṛpādīnāṃ saptatyā sahite kṛte* || 152 ||
> *vyāse caturdaśahṛte śālāmānaṃ vinirdiśet* |
> *pañcatryaṃśahṛte 'nyatrālindamānaṃ bhavec ca tat* || 153 ||

152. '[...] If 70 is added to [the width of the house] of *senāpati*, king, etc;
153. [and] the width be divided by 14, one shall [thus] determine the size of the *śālā*; divided in separate [calculation] by 35 – that shall be the size of the *alinda*.'

Cf. also 1.6 above.

19.23:
tasyāḥ ṣoḍaśahaste syāt pañcamāṃśadvayena vā |
saptamāṃśatrayena syād dvayor aparaveśmanoḥ ||

a) *tasyāṃ* (Ka)
anuṣṭubh (pathyā)

'Or, in case it has [a width of] sixteen cubits, [the width of the *alinda* shall be] two-fifths; it shall be three-sevenths for the two other dwellings.'

The feminine genitive in the first quarter indicates that sixteen cubits here is the width of the *śālā*, not of the entire plot; a *śālā* of these dimensions is to be expected in the case of a *vāstu* having a width of sixty-four cubits – the one prescribed for a *senāpati* and for a *purodhasa* in 19.15; such a dwelling would thus have an *alinda* with a width of 6 2/5 cubits. The 'two other dwellings' may be taken to be identical with the first two smaller buildings alluded to in BṛS 52.05 quoted in the note on SAS 19.15 above. Accordingly, an edifice with a width of fifty-eight cubits has a *śālā*-width of fourteen and a half cubits, while in the case of a fifty-two-cubit-plot the *śālā* is thirteen cubits wide. If the rule of SAS 19.23 is applied, we arrive at a width of the *alinda* of 6 3/14 cubits and 5 4/7 cubits respectively. It must be pointed out, however, that the application of this rule from SAS to buildings described in BṛS is entirely based on speculation; there is no conclusive evidence that *dvayor aparaveśmanoḥ* in 19.23cd actually refers to the next smaller of the five dwellings prescribed for the *senāpati*, nor is it in any way safe to assume that the author of SAS would also have had the *senāpati*'s house diminished in steps of six cubits. As we have already seen, SAS and BṛS also disagree on the steps in which the house of a king should be diminished; cf. above, SAS 19.16.

19.24:
antyayor hastayoḥ sa syāc caturbhir navamāṃśakaiḥ |
pañcabhiḥ ṣaḍbhir ebhiś ca sārdhaiḥ sāṅghrinagaiḥ karaiḥ ||
anuṣṭubh (pathyā)

'For those two with the lowest [number of] cubits it shall [measure] four-ninths; and these five and seven elevenths and a half cubits [?]'

If we continue our calculation with the plot widths from BṛS 52.5, a *vāstu* forty-six cubits wide would have a *śālā*-width of

11 1/2 cubits, and a *vāstu* with a width of forty cubits would have a *śālā* with a width of ten cubits; their respective *alindas* would be 5 1/9 cubits and 4 4/9 cubits in width. As stated above, these calculations are purely speculative.

The second half of this stanza is rather problematic; I have no satisfactory explanation to offer. The (*dvandva*-?)compound *sāṅghrinaga* could be a code for the number eleven: *sāṅghri* 'with feet (four in the case of an animal)' + *naga* 'mountain; the number seven.' Indeed, five-elevenths would be next logical step in the series of fractions beginning with two-fifths used in computing the width of the *alinda*. Still, the whole line remains rather cryptic.

19.25-26:
dairghyaṃ syād daśabhiḥ sārdhaiḥ śālāyāḥ ṣoḍaśādiṣu |
***niveśadaśamāṃśo yaḥ sa yutaḥ saptabhiḥ karaiḥ* || 25 ||**
anuṣṭubh (pathyā)

śālāyā vistaraḥ proktaḥ śreṣṭhānām iha veśmanām |
***alindamānaṃ prāg eva proktaṃ nikhilaveśmanām* || 26 ||**
anuṣṭubh (ma-vipulā)

25. 'The length of the *śālā*s shall be fifteen (or: ten and a half) in [the case of houses measuring] sixteen [cubits] and so on; to that which is one-tenth of the dwelling shall be added seven cubits.

26. The width (or: subject) of *śālās* has thus been explained with reference to the largest dwellings; the dimensions of the *alindas* have already been explained with reference to all dwellings.'

The first of these two stanza seems to be in contradiction to 19.22; I have not been able to find any parallel in the three older texts. It may perhaps be pointed out that the method given in 19.25cd yields a *śālā* which, at 10 1/5 and 8 3/5 cubits respectively, is rather narrow in the case of the largest (32 cubits), and rather wide in the case of the smallest plot (16 cubits).

Yet another rule governing the width of the *śālā* is supplied in 28.18:

> *jyeṣṭhe bhavet saptadaśahastāc chālā pravistṛtā |*
> *madhyame daśahastāt tu pañcahastāt kanīyasi ||*

'In the largest [dwelling], the *śālā* shall be seventeen cubits wide, but in a middle-sized one [it shall be] ten cubits [wide], [and it shall be] five cubits [wide] in the smallest [dwelling].'

19.27:
yac chālālindayoḥ śeṣaṃ bhaved garbhagṛhaṃ hi tat |
mūṣāvacchinnam icchanti śālādairghyaṃ vipaścitaḥ ||

c) *mūṣāvicchinnam* (Ka)

anuṣṭubh (pathyā)

'That which is the remainder of [the plot after deducting the area covered by] *śālā* and *alinda* – that shall be the *garbhagṛha*; the learned know the length of the *śālā* to be subdivided by *mūṣā*s.'

The technical term *garbhagṛha* thus appears to be a synonym for *aṅgaṇa*, unless the latter refers to both *garbhagṛha* and *alinda*. Either way, it seems to be congruent with *gṛhanābhi* in 19.13 – cf. 1.5.1 above; for *mūṣā*, cf. 1.5.8.

19.28:
śālāvyāsapramāṇā syāt sarveṣām avakosimā |
diśāsu bhavane śālā vidiśākarṇasāmayaḥ ||

anuṣṭubh (pathyā)

'The *avakosimā* shall have a length and width equal to the width of the *śālā* in all instances; an abode [shall have] the *śālā*s in the cardinal directions, the corner-rooms [shall be] in the intermediate directions.'

Avakosimā is a common technical term for that *śālā* which is located in one of the corners of the dwelling and has no direct access to the courtyard; it is constituted by the intersection of two of the principal *śālā*s. The word *pramāṇa* can have the special meaning 'side of a square', which is arguably the meaning intended here. No *karṇaśālā*s or *avakosimā*s are mentioned in BṛS, MP, or VP.

Karṇasāmayaḥ appears to be the nominative plural of a not otherwise attested **karṇasāmi*.

2.3 *adhyāya* 20

20.01:

agrataḥpr̥ṣṭhataḥśabdau dvāreṇa niyatau gr̥he |
yato dvāraṃ tad agraṃ syāt pr̥ṣṭhaṃ pr̥ṣṭham udāhr̥tam ||
anuṣṭubh (pathyā)

'With reference to the house, the two expressions 'in front' and 'in the back' [are dependent] on [the position of] the door; where there is the door, that shall be the front, the backside is called the back.'

The participle *niyata* in its special meaning 'depending on' is usually construed with the locative rather than the instrumental. One might be tempted to emend **dvāreṣu*, but in absence of any variant readings, it seems more likely that the instrumental *dvāreṇa* is actually the original wording – see above.

20.02-03:

dravyāyāmodayavyāsaiḥ śālā yatrādhikā bhavet |
vāmā vā dakṣiṇā vāpi agrataḥ pr̥ṣṭhato 'pi vā || 02 ||
anuṣṭubh (pathyā)

hanti dravyādhikā dravyam āyāmābhyadhikā kulam |
ucchrāyābhyadhikā pūjāṃ saṃtatiṃ vistarādhikā || 03 ||
anuṣṭubh (pathyā)

02. 'Where the *śālā* may be excessive in its [individual] building elements, its width, height, or length – either the left or the right hand [*śālā*], or [the one] in front or in the back –

03. [there a *śālā*] excessive in [size or number of its individual] elements destroys the property, [one that is] excessive in width [destroys] the household; [one that is] excessive in height [destroys] the *pūjā*, [one that is] excessive in length [destroys] the lineage.'

The adjectives *vāmā* and *dakṣiṇā* in 20.02c) obviously refer to *śālā* in the preceding quarter, which implies that *agrataḥ* and *pr̥ṣṭhataḥ* also refer to the position of the *śālā* with reference to the *vāstu*; this seems to suggest either (1) that the specifications of 20.02f. apply to *catuḥśāla*s in particular; or (2) that the position of the *śālā* in the plot is of no consequence for the auspicious or inauspicious effects of its dimensions. Note, however, that the position of *śālā*s is not usually expressed through the opposition of 'front/back, left/right' but rather with reference to the cardinal directions.

The term *vyāsa* for 'width' does not normally occur in SAS with the exception of some passages in the 10th *adhyāya*, see above. – For the elision of *sandhi* between the third and fourth quarters cf. 1.3.1.

It is not clear whether *dravyādhika-* refers to an excessive size of any of the individual building elements, or to an excess in their total number. The term *dravya* is also ambiguous insofar as it usually refers to building **elements** such as posts or beams, but at least in the context of the 16th *adhyāya* should better be translated as building **material**.

The contents of this stanza is repeated almost verbatim in 48.132:

> *dravyaṃ dravyādhikaṃ hanti kulam āyāmato 'dhikam |*
> *ucchrayābhyadhikaṃ pūjāṃ santatiṃ vistarādhikam ||*

'Excess of building elements destroys the property, excess of width the household; excess of height, the *pūjā*, excess of length, the lineage.'

For this parallel, cf. 1.3.3; cf. perhaps also Br̥S 52.113:

> *prāguttaronnate dhanasutakṣayaḥ sutavadhaś ca durgandhe |*
> *vakre bandhuvināśo na santi garbhāś ca diṅmūḍhe ||*

'In [a house] elevated on the north-eastern side, there is loss of wealth and sons, death of a son in one of bad smell; in a crooked [house], there is annihilation of relatives, no children are born in one not aligned to the cardinal directions.'

In contrast to SAS 20.02-03, the bad consequences given in BṛS 52.113a do not depend on the position of the door, but on the cardinal directions.

20.04-07:

yasya nimnā bhaved bhūmir vāmā dakṣiṇakā sthalā |
bahudoṣaṃ hi tad vāstu putrapautravināśakam || 04 ||

a) *prāyo nimnā* (Kha Da); b) *dakṣiṇakāsthalā* (Śa Śu)
anuṣṭubh (pathyā)

yasya dakṣiṇakā nimnā bhūmir vāmā sthalā bhavet |
yatnenāpi kṛtaṃ tat syād bhartur alpaphalodayam || 05 ||

b) *vāmāsthalā* (Śa Śu)
anuṣṭubh (pathyā)

paścimena bhaven nimnā bhūmiḥ sthūlatarāgrataḥ |
yatra tat sarvavarṇeṣu sarvakāmapradaṃ gṛham || 06 ||

anuṣṭubh (pathyā)

agrataś ca yadā hīnaṃ pṛṣṭhataś cocchritaṃ bhavet |
bhavanaṃ svāmino hy āśu virāgavyasanāya tat || 07 ||

anuṣṭubh (pathyā)

04. 'That *vāstu* the ground on the left of which may be depressed [and the ground] on the right [of which may be] an elevation – that is indeed full of faults, [and] brings about the destruction of sons and grandsons.

05. [That *vāstu*] the ground on the right [of which] is depressed, and [the ground] on the left [of which] is an elevation – even if it were built with care, [would bring] little reward for the master [of the house].

06. Where the ground may be depressed in the back, [and] more massive in front [of the *vāstu*] – that house brings [fulfilment of] all desires for all *varṇas*.

07. If the abode were low in front and high in the back, it would quickly lead to loss of equanimity for the master [of the house].'

The expression *dakṣiṇaka-* in this and the following stanza is obviously a metrical extension of *dakṣiṇa-*; SHASTRI and AGRAWALA seem to have supposed the mss' *dakṣiṇakāsthalā* to represent *dakṣiṇakā *asthalā*, which is rather unlikely; although an adjective *a-sthala-* could easily be formed either from *sthalā* or from *sthalam*, both roughly meaning 'elevation,' this interpretation would render the contents of this stanza virtually identical with that of the following one. SHUKLA has adopted this error in his edition ([2]2001:128) and translates: 'The house whose southern site-ground is depressed on the left-hand side [...]' (*jis ghar ke dakṣiṇ kī sthal-bhūmi bāyīṃ or nimna hoti hai*).

It is obvious that *paścimena* in 20.06a cannot refer to the cardinal direction here, but rather is used as a synonym for *pṛṣṭhataḥ*; cf. also 20.17 below.

From the context it is clear that *hīna-* and *ucchrita-* in 20.07ab refer not to the building itself, but to the grounds, as in the preceding three stanzas. It is awkward that this fact is not reflected in the structure of the stanza. The compound *virāgavyasana* is difficult to construe; the conventional meaning of *virāga* is 'indifference to worldly attachments,' and *vyasana* usually means 'loss, destruction' or 'calamity.' As the opposition to the preceding stanza suggests a negative *phala* for a house the grounds of which are raised in the back and depressed in front, it seems fitting to render *virāga* with the less specific 'equanimity.'

– For the parallel of 20.04-07 in 48.02-04, cf. 1.3.3; it should be noted that in contrast to 48.02-04, no mention here is made of a depression in the centre of the building grounds.

The proclivities of the building grounds are also the subject of BṛS 52.114-115:

icched yadi gṛhavṛddhiṃ tataḥ samantād vivardhayet tulyam |
ekoddeśe doṣaḥ prāg athavā 'py uttare kuryāt || 114 ||
prāg bhavati mitravairaṃ mṛtyubhayaṃ dakṣiṇena yadi vṛddhiḥ |
arthavināśaḥ paścād udagvivṛddhir manastāpaḥ || 115 ||

114. 'If one wishes for prosperity of the house, then one shall raise [the ground] to an equal height on all sides; [if] a fault in one direction [cannot be avoided, then it] shall be made in the east or in the north.
115. [If] there is an elevation in the east, [the result is] enmity with friends, if in the south, danger of death; loss of wealth in the west, a proclivity in the north [causes] heartache.'

Cf. also BṛS 52.89:

udagādiplavam iṣṭaṃ viprādīnāṃ pradakṣiṇenaiva |
vipraḥ sarvatra vased anuvarṇam atheṣṭam anyeṣām ||

'A declivity in the north etc. is fit for brahmans etc. in clockwise direction; according to others, a brahman may dwell anywhere, [the others] according to *varṇa*.'

It is quite obvious that the rules given in SAS 20.04-07 and 48.02-04 are unrelated to the ones given in BṛS. While MP seems to contain no corresponding passage at all, the somewhat cryptic text of VP 01.32cd-33 bears a faint resemblance with BṛS 54.114 quoted above:

[...] *gambhīrā brāhmaṇī bhūmir nṛpāṇāṃ tuṅgam āśritā* || 32 ||
vaiśyānāṃ samabhūmiś ca śūdrāṇāṃ vikaṭā smṛtā |
sarveṣāṃ caiva varṇānāṃ samabhūmiḥ śubhāvahā || 33 ||

32. '[...] The ground for a brahman [shall be] low, that for a king [i.e., *kṣatriya*] situated on an elevation.
33. The ground for a *vaiśya* [shall be] even, that for a *śūdra* is known to be excessive [?]; and for all *varṇa*s, an even ground is auspicious.'

20.08-10:

sacchatraṃ ca sakakṣaṃ ca tathaiva saparikramam |
***saprabhaṃ ca samākhyātaṃ gṛham atra caturvidham* || 08 ||**

anuṣṭubh (pathyā)

bāhyodakaṃ ca sacchatraṃ sakakṣam ubhayodakam |
sāvaśyāyaṃ tu yad veśma tad vidyāt saparikramam || 09 ||
anuṣṭubh (pathyā)

ekenāpy atra mukhataḥ pṛṣṭhataḥ pārśvato 'pi vā |
saprabhaṃ syād alindena lakṣaṇaṃ tu pṛthak pṛthak || 10 ||
anuṣṭubh (na-vipulā)

08. '*Sacchatra* and *sakakṣa*, also *saparikrama*, and *saprabha* – [thus] is called the four-fold house.

09. And [a dwelling that] has water on its outside [is called] *sacchatra*, *sakakṣa* [is called a dwelling that] has got water on both sides; a dwelling that is endowed with *avaśyāya* – that shall be known as *saparikrama*.

10. [That dwelling which] has got one single *alinda*, in front, in the back, or on the sides – that shall be [called] *saprabha*, [its] qualities, though, [shall be enumerated] in due order.'

SAS 20.08 supplies the names and descriptions of four house types; as we shall see in the following stanzas, the precise nature of this fourfold distinction is far from clear. Translated literally, the four houses presented here are referred to as (1) 'having an umbrella or parasol,' (2) 'having an enclosure or inner chamber,' (3) 'having circumambulation,' and (4) 'having light or splendour.' In 20.09, a house of the type of *sacchatra* is defined as 'having water on its outside' (*bāhyodaka-*), whereas a *sakakṣa*-house is said to have water on both sides (*ubhayodaka-*), i.e. inside and out. In the absence of any further explanation, one can only assume that *sacchatra* refers to an edifice that is covered in its entirety by a roof (as if covered by an umbrella) which keeps out the rain water, whereas a house with an inner courtyard (or 'enclosure') receiving part of the rain water would be called *sakakṣa* (cf. the Graeco-Roman atrium house of the *impluviatum*-type, KOEPF [3]1999 s.v. Atrium).

The third type is particularly puzzling; from its name, one would expect a house with some sort of uninterrupted passage running around either its outside or its interior courtyard. But in 20.09, it is described as 'having dew' (*sāvaśyāya-*)! The fourth type, *saprabha*, is more thoroughly explained in 20.10 as 'having got one single *alinda*' (*ekenāpi* [...] *saprabhaṃ syād alindena*). A loose connection between its designation and its description can be established insofar as an open verandah is exposed to the daylight. This is the only of the four house types mentioned in this stanza described at greater length in the following stanzas (20.11-12), whereas a house with two *alinda*s (see 20.13-18) seems not to be implied here at all.

If *sacchatra* and *sakakṣa* can be taken as opposites of a kind, then one may well speculate about a similar opposition between *saparikrama* and *saprabha*; perhaps the former refers to a building with an interior courtyard surrounded by an uninterrupted *alinda* ('circumambulating' it) – in effect, a *catuḥśāla* –, while the latter describes an edifice with an *alinda* on its outside. If that is the case, then *sacchatra* is more or less synonymous with *hīnavāstu* (cf. 24.25 below), while *sakakṣa* refers to any house with an interior courtyard, i.e. a *catuḥ-* to *daśaśāla.*

In BṛS 52.20-21 we find an alternative fourfold distinction regarding the position not of the *alinda*, but of the passage known as *vīthikā* 'footpath' (cf. pd s.v. *vīthi* '*Strasse, Weg* [...] **Terrasse, der freie Raum zwischen Haus und Strasse*'):

> *śālātribhāgatulyā kartavyā vīthikā bahir bhavanāt* |
> *yady agrato bhavati sā soṣṇīṣaṃ nāma tad vāstu* || 20 ||
> *sāyāśrayam iti paścāt sāvaṣṭambhaṃ tu pārśvasaṃsthitayā* |
> *susthitam iti ca samantāc chāstrajñaiḥ pūjitāḥ sarvāḥ* || 21 ||

20. 'Outside the dwelling, a *vīthikā* shall be made, equal [in width] to one-third of the *śālā*; if it is [situated] in front [of the dwelling], the *vāstu* is called *soṣṇīṣa* ('having a diadem');

21. *sāyāśraya* ('evening shelter'), [if the *vīthikā* is situated] in the back, *sāvaṣṭambha* ('having a support or prop') on account of its being situated on the sides; and *susthita* ('well-placed'), [if it is] all around; that is praised by all who are conversant with the *śāstra*.'

Cf. also MP 254.37-38:

śālāyās tu tribhāgena yasyāgre vīthikā bhavet |
soṣṇīṣaṃ nāma tad vāstu paścāc chreyocchrayaṃ bhavet || 37 ||
pārśvayor vīthikā yatra sāvaṣṭambhaṃ tad ucyate |
samantād vīthikā yatra susthitaṃ tad ihocyate || 38 ||

'That *vāstu* which may have a *vīthikā* in front, [measuring] one-third of the *śālā* [in width] is called *soṣṇīṣa*, [if it is located] in the back, it shall be [called] *śreyocchraya* [sic!]. That [*vāstu*] which has got a *vīthikā* on the sides is called *sāvaṣṭambha*, that which has got a *vīthikā* all around is here called *susthita*.'

An identical statement can be found in VP 02.154-155ab:

śālātribhāgatulyā ca kartavyā vīthikā bahiḥ |
bhavanāt pūrvato 'ṣṇīṣaṃ paścā?(s vā)t sā(pā)yāśrayaṃ bhavet ||
sāvaṣṭambhaṃ pārśvayos tu sarvatra susthitaṃ bhavet |

'Outside, a *vīthikā* shall be made equal to one-third of the *śālā* [in width]; [if it is situated] in front of the dwelling, [the latter] shall be [called] *uṣṇīṣa* [sic!], [if] in the back, [it shall be called] **sāyāśraya*; *sāvaṣṭambha*, though, [if it is] on both sides, [if the *vīthikā* is] all around, [the dwelling] shall be [called] *susthita*.'

In the face of this considerable agreement, it is interesting to note that the *vīthikā* does not have a very prominent place in SAS; it is mentioned only twice in stereotyped statements about the innumerable varieties of *catuḥ*- and *dviśāla*s respectively; cf. SAS 19.38-40ab:

mūṣābhedāś catuḥśāle ṣaṭpañcāśacchatadvayam |
alindavīthīpragrīvaniryūhakagavākṣakaiḥ || 38 ||
tamaṅgabhadravinyāsaracanābhir anekadhā |
aparasparasaṃbādhāt saṃvṛtair vivṛtair api || 39 ||
gṛhabhedāḥ prasūyante yeṣāṃ saṃkhyā na vidyate |

38. 'In the case of the *catuḥśāla*, there are 256 divisions according to [the position of] the *mūṣās*; by [adding] *alindas*, *vīthīs*, fences, *niryūhakas*, [and] *gavākṣas*;
39. by the arrangement and distribution of *tamaṅgas* and *bhadras*, [the divisions are] multiple. Because they are covered and overlap by obstructing each other:
40. divisions of the house arise the number of which is not known. [...]'

It is perhaps no coincidence that these stanzas occur at the end of the passage in the 19th *adhyāya* discussed under 1.8.2 above; cf. also SAS 22.03-04:

> *anekabhedabhinnāni laghuprastārayogataḥ* |
> *mūṣābhedakrameṇa syur bhedābhedakrameṇa tu* || 03 ||
> *tathā nilīnakaraṇād vīthikālindamārgataḥ* |
> *prāggrīvādividhānena dvaiśālyādiviparyayāt* || 04 ||

03. 'The divisions shall be divided variously by application of the *laghuprastāra*; by the divisions according to [the positions of] the *mūṣās*, and by the divisions of the divisions.
04. Also because of concealing [?], [and] because of the *vīthikā*, the *alinda*, and the road [or: because of the passage that is constituted by *vīthikā* or *alinda*], by erecting fences etc., and because of inversion of *dvaiśālya* [?] etc.'

Note that in both passages, *vīthī*/*vīthikā* and *alinda* are mentioned together, which shows that they cannot refer to the same thing. For *nilīna*- in 22.04a, cf. note on 20.35 below.

20.11-12:

***eko 'lindas tu kartavyo mukhato dakṣiṇena vā* |**
***mukhe rājaprasādāya dakṣiṇe 'rthavivardhanaḥ* || 11 ||**
anuṣṭubh (pathyā)

***vāmatas tu na kartavya eko 'lindo na pṛṣṭhataḥ* |**
***vāmato 'rthavināśāya pṛṣṭhato mriyate gṛhī* || 12 ||**
anuṣṭubh (pathyā)

11. 'One *alinda* shall be built in front or on the right; if [it is situated] in front, [it leads] to the king's favour, if [it be built] on the right, [the result shall be] increase of wealth.

12. A single *alinda* shall not be built on the left, nor in the back; [if it is built] on the left, [it leads] to destruction of wealth, [if it is built] in the back, the householder will die.'

These prescriptions apply to houses of the type of *saprabha* as defined in 20.10 above; as already indicated in the introduction (1.3.3), these and the following stanzas describe ten of the sixteen basic varieties of a single *śālā* introduced in 23.04-12ab:

vidyād alindān sarveṣu laghusthāneṣu paṇḍitaḥ |
savyāvartaṃ gr̥hamukhād etāṃś ca viniyojayet || 04 ||
eṣām alindasaṃyogād bhavanānāṃ pr̥thak pr̥thak |
nāmāni guṇadoṣāś ca vakṣyante 'nukramāt ataḥ || 05 ||
dhruvaṃ dhanyaṃ jayaṃ nandaṃ kharaṃ kāntaṃ manoramam |
sumukhaṃ durmukhaṃ krūraṃ supakṣaṃ dhanadaṃ kṣayam || 06 ||
ākrandaṃ vipulaṃ caiva vijayaṃ gr̥ham uttamam |
dhruve jayam avāpnoti dhanye dhānyāgamo bhavet || 07 ||
jaye sapatnāñ jayati nande sarvāḥ samr̥ddhayaḥ |
kharam āyāsadaṃ veśma kānte ca labhate śriyam || 08 ||
āyurārogyam aiśvaryaṃ tathā vittasya sampadaḥ |
manorame manstuṣṭir gr̥habhartuḥ prakīrtitā || 09 ||
sumukhe rājyasanmānaṃ durmukhe kalahaḥ sadā |
krūravyādhibhayaṃ krūre supakṣaṃ gotravr̥ddhikr̥t || 10 ||
dhanade hemaratnādi gāś caiva labhate pumān |
kṣayaṃ sarvakṣayaṃ geham ākrandaṃ jñātimr̥tyudam || 11 ||
ārogyaṃ vipule khyātir vijaye sarvasampadaḥ |

04. 'The expert shall know the *alinda*s to be in all *laghu*-positions [of the *prastāra*]; one shall set them down beginning from the front side of the house moving left [i.e., in clockwise direction].
05. The names, as well as the merits and defects of the houses according to the application of the *alinda*s are now enumerated in due order, one after the other.

06. (1) *dhruva*, (2) *dhanya*, (3) *jaya*, (4) *nanda*, (5) *khara*, (6) *kānta*, (7) *manorama*; (8) *sumukha*, (9) *durmukha*, (10) *krūra*, (11) *supakṣa*, (12) *dhanada*, (13) *kṣaya*;
07. (14) *ākranda*, (15) *vipula*, and (16) *vijaya*, the best house. In a *dhruva*, one gains victory, in a *dhanya*, there shall be aqcuisition of grain.
08. In a *jaya*, one vanquishes the enemy, in a *nanda*, there are all [kinds of] success; the dwelling [called] *khara* brings fatigue, in a *kānta*, one gains prosperity.
09. In a *manorama*, there is known to be [long] life, good health, power, abundance of riches, and contentment for the master of the house.
10. In a *sumukha*, there is royal favour, in a *durmukha*, there is strife at all times; danger of terrible disease [dwells] in a *krūra*, a *supakṣa* causes the clan [or: cattle shed] to prosper.
11. In a *dhanada*, a man gains gold, jewels, and cows; a house [called] *kṣaya* causes ruin of everything, an *ākranda* causes death of relatives.
12. There is good health in a *vipula*, abundance of everything is known to be in a *vijaya* [...] .'

It will not be necessary here to recount the position of the *alinda*(s) in each of these houses, as they can be taken from fig. 8ab. What is significant in this context is that the four positions of a single *alinda* given in 20.11-12 correspond to *dhanya*, *jaya*, *durmukha*, and *khara* respectively; and although there is no direct correspondence between the *phala*s given in these two passages, there is an overall agreement concerning the auspicious or inauspicious nature of the respective position of the *alinda*.

It seems that 23.02-12ab has its origin in VP 02.101-107, which shows some variations:

guror adho laghuḥ sthāpyaḥ purastād ūrdhvavan nyaset |
gurubhiḥ paścime pūr(ve)ṇe sarvalaghvavadhir vidhiḥ || 101 ||
syād alindo laghusthāne nālind(aṃ)o gurum āśrit(am)aḥ |
pradakṣiṇair gr̥hadvārād (ā)alindair daśaṣaḍvidhā || 102 ||
dhruvasaṃjñaṃ gr̥haṃ tv ādyaṃ dhanadhānyasukhapradam |
dhānyaṃ dhānyapadaṃ nr̥ṇāṃ jayaṃ syād vijayapradam || 103 ||

nandaṃ strīhānidaṃ [?] *nūnaṃ kharaṃ sampadvināśanam* |
putrapautrapradaṃ kāntaṃ śrīpadaṃ syān manoharam || 104 ||
suvaktraṃ bhogadaṃ nūnaṃ durmukhaṃ vimukhapradam |
sarvaduḥkhapradaṃ krūraṃ vipulaṃ [sic!]
śatrubhītidam [?] || 105 ||
dhanadaṃ dhanadaṃ gehaṃ kṣayaṃ sarvakṣayāvaham |
ākrandaśokajanakaṃ vipulaṃ śrīyaśaḥpradam || 106 ||
vipulaṃ nāma sadṛśaṃ dhanadaṃ vijayābhidham || 107 ||

101. 'Underneath the *guru* [in the first column], *laghu* shall be set down, afterwards [*guru*] shall be written as above; when the last [position] is filled in with *gurus*, the last [line consists of] *laghus* entirely – [this is] the rule.
102. There shall be an *alinda* in [each] *laghu*-position, there shall be no *alinda* in a *guru*; by [placing] the *alindas* in clockwise direction beginning from the front door, [there is a] sixteenfold [division].
103. The first house is called *dhruva*, it causes the happiness of wealth and grain; a *dhānya* is a receptacle of grain for men, a *jaya* shall cause victory.
104. A *nanda* verily causes death of women [?], a *khara* destroys wealth; a *kānta* bestows sons and grandsons, a *manohara* shall be an abode of prosperity.
105. A *suvaktra* verily causes pleasure, a *durmukha* causes adversity; a *krūra* causes all [kinds of] suffering, a *vipula* [sic!] causes danger from enemies [?].
106. A house [called] *dhanada* bestows wealth, a *kṣaya* brings about ruin of everything; an *ākranda* produces sorrow, a *vipula* causes prosperity and fame.
107. Like the [house] called *vipula*, the one called *vijaya* causes wealth.'

Again, the positive or negative properties of the respective houses generally differ in detail only – with the obvious exception of *kānta* and *vipula*, which latter word might be a corruption of **vipakṣa* (for *supakṣa*); I am inclined to blame these differences on an error in the textual transmission.

There appears to be a system at work here, a set of three principles governing the auspicious and inauspicious effects of a *śālā* depending on the position of its *alinda*(s) with reference to the front door; these can be stated as follows:

(1) an *alinda* in front or on the right hand side is auspicious, an *alinda* in the back or on the left is inauspicious – cf. the text;
(2) an auspicious *alinda* cancels out the ill effects of its direct opposite (cf. *kānta*, *supakṣa*);
(3) the opposition left – right is more significant than the opposition front – back: an *alinda* on the right is capable of overriding the effects of an *alinda* in the back or on the left (cf. *manorama*, *supakṣa*) or even both (cf. *vipula*), whereas an *alinda* in front can only cancel out the undesirable effects of an *alinda* in the back, but not those of an *alinda* on the left (cf. *kānta*, *krūra*).

20.13-18:

***yasya syātām alindau dvau gr̥hasyobhayapārśvayoḥ* |**
***dhanalābhaṃ vijānīyāt tatpraveśe kuṭumbinaḥ* || 13 ||**
anuṣṭubh (pathyā)

***yasya syātām alindau dvāv agrataḥ pr̥ṣṭhatas tathā* |**
***dhanadhānyam avāpnoti saubhāgyaṃ cāpi tadgr̥hī* || 14 ||**
anuṣṭubh (pathyā)

***yasya vā halakālindo mukhato dakṣiṇena vā* |**
***rājaprasādais tatsvāmī dhanadhānyaiś ca vardhate* || 15 ||**
anuṣṭubh (ma-vipulā)

***vāmato halakālindo mukhataś ca kr̥to yadi* |**
***rājadaṇḍabhayaṃ vidyāt patnī cāsya vinaśyati* || 16 ||**
anuṣṭubh (pathyā)

***dakṣiṇo halakālindaḥ paścimaś ca kr̥to yadi* |**
***tataḥ parāpi vr̥ddhiḥ syāt saubhāgyaṃ ca paraṃ bhavet* || 17 ||**
anuṣṭubh (pathyā)

pṛṣṭhato halakālindo vāmataś ca kṛto yadi |
kalatramaraṇaṃ tatra bhaved durbhagatāpi ca || 18 ||

anuṣṭubh (pathyā)

13. '[The dwelling which] has got two *alinda*s, [one] on either side of the house – on entering that, the householder shall experience gain of wealth.

14. [That house which] has got two *alinda*s, [one each] in front and in the back – the master of that [house] gains wealth and grain, and also good fortune.

15. Or [that building] which has got a *halakālinda* in front or on the right – the master of that [house] prospers through the favour of the king, and through wealth and grain.

16. If a *halakālinda* is built in front and on the left [of the building, then] he shall know danger of punishment by the king, and his wife will perish.

17. If a *halakālinda* is built on the right and in the back [of the building], then there shall be great success, and excellent good fortune [for the master of the house].

18. If a *halakālinda* is built in the back and on the left [of the building], there shall be death of the wife, and also bad fortune.'

20.13-18 contain the rules for houses with two *alinda*s, on opposite sides of the house in the case of 20.13-14 (corresponding to the *supakṣa* and the *kānta* of 23.04-12ab), and adjacent to each other in 20.15-18 (*nanda*, *krūra*, *manorama*, and *kṣaya* respectively). These latter are referred to as *halakālinda*, literally 'plough-verandahs'. The word *hala*/*-ka* is generally used to describe architectural objects situated at right angles to each other, cf. 24.01-18ab, where the synonymous *lāṅgala*/*-ka* is also used in the same sense. It is remarkable that the four house types referred to in

20.08 do not seem to include a house with more than one and less than four *alinda*s, and also that no mention is made in this *adhyāya* of a house with three *alinda*s; the latter are only implicitly contained in the *prastāra*s of the 23rd *adhyāya*. With the exception of the parallel passage in VP 02.103-107 quoted in the preceding note, none of the three anterior texts contains any information about positive or negative results of the number and position of the *alinda*s.

– For *paścima* in 20.17b cf. note on 20.06 above; note also the uniformity of the first lines of 20.16-18.

20.19-20:

pr̥ṣṭhato vāmataś caiva purato dakṣiṇena vā |
alindasya kr̥tasyātha vakṣyāmo 'nukramāt phalam || 19 ||

anuṣṭubh (pathyā)

pr̥ṣṭhato dāranāśāya dhanalābhāya dakṣiṇe |
agre rājaprasādāya vāmato 'rthavināśanaḥ || 20 ||

b) *dhananāśāya* (Kha Da)
anuṣṭubh (pathyā)

19. 'We will now pronounce the result of an *alinda* built in the back, on the left, in front, or on the right in due order.

20. [If an *alinda* is built] in the back, [it leads] to loss of a wife, to acquisition of wealth [if it is built] on the right; [if it is built] in front [it leads] to the king's favour, [if it is built] on the left, [its result is] destruction of wealth.'

These two stanzas are an almost verbatim repetition of 20.11-12, cf. 1.3.3.

20.21-23:

samāpitaṃ tu yad vāstu sarvataḥ pariśodhitam |
svāminas tad bhaved dhanyaṃ sthapateś ca yaśaskaram || 21 ||

anuṣṭubh (pathyā)

arjitaṃ vardhate tasya vṛddhiś ca syān nṛpaśriyā |
dharmakāmāś ca vardhante kīrtir āyur yaśo balam || 22 ||

a) *arcitaṃ* (Kha Da); c) *dhanakāmāś ca* (Kha Da)
anuṣṭubh (pathyā)

nityaṃ prakrīḍitajanaṃ nityaṃ saṃnihitaśri tat |
nṛtyavāditragītaiś ca nityāmodaṃ nirāmayam || 23 ||

b) *hitaṃ saṃnihita°* (Kha Da)
anuṣṭubh (na-vipulā)

21. 'That finished *vāstu* which is purified on all sides – that is auspicious for the owner, and glorious for the *sthapati*.

22. What he has obtained, shall increase, and there shall be prosperity by the blessing of the king; and [his] righteousness and desires thrive, [also his] fame, life[-span], reputation, and power.

23. It shall always have playful inmates, Śrī shall always be near to that [dwelling]; always shall it be delightful with dance, instrumental music, and song, and free from illness.'

These stanzas elaborate on the positive results of adhering to what SHUKLA (1958:324sqq.) has referred to as the 'building bye-laws' of *vāstuvidyā*: a *vāstu* that on being completed is found to be perfectly in accord with the regulations is conducive to the owner's material wellbeing, and beneficial for the reputation of the builder.

The second line of 20.22 seems to contain an allusion to the three conventional goals of human life, *dharma, artha*, and *kāma*; whereas *dharma* and *kāma* are expressly mentioned, *artha* is implied by the four terms in the last quarter (*kīrti, āyus, yaśas, bala*).

20.24-26:

tatra naikaprakārāṇi triśālāny upalakṣayet |
prakāreṣu ca sarveṣu nindyau yāmyāparojjhitau || 24 ||

anuṣṭubh (pathyā)

ekasmin svāmino mṛtyur aparasmin dhanakṣayaḥ |
***pūrvottarojjhitau dhanyau saṃjñāś caiṣāṃ prakārataḥ* || 25 ||**

c) *pūrvottarau sthitau* (Kha Da)

anuṣṭubh (pathyā)

syur udakpūrvayāmy*ādya*śālāhīnāny anukramāt |
***hiraṇyanābhasukṣetracullīpakṣaghnanāmabhiḥ* || 26 ||**

a) °*apy a*° (Ka Kha Ga Da Śa Śu).

anuṣṭubh (pathyā)

24. 'There, one shall describe the [buildings of the type of] *triśāla* [which are] of many diverse types; of all types, those two that have no souther [or] western [*śālā*] are to be frowned upon.

25. In the one, [there is] death for the master [of the house], in the other, [there is] loss of wealth; those two that have no eastern [or] northern [*śālā*] are auspicious, and their [respective] designations according to their type [are now enumerated].

26. They shall be – [according as they are] lacking the northern, eastern, southern etc. *śālā*, in this order – *hiraṇyanābha*, *sukṣetra*, *cullī*, [and] *pakṣaghna* by name.'

The parallel of 20.24-26 in 22.07-10ab has already been discussed under 1.3.3 and 1.3.4 above. There are two reasons for the emendation *°*ādya*° for °*āpy a*° in 20.26ab (which was suggested by Roland STEINER in a private communication): (1) beside the fact that the compound *aśālāhīna-* would be rather difficult to construe ('diminished by lacking a *śālā*'), it would also violate the caesura (*a*|*śālā*°); (2) as the compound contains no equivalent of 'west(ern),' and as the phrase *udakpūrvayāmya api aśālāhīnāny* [*gṛhāṇi*] would be ungrammatical, the emendation *°*dya*° for the graphologically similar °*pya*° is the least intrusive solution.

Cf. BṛS 52.37-38:

uttaraśālāhīnaṃ hiraṇyanābhaṃ triśālakaṃ dhanyam |
prākśālayā viyuktaṃ sukṣetraṃ vṛddhidaṃ vāstu || 37 ||
yāmyāhīnaṃ cullī triśālakaṃ vittanāśakaram etat |
pakṣaghnam aparayā varjitaṃ sutadhvaṃsavairakaram || 38 ||

37. 'A *triśāla* without a northern *śālā* is the wealth-bestowing *hiraṇyanābha*; without an eastern *śālā*, it is the prosperous *vāstu* [called] *sukṣetra*.
38. a *triśāla* without a southern [*śālā*] is [called] *cullī*, that causes destruction of property, [it is called] *pakṣaghna* [if] it has no eastern [*śālā*], it causes loss of sons, and enmity.'

The corresponding passage in MP 254.04cd-08ab has some slight variations, including the omission of the name *cullī*:

saumyaśālāvihīnaṃ yat triśālaṃ dhanyakaṃ ca tat || 04 ||
kṣemavṛddhikaraṃ nṛṇāṃ bahuputraphalapradam |
śālayā pūrvayā hīnaṃ sukṣetram iti viśrutam || 05 ||
dhanyaṃ yaśasyam āyuṣyaṃ śokamohavināśanam |
śālayā yāmyayā hīnaṃ yad viśālaṃ tu śālayā || 06 ||
kulakṣayakaraṃ nṛṇāṃ sarvavyādhibhayāvaham |
hīnaṃ paścimayā yat tu pakṣaghnaṃ nāma tat punaḥ || 07 ||
mitrabandhūn sutān hanti tathā sarvabhayāvaham |

04. '[...] That *triśāla* which has no northern *śālā* – that is called *dhanyaka* [sic!];
05. it causes security and prosperity for men, [and] has the result of many sons. Without an eastern *śālā*, it is called *sukṣetra*:
06. [it causes] wealth, fame, [and long] life, [and] destroys grief and delusion. That which is lacking a southern *śālā*, but extensive on account of a *śālā* [?]:
07. [that] causes loss of the household for men, and brings about all [kinds of] diseases and dangers. But that which has no western *śālā* – that is called *pakṣaghna*;
08. it kills friends, relatives, and sons, and brings about all [kinds of] dangers. [...]'

Cf. also VP 02.186-190:

> *uttaradvārahīnaṃ yat triśālaṃ dhanadhānyadam |*
> *hiraṇyanābhanāmānaṃ* [sic!] *rājñāṃ*
> *saukhyavivardhanam* || 186 ||
> *prāgdvāraśālahīnaṃ tu sukṣetraṃ nāma tad gṛham |*
> *vṛddhidaṃ putrapautrāṇāṃ dhanadhānyasamṛddhidam* || 187 ||
> *yāmyaśālāvihīnaṃ ta(hli)t triśālaṃ cu(ttri)llisaṃjñakam |*
> *vināśanaṃ dhanasyāpi putrapautrādināśanam* || 188 ||
> *pratyak(chā)śālāvihīnaṃ tu pakṣaghnaṃ nāma tad gṛham |*
> *putrāṇāṃ doṣadaṃ caiva paraṃ ca puravāsinām* || 189 ||
> *catvāro 'mī mayā proktā bhedāś caiva caturdaśa |*
> *tasmād vicārya kurvīta gṛhakarmaṇi kovidaḥ* || 190 ||

186. 'The wealth- and grain-bestowing *triśāla* that has no northern door – that is called *hiraṇyanābha*, and makes the happiness of kings increase.
187. Without an eastern door and *śālā*, the house is called *sukṣetra*; it causes prosperity for the sons and grandsons, and causes abundance of wealth and grain.
188. A *triśāla* without a southern *śālā* is called **cullī*; it destroys the property, and destroys sons, grandsons, etc.
189. Without a western *śālā*, the house is called *pakṣaghna*; it has bad consequences both for the sons and for the other inhabitants of the city.
190. These four [types of *triśāla*] have been declared by me, and also the fourteen divisions [?]; the expert should go about building a house accordingly.'

20.27:

viniyogo yathālindam alindavyūḍhir icchayā |
veśmāny atha dviśālāni kīrtyante ṣaḍ yathākramam ||

anuṣṭubh (pathyā)

'[Their] layout [shall be executed] according to the *alinda*, the breadth [?] of the *alinda* [shall be] as one desires; now the six dwellings [of the type of] *dviśāla* are enumerated in due order.'

20.28-32:
dikkarṇeṣu dviśālāni tatkarṇānyeṣu nirdiśet |
saṃmukhe dve sametāni ṣaḍ etāny upalakṣayet || 28 ||
b) *tatkartānyeṣu* (Kha Da)
anuṣṭubh (pathyā)

siddhārthaṃ dakṣiṇāpratyag bhavanty atrārthasiddhayaḥ |
yamasūryam udakpratyak tatra mṛtyubhayaṃ sadā || 29 ||
anuṣṭubh (pathyā)

prāgudīcyos tu daṇḍaḥ syād daṇḍas tatra sadā bhavet |
prāgyāmyayos tu vātākhyaṃ vāstu tat kalahottaram || 30 ||
anuṣṭubh (pathyā)

udagdakṣiṇasāṃmukhye dviśālaṃ kācavāstv iti |
tatra jñātivirodhaḥ syān na tat kuryāt kadācana || 31 ||
anuṣṭubh (pathyā)

prākpratīcyos tu sāṃmukhye cullīvāstu vinirdiśet |
tatra vittakṣayo ghoraḥ kadāpy etan na kārayet || 32 ||
anuṣṭubh (pathyā)

28. 'The *dviśāla*s [are situated] in the intermediate directions, one shall specify [their *phala*s] in those [directions] across from their [inner] angles; two [of them have wings] facing each other, all in all one shall know these six:

29. [the *śālā*s of a building of the type of] *siddhārtha* [are situated in] the south [and in] the west, here is found fulfilment of worldly goals; [the *śālā*s of a building of the type of] *yamasūrya* [are situated in] the north [and in] the west, always [there is] mortal danger there.

30. But in case [the *śālā*s are situated in the directions of] east and north, it shall be [called] *daṇḍa*, always there shall be punishment there; but in case [the *śālā*s are situated in the

directions of] east and south it is called *vāta*, that *vāstu* [causes] the worst kind of strife.

31. If it faces north and south, the *dviśāla* [is known as] a *vāstu* [of the type of] *kāca*; there, there shall be enmity with close relatives, never shall that [type of house] be built.

32. But [that building] which faces east and west – [that] one shall know as a *vāstu* [of the type of] *cullī*; [there is] terrible loss of wealth there, never shall one cause that [type of house] to be built.'

The first half of 20.28 is rather cryptic, and accordingly my translation is only tentative: *tatkarṇānya-* seems to refer to the fact that the auspicious or inauspicious properties of a *hīnaśāla* are determined not so much by the quarters in which the main body of the edifice is situated, but rather by the quarters to whose good or bad influences the building is exposed by the absence of a *śālā*. Accordingly, a *siddhārtha*, being exposed to the beneficient influences of the north and the east, bodes well for its owner, while a *daṇḍa*, which is exposed to the bad influences of the south and the west, causes his death etc. *Saṃmukha-* clearly refers to *kāca* and *cullī*, whose *śālā*s are face to face, and not at right angles with each other as in the case of the other four *dviśāla*s.

For the parallel in 22.07-10ab, cf. 1.3.3 and 1.3.4 above; cf. also BṛS 52.39-41:

> *siddhārtham aparayāmye yamasūryaṃ paścimottare śāle* |
> *daṇḍākhyaṁ udakpūrve vātākhyaṃ prāgyutā yāmyā* || 39 ||
> *pūrvāpare tu śāle gṛhacullī dakṣiṇottare kācam* |
> *siddhārthe 'rthāvāptir yamasūrye gṛhapater mṛtyuḥ* || 40 ||
> *daṇḍavadho daṇḍākhye kalahodvegaḥ sadaiva vātākhye* |
> *vittavināśaś cullyāṃ jñātivirodhaḥ smṛtaḥ kāce* || 41 ||

39. 'The *siddhārtha* [consists of] a western and a southern [*śālā*], the *yamasūrya* [of] a western and a northern *śālā*; [the house] called

daṇḍa [consists of] a northern and an eastern [*śālā*], the one called *vāta* [of] a southern [*śālā*] added to an eastern one.
40. An eastern and a western *śālā* [constitute] the *gr̥hacullī*, a southern and a northern one the *kāca*; in a *siddhārtha*, there is acquisition of wealth, in a *yamasūrya*, death of the householder.
41. Corporal punishment in the one called *daṇḍa*, strife and alarm always [reside] in the one called *vāta*; loss of property in a *cullī*, hostility of relatives is known [to reside] in a *kāca*.'

Cf. also, again with some omissions, and probably more than a fair deal of textual corruption, MP 254.08cd-14ab:

yāmyāparābhyāṃ śālābhyāṃ dhanadhānyaphalapradam || 08 ||
kṣemavr̥ddhikaraṃ nr̥̄ṇāṃ tathā putraphalapradam |
yamasūryaṃ ca vijñeyaṃ paścimottaraśālikam || 09 ||
rājāgnibhayadaṃ nr̥̄ṇāṃ kulakṣayakaraṃ ca yat |
udakpūrve tu sālehaṃ daṇḍākhye yatra tad bhavet || 10 ||
akālamr̥tyubhayadaṃ paracakrabhayāvaham |
(dhanā)vātākhyaṃ pūrvayāmyābhyāṃ śālābhyāṃ yad
<d>viśālakam || 11 ||
tac chastrabhayadaṃ nr̥̄ṇāṃ parābhavabhayāvaham |
cullī pūrvāparābhyāṃ tu sā bhaven mr̥tyusūcinī || 12 ||

vaidhavyadāyakaṃ strīṇām anekabhayakārakam |
kā(rya)cam uttarayāmyābhyāṃ śālābhyāṃ
bhayadaṃ nr̥ṇām || 13 ||
siddhārthavajravarjyāṇi viśālāni sadā budhaiḥ |

08. [...] [A house constituted] by a southern and a western *śālā* has wealth and grain as its consequence;
09. it causes security and prosperity for men, [and] has the result of sons. It is known as *yamasūrya* [if] it has a western and a northern *śālā*;
10. it causes danger for men from the king's side, and from fire; and that which causes destruction of the household – that is the one with a northern and an eastern *śālā*, which [together] are called *daṇḍa*;
11. it causes the danger of untimely death, and brings about danger from a foreign army. That *dviśāla* called **vāta*, which [is constituted] by an eastern and a southern *śālā*:

12. that causes danger from weapons for men, and brings about the danger of subjugation by others. But the *cullī*, [which is constituted] by an eastern and a western [*śālā*] – that shall be the needle of death [itself];
13. it causes widowhood for women, and causes multiple kinds of danger.The **kāca* [that is constituted by] a northern and a southern *śālā* causes danger for men.
14. The *viśālas* [?] shall always be kept free of *siddhārthavajra* by the wise [?]. [...]'

Cf. also VP 02.171-185, which differs considerably from the other texts – among other things, by using the specific names of the sixteen kinds of single *śālā*s (cf. fig.10):

yāmyaśālā nyased ādau dvitīyā paścime tataḥ |
tṛtīyā cottare sthāpyā caturthī pūrvapaścimā || 171 ||
dakṣiṇe durmukhaṃ kṛtvā pūrve ca kharasaṃjñakam |
tad vātākhyaṃ bhaved gehaṃ vātarogapradaṃ smṛtam || 172 ||
dakṣiṇe durmukhaṃ gehaṃ paścime dhānyasaṃjñakam |
siddhārthākhyaṃ dviśālaṃ ca sa<r>vasiddhikaraṃ
nṛṇām || 173 ||
paścime dhānyanāmānam [sic!] *uttare jayasaṃjñakam* |
(maya)yamasūryaṃ dviśālaṃ tan mṛtyudaṃ nāśạdaṃ
smṛtam || 174 ||
pūrve tu kharanāmānam uttare dhānyasa<ṃ>jñakam |
daṇḍākhya tad dviśālaṃ syād daṇḍaṃ kuryāt punaḥ
punaḥ || 175 ||
durmukhaṃ dakṣiṇe kuryād uttare jayasaṃjñakam |
vātākhyaṃ tad dviśālaṃ tu bandhunāśaṃ dhanakṣayam || 176 ||
kharaṃ ca pūrvadigbhāge paścime dhānyasaṃjñakam |
gṛhaṃ cu(lkī)llī dviśālaṃ tat paśuvṛddhi dhanapradam || 177 ||
vipakṣaṃ dakṣiṇe bhāge paścime krūrasa<ṃ>jñakam |
śobhanākhyaṃ dviśālaṃ tad dhandhānyakaraṃ param || 178 ||
vijayaṃ dakṣiṇe bhāge vijayaṃ caiva paścime |
dviśāla<ṃ tat> kumbhākhya<ṃ syāt>
pu(trā)tradārādisaṃyutam || 179 ||
dhanaṃ ca pūrvadigbhāge dhānyaṃ caiva tu paścime |
nandākhyaṃ tad dviśāla<ṃ> ca dhanadaṃ śobhanaṃ
smṛtam || 180 ||

vijayaṃ sarvadigbhāge dviśālākhyaṃ tad eva hi |
śaṅkākhyaṃ nāma tad gehaṃ śubhadaṃ ca nṛṇāṃ bhavet || 181 ||
vipulaṃ sarvadigbhāge dviśālaṃ tat prajāyate |
tāni saṃpuṭasaṃjñāni dhanadhānyapradāni ca || 182 ||
dhanadaṃ sarvadigbhāge suvaktraṃ vā manoramam |
kāntaṃ nāma tu tad gehaṃ sarveśāṃ śobhanaṃ smṛtam || 183 ||
dviśālānāṃ tadgṛhāṇāṃ bhedāś caiva trayodaśa |
phalapākārtham eteṣāṃ mayā proktaṃ suvistarāt || 184 ||
pūrvayāmyam atha yāmyapaścimaṃ paścimottaram athottarapūrvakam |
prākpratīcam atha dakṣiṇottaraṃ vāstu ṣaḍvidham ida<ṃ> dviśālakam || 185 ||

171. 'First, one shall set down [or: build?] the southern *śālā*, then the second in the west; and having built the third one in the north, [one shall set down] the fourth and last [?] [*śālā*] in the east.
172. Having made [a *śālā* of the type of] *durmukha* in the south, and the one called *khara* in the east – that house shall be called *vāta*, it is known to cause diseases of *vāta*.
173. A *durmukha*-house in the south, [and] in the west the one called *dhānya* – that *dviśāla* is called *siddhārtha*, and it causes success in all things for men.
174. In the west, the one called *dhānya*, in the north, the one called *jaya* – that *dviśāla* [is called] **yamasūrya*, it is known to cause death and ruin.
175. In the east, the one called *khara*, in the north, the one called *dhānya* – that *dviśāla* shall be known as *daṇḍa*, it may cause repeated punishment.
176. A *durmukha* shall be made in the south, in the north, the one called *jaya* – that *dviśāla* is known as *vāta*, it kills relatives and destroys wealth.
177. A *khara* in easterly direction, in the west, the one called *dhānya* – that *dviśāla* is the *cullī*-house, it causes [acquisition of] cattle, success, and wealth.
178. A *vipakṣa* on the southern tract, in the west, the one called *krūra* – that *dviśāla* is called *śobhana*, it bestows supreme wealth and grain.
179. A *vijaya* on the southern tract, and a *vijaya* in the west as well – [that] *dviśāla* is called *kumbha*, it is endowed with sons, wives, etc.

180. A *dhana*[-*da*? *dhānya*?] on the eastern tract, and a *dhānya* in the west [as well] – that *dviśāla* is called *nanda*, and it is considered beautiful and to cause wealth.
181. A *vijaya* in any direction – that [type of] house [which] is known as *dviśāla* [?] is called *śaṅka*, and it shall be auspicious for men.
182. A *vipula* in any direction – that is called *dviśāla* [?], [and] these [varieties] known as *sampuṭa* bestow wealth and grain.
183. A *dhanada* in any direction, or a *suvaktra*, or a *manorama* – that house is called *kānta*, it is auspicious for all.
184. I have enumerated the thirteen divisions of the houses of the *dviśāla*s [?] extensively in order to make their results ripen.
185. East and south, and south and west, west and north, and north and east; east and west, and south and north – that six-fold *vāstu* is the *dviśāla*.'

This rather lengthy passage has been quoted *in extenso*, because it seems to be widely independent of the other two sources as it differs from them in two important points: (1) the order in which the six basic varieties are given is different (starting from the south-east, rather than the south-west), and (2) it admits of thirteen rather than six varieties. But whereas SAS 22 knows of 52 varieties all of which can be auspicious or inauspicious, VP only gives the names and setups of those in addition to the six basic types of *dviśāla* that are considered auspicious, betraying, as it were, a greater sense of pragmatism. Cf. also 1.7.2 above.

20.33-34:

catuḥśālaṃ triśālena prāntam prākāravartinā |
pūrveṇa saptaśāleṣu maṇicchanda iti smṛtam || 33 ||
anuṣṭubh (pathyā)

anyāni caivaṃ triṇy āhuḥ prāntam eva pradakṣiṇam |
aparaṃ paridhānaṃ ca sapakṣam iti tāni ca || 34 ||
anuṣṭubh (ma-vipulā)

33. 'A *catuḥśāla* [joined] on end [?] with an eastern *triśāla* with a compound wall – that is called the *maṇicchandas* among the *saptaśāla*s.

34. And thus they call the other three [that are joined] on end [?] in clockwise direction; they are [called] *apara*, *paridhāna*, and *sapakṣa*.'

Tab. 5 – The types of *saptaśāla* mentioned in SAS 20.33-34 and SAS 25.75-90

Combination:	SAS 20.33-34:	SAS 25.75-90:
catuḥśāla + *hiraṇyanābha*	*apara*	*śrīvatsa, śrīvāsa, śrīkula, śrīsamudgaka, śrīkaraṇḍaka*
catuḥśāla + *sukṣetra*	*paridhāna*	*śrīvṛkṣa, śrīnivāsa, śrīgokula, śrīnanda, śrībhāṇḍāgāra*
catuḥśāla + *cullī*	*sapakṣa*	*śrīpāla, śrībhūṣaṇa, śrīsthāvara, śrī-hrada, śrīnilaya*
catuḥśāla + *pakṣaghna*	*maṇicchandas*	*śrīkaṇṭha, śrī-maṇḍana, kumbha, śrīdhara, śrīniketana*

It is not clear whether *prāntam* is to be construed as an attribute of *catuḥśālam*, or as an adverb; its precise meaning remains obscure in either instance. Cf. SAS 25.75-90, where the *saptaśālas* consisting of one *catuḥśāla* joined with one *triśāla* are described; none of the four names given in 20.33-34 are mentioned there.

Instead, there are said to be 20 varieties of *saptaśāla* consisting of a *catuḥ-* and a *triśāla*, arising from the combinations of the five basic types of *catuḥśāla* (*sarvatobhadra* etc. – cf. note on 24.44 below) and the four basic types of *triśāla* (*hiraṇyanābha* etc. – cf. note on 20.24-26 above). The correspondence of 20.33-34 and 25.75-90 can be presented in tabular form as above.

20.35:
ekabhittī tu śāle dve gr̥hasaṅghaṭṭa ucyate |
na taṃ kuryāt sa hi sadā bandhadoṣavadhapradaḥ ||
anuṣṭubh (na-vipulā)

'Two *śālā*s having one wall [in common] - [that] is called *gr̥ha-saṅghaṭṭa*; it should not be done, [because] it always causes bondage, fault, [and] murder.'

It is to be assumed that *śālā* for once does not refer to the individual chambers of one and the same house, but rather to a) two *śālā*s belonging to different houses, or b) to two different houses in their entirety; in the latter case, this would be the only instance in the text of SAS where *śālā* is used as a synonym for *gr̥ha* (cf. also 1.5.5 above and the note on SAS 39.06 below).

Cf. the occurrence of *saṅghaṭṭa* in SAS 19.13:

gr̥hamālātha saṅghaṭṭo gr̥hanābhir gr̥hāṅgaṇam |
udbhinnaṃ bhinnakakṣaṃ ca nilīnaṃ pratipāditam ||

'The *gr̥hamālā* (lit.'wreath of the house' [or: of houses]) is the *saṅghaṭṭa* (lit.'connection'), the *gr̥hanābhi* (lit.'navel of the house') is the courtyard of the house; [this is either] outwardly visible [or] has a distinct enclosure, and is [either] concealed [or] exposed.'

This stanza requires some explanation: Apparently, *gr̥hamālā* and *saṅghaṭṭa* are a reference to the covered part of the structure surrounding the courtyard on all four sides in a *catuḥśāla*. The four expressions in the second line – which can be interpreted either as adverbs or as attributes of *gr̥hāṅgaṇa* – are not altogether unproblematic; the basic meaning of *ud-bhid* is 'to come forth, become visible, split open (as a blossom);' *ni-lī* means 'to be stuck, attached to, be hidden, concealed'; the causative of *prati-pad* means 'to lead to, provide, bestow, make known, declare, explain'. These last three seem to be most appropriate as they supply us with the opposite of *ni-lī*. In the usage of SAS, *kakṣā* usually refers to the courtyard (cf. note on 20.08-12 above).

The meaning of the second line becomes apparent when one compares MM 27.11:

> *gṛhakriyā hi dvividhā bhinnābhinnaprakārataḥ* |
> *bhinnaṃ ca piṇḍabhedaṃ ca vakṣye sphuṭataraṃ yathā* ||

> '*Il y a deux façons de construire une maison: selon le mode disjoint ou selon le mode joint. De façon plus claire on dit qu'il s'agit de maisons (à éléments) séparés ou de maisons formant bloc.*' [Tr. DAGENS]

If the individual *śālā*s are are not connected, the courtyard is visible from the outside (*udbhinna-* and *pratipādita-*), but if they form an uninterrupted row, the courtyard is concealed from outside view (*nilīna-* and *bhinnakakṣa-*).

A comparison with the parallel of SAS 19.13 in AP 100.12-16, confused as it may be, seems to point in the same direction:

> *gṛhamālā gṛhanābhir gṛhasaṅghaṭṭa eva ca* |
> *gṛhāṇaka iti proktaṃ gṛhabhedacatuṣṭayam* || 12 ||
> *kukṣau caivāgrataḥ pṛṣṭhe paṅktau caiva gṛhāḥ sthitāḥ* |
> *gṛhamāleti nāmnā vai praśastā chandasambhavā* || 13 ||
> *vidikṣu dikṣu pṛṣṭhāgre* [sic!] *kukṣau veśmāni sarvataḥ* |
> *gṛhasaṅghaṭṭanāmāsau samproktaḥ śāstrakovidaiḥ* || 14 ||
> *gṛhamadhye* <'>*pavarakā nānākārā hy alindakāḥ* |
> *alindaiś cāpavarakair gṛhanābhir itīryate* || 15 ||
> *adho bhūmau suvistīrṇa uparyupari vai punaḥ* |
> *gṛhāṇaka iti proktā gṛhā vai vedasaṅkhyayā* || 16 ||

12. '*Gṛhamālā*, *gṛhanābhi*, and *gṛhasaṅghaṭṭa*, [and] *gṛhāṇaka* – thus is called the four-fold division of the house.

13. Houses are standing in the'belly' [?] and in front, in the back and in the line [?] – that is called *gṛhamālā*, it is recommended [if] arisen from [application of] *chandas*.
14. There are dwellings in the intermediate and cardinal directions, in the back and in front, [and] in the 'belly' [?] – that is called *gṛha-saṅghaṭṭa* by those conversant with the *śāstra*.
15. There are all kinds of chambers and *alinda*s in the middle of the house – because of the *alinda*s and chambers, it is called *gṛhanābhi*.
16. It is very spacious below on the ground, and again further up [? or: on each consecutive storey] – [that is called] *gṛhāṇaka*; by this four-fould [distinction], the houses are explained.'

Obviously *gṛhāṇaka*, a word without apparent meaning, is a corrupt reading for *gṛhāṅgaṇa*. – For *mālā* in *gṛhamālā* cf. perhaps also *vitardikāṣṭhamālā* in 18.16.

20.36:
ity uccanīcagṛhabhāgaphalaṃ pradiṣṭam
asminn alindaphalam apy aśubhaṃ śubhaṃ ca |
yad dvitriśālagṛhalakṣma tad apy amuṣmin
sāmānyato dvitayayogabhavaṃ ca samyak ||
vasantatilakā

'Thus is explained the fruit of high and low portions of the house, also the auspicious and inauspicious fruit [respectively] of the *alinda* [are explained] in this [chapter]; that which is the [distinctive] quality of the *dvi-* and *triśāla* [respectively] – that also [has been explained] in this [chapter], and in the same manner [their] property as *dvitayayoga* [?] [has been explained] thoroughly.'

iti mahārājādhirājaśrībhojadevaviracite samarāṅgaṇa-sūtradhārāparanāmni vāstuśāstre nimnoccaphala*sa-cchatrādi*saṃjñālindaphalasadvāstuphaladviśāla-triśālagṛhasaṅghaṭṭalakṣaṇaphalāni nāma viṃśo 'dhyāyaḥ |

°*cchatrādi*° (Ka Kha Ga Da Śa Śu)

'Thus [ends] the twentieth chapter in the *vāstuśāstra* composed by Mahārājādhirāja Śrībhojadeva also called *Samarāṅgaṇa-sūtradhāra*, called 'The fruits of depressions and elevations, the designations '*sacchatra*' etc., the fruits of *alindas*, the fruits of a good *vāstu*, the [distinctive] qualities of *dviśālas*, *triśālas*, and of the *gṛhasaṅghaṭṭa*."

2.4 *adhyāya* 24

24.01-03:

karṇaśālānibaddhāni maṇḍapair antarasthitaiḥ |
asambādhājirāṇi syur halāni daśa pañca ca || 01 ||

anuṣṭubh (pathyā)

īśvaraṃ vṛṣabhaṃ candraṃ rogaṃ pāpaṃ bhayapradam |
nandanaṃ khādakaṃ dhvāṅkṣaṃ vikṛtaṃ vilayaṃ kṣayam || 02 ||

d) *kṣamam* (Da)
anuṣṭubh (pathyā)

yāmyaṃ ca viparītaṃ ca bhadrakaṃ ceti nāmataḥ |
etāni halakākhyāni vidyāt gehāni yatnataḥ || 03 ||

anuṣṭubh (pathyā)

01. 'There shall be fifteen *hala*s, having spacious courtyards, joined together with *karṇaśālā*s, with *maṇḍapa*s situated on the inside [of the courtyard].

02. (1) *Īśvara*, (2) *vṛṣabha*, (3) *candra*, (4) *roga*, (5) *pāpa*, (6) *bhayaprada*; (7) *nandana*, (8) *khādaka*, (9) *dhvāṅkṣa*, (10) *vikṛta*, (11) *vilaya*, (12) *kṣaya*;

03. and (13) *yāmya*, and (14) *viparīta*, and (15) *bhadraka* by name: these houses called *halaka* one shall know thoroughly.'

Apparently, a *hala* or *halaka* (or *lāṅgala*/*lāṅgalaka*) is a type of *catuḥśāla* whose *karṇaśālā*s (cf. 19.29) protrude from the corpus of the main edifice, or to whose *karṇaśālā*s such protrusions in the shape of an extra *śālā* (cf. 24.11) are added. There is an entry in ACHARYA (1993: 441) for *lāṅgalākāra*: 'Anything shaped like the plough, a pavilion with three faces, a type of hall'. This is based on MS 34.277ab:

trivaktraṃ lāṅgalākāraṃ nandyāvartaṃ caturmukham |

'The three-faced pavilion are shaped like the plough (*lāṅgala*); and the *Nandyāvarta* pavilions should be four-faced.' [Tr. ACHARYA]

It is hard to see how this can fit the meaning apparently intended in our text. MS 35.34ab comes closer:

lāṅgalaṃ svāstikaṃ caiva dviśālā ca(lāyā) paryākhyakam |

'The *Svastika* mansion is plough-shaped, and synonymous with *dviśālā* (two rows of buildings).'

The word thus refers to any building or building element that is vaguely L-shaped in plan – cf. the *halakālinda* in 20.13-18 above. In this context, the term *hala* can refer to either the main edifice – as is the case in this stanza – or the protruding *śālā*.

The names assigned to the individual edifices are usually indicative of their auspicious or inauspicious properties, as will be seen below.

24.04:
agnirakṣonileśānakoṇagānāṃ yathākramam |
ekadvitricaturthākhyā halakānāṃ prakalpayet ||

ab) °*koṇe bhāgāṃ* (Da)
anuṣṭubh (pathyā)

'For the *halaka*s situated in the intermediate directions (lit. 'corners') [associated with] Agni, Rakṣas, Anila, and Īśāna respectively one shall establish the designations 'first', 'second', 'third', and 'fourth' [respectively].'

Here *halaka* refers not to the main edifice, but to the protruding portion of the building. The assignment of the four intermediate directions to the four deities Agni, Rakṣas, Anila, and Īśāna, though insuspicious at first glance, is not entirely unproplematic in the context of SAS, and a brief discussion will be in order:

1) Agni is usually associated with the southwestern direction, hence the adjective *āgneya*, 'southwestern'. In the *vāstupuruṣa*-

maṇḍala described in the SAS, though, Agni is placed in the north-eastern *pada*, otherwise the domain of Īśa (cf. SAS 11.07); the same is the case in BṛS 52.43, MP 253.23-24, and VP 05.04. But for practical reasons one needs to assume that in this chapter, Agni is placed in the southwestern corner. What is unusual about this is not only the discrepancy between SAS 11 and SAS 24, but also the fact that customarily, any enumeration of deities with reference to the cardinal and intermediate directions begins in the northeast, not in the southeast.

2) Rakṣas is customarily identified with Nirṛti or Nairṛta (cf. pd q.v.), who is traditionally associated with the southwest. The fact that Rakṣas follows Agni in 24.04 is in perfect keeping with the general rule that deities associated with the directions are usually enumerated clockwise.

3) Following this rule, Anila or Vāyu needs to be placed in the northwest, which is perfectly conventional, cf. the adjective *vāya-vya*, 'northwestern' (pd, q.v.). Yet in any *vāstupuruṣamaṇḍala* known to me, the northwestern *pada* is usually occupied by Roga, Vāyu being assigned to the southeastern *pada* in SAS, BṛS, MP, and VP.

4) Īśāna, then, occupies the northeastern corner, which is in keeping with tradition, and also with the *vāstupuruṣamaṇḍala* as described in MM, MS etc, though not that of SAS and BṛS and MP. What is also unusual is that Īśāna is mentioned last (see above), and assigned the fourth position instead of the first.

24.05:
anena kramayogena cchandobhedā bhavanti ca |
tatrādyeneśvaraṃ nāma halakena gṛhaṃ bhavet ||
anuṣṭubh (pathyā)

'By applying this order, the divisions of *chandas* arise; thus, there shall be the house called (1) *īśvara*, because it has got the 'first' *halaka*.'

For the position of the respective protrusion, see fig.9ab; for *chandas*, cf. 1.5.7 above.

In the case of a *halaka* with four positions which can be either *laghu* or *guru*, i.e. can have one or no protrusion, the *prastāra* of 4^2 = 16 possible results applies. As we have seen, there are only fifteen different types of *halaka*s, because the zero-option of four *guru*s – effectively an edifice without protrusions – would not qualify as a *halaka*.

24.06:

sarvalakṣaṇasaṃyuktaṃ sarvavṛddhiphalapradam |
vṛṣabhaṃ tu dvitīyena putradāravivardhanam ||

anuṣṭubh (pathyā)

'It is endowed with all [auspicious] signs, and bestows all fruits of prosperity; the [house that is called] (2) *vṛṣabha* on account of [its having] the 'second' [*halaka*], though, makes sons and wives prosper.'

The contents of the first half of this stanza obviously belongs to the preceding stanza.

24.07:

prathamaṃ ca dvitīyaṃ ca gṛhe tu halakaṃ yadi |
candraṃ vṛddhikaraṃ nṝṇāṃ sarvalakṣaṇasaṃyutam ||

c) *nṛṇāṃ* (Śa)

anuṣṭubh (pathyā)

'But if there are both the 'first' and 'second' *halakas* in a house, [it is called] (3) *candra*, [and] causes prosperity for men, being endowed with all [auspicious] signs.'

By the contingencies of the metre, the vocalic *ṛ* in *nṛṇāṃ* needs to be long; either form is grammatically permissible. Whether the metrically wrong form is original to the mss could not be ascertained as SASTRI quotes no variant readings; in all probability it is a simple printing error. SHUKLA (2001:142) has the metrically correct form.

24.08:

vāyavyaṃ halakaṃ yatra rogaṃ rogavivardhanam |
prathamaṃ ca tṛtīyaṃ ca gṛhe tu halakaṃ yadi ||

b) *rogabhayapradam* (Kha)
anuṣṭubh (pathyā)

'Where there is a *halaka* in the intermediate direction associated with Vāyu, [that house is called] (4) *roga*, [and] it increases disease. But if there are both the 'first' and the 'third' *halaka* in an house:'

The second half of this stanza needs to be construed with the first half of the following stanza.

24.09:

pāpaṃ tan nāmato vāstu sarvapāpaprayojakam |
pitṛrogoktakoṇābhyāṃ bhayadaṃ rogamṛtyave ||

a) *pāpakaṃ nāmato* (Ka)
anuṣṭubh (pathyā)

'that *vāstu* is (5) *pāpa* by name, [and] brings about all [kinds of] sin. Because [it has got *halakas*] in the intermediate directions called Pitṛ [and] Roga, it is called (6) *bhayada*, [and] it leads to disease and death.'

The taxonomy of the four intermediate directions introduced in 24.04 is deviated from in this stanza. Pitṛ (or Pitṛgaṇa) and Roga have not been mentioned in this chapter so far; in the *vāstupuruṣamaṇḍala* they customarily occupy the southwestern and northwestern *padas* respectively.

24.10:
pitṛrogāgnikoṇeṣu nandanaṃ gṛham ādiśet |
sukham arthapradaṃ śāntaṃ halakaṃ parikīrtitam ||
anuṣṭubh (pathyā)

'In case [it has got *halakas*] in the intermediate directions associated with Pitṛ, Roga, and Agni, the house shall be called (7) *nandana*; it is praised as an auspicious, peaceful *halaka* leading to worldly success.'

Obviously, the harmful or auspicious properties of the buildings are not dependent on the situation of the individual protrusions, but rather on their combination; cf. this and the preceding stanzas.

24.11:
īśānyāṃ tu caturthena khādakaṃ khādakaṃ gṛham |
lāṅgalādyā yadā śālā īśānyāṃ ca yadāparā ||
anuṣṭubh (pathyā)

'Because [it has got] the 'fourth' [*halaka*] in the intermediate direction associated with Īśāna, the house [is called] (8) *khādaka*, [and it is] devouring. If it has the 'first' of the *lāṅgalas* (halakas), and the other *śālā* in the intermediate direction associated with Īśāna:'

Here, we have the only indication that the protruding portion of the edifice is actually an additional room or *śālā*. Note also that once more the division of the stanzas does not reflect the division of the contents.

24.12:
dhvāṅkṣaṃ tan nāmato vāstu daridrāṇāṃ vidhīyate |
dvitīyā ca caturthī ca śālā lāṅgalake yadi ||
anuṣṭubh (pathyā)

'that *vāstu* is known as (9) *dhvāṅkṣa*, [and] it is made for the poor. If there are the 'second' and the 'fourth' *śālā* in a *lāṅgalaka*:'

In the last quarter of this stanza, *lāṅgalaka* refers to the main edifice, not to the protruding *śālā*.

24.13:
vikr̥taṃ vikr̥tāvāsaṃ pravāso 'tra kuṭumbinaḥ |
ādyā śālā dvitīyā ca caturthī ca yadā punaḥ ||
anuṣṭubh (pathyā)

'[it is called] (10) *vikr̥ta*, [and] it is an abode of change [for the worse; or: of disfigurement], [and] here there is absence from home for the master of the house. And if [it has got] the 'first' *śālā*, and the 'second' and the 'fourth':'

24.14:
vilayaṃ hānidaṃ nityaṃ gr̥haṃ tad vittanāśanam |
vāyavyaṃ halakaṃ yasminn aiśānyāṃ ca yadā punaḥ ||
d) *īśānyāṃ* (Ka)
anuṣṭubh (pathyā)

'that house [called] (11) '*vilaya*' is always detrimental, [and] it destroys wealth. But where [there is] the *halaka* associated with Vāyu, and [another one] in the direction associated with Īśāna:'

24.15:
kṣayaṃ kṣayakaraṃ nityaṃ halakeṣu guhaṃ bhavet |
agnivāyumaheśānāṃ śālā lāṅgalake yadi ||
a) *jñeyaṃ* (for nityaṃ; Kha, Da)
anuṣṭubh (pathyā)

'[that is called] (12) '*kṣaya*', [and] always causes ruin; it shall be the 'cave' [?] among the *halakas*. If there are *śālās* [in the intermediate directions] belonging to Agni, Vāyu, and Maheśāna in a *lāṅgalaka*:'

I am not familiar with the use of the word *guha*, 'cave' as denoting something exceedingly low or bad, which apparently is the sense intended here.

24.16:
yāmyaṃ mr̥tyukaraṃ nr̥ṇāṃ na tat kuryāt kadācana |
mārute nairr̥taiśānyoḥ śālākarṇeṣu lāṅgalam ||

anuṣṭubh (pathyā)

'[it is called] (13) '*yāmya*', [and] it brings about death for men; never shall that [house] be built. [If there is] a *lāṅgala* in the intermediate direction associated with Māruta (Vāyu), and in those associated with Nairr̥ta and Īśāna with reference to the *śālā*-corners:'

24.17:
viparītaṃ vyādhikaraṃ nr̥ṇāṃ nāśakaraṃ tathā |
catasro halake yatra prādakṣiṇyamukhāḥ sthitāḥ ||

d) °*mukhās tathā* (Kha Da)
anuṣṭubh (bha-vipulā)

'[It is called] (14) '*viparīta*', [and] it causes disease for men, [and] it is ruinous. Where there are [all] four [*śālās*] in a *halaka*, positioned with their front sides in clockwise direction:'

The adjective *prādakṣiṇyamukha* in d) indicates the way in which the *halakas* are added to the main edifice (cf. fig. 9ab).

24.18-20:
bhadrakaṃ nāma tad vāstu sarvabhadraprayojakam |
dvārocchrāyaṃ savistāraṃ talocchrāyaṃ ca veśmanām || 18 ||

anuṣṭubh (pathyā)

pīṭhasya ca samutsedhaṃ bhittivistāram eva ca |
tathā dārukalā caiva yā proktā gr̥hakarmaṇi || 19 ||

c) *dārukalāṃ* (Ka Kha Ga Da)
anuṣṭubh (pathyā)

eka**śālavidhānaṃ ca teṣāṃ nāmāni yāni ca |
***tat saṃprati pravakṣyāmo yathāvad anupūrvaśaḥ* || 20 ||**

a) *ekaśālāvidhānaṃ* (Kha Kha Ga Da Śa Śu)
anuṣṭubh (pathyā)

18. 'that *vāstu* is called (15) '*bhadraka*', [and] it brings about all that is auspicious. The height of doors, along with their width, and the height of the storeys of dwelling-places;

19. and the height of the *pīṭha*, and also the width of the walls, as well as that which is called wood-carving with reference to house-construction;

20. and the prescriptions for *ekaśāla*s, as well as that which is their names: that I shall presently declare in due order.'

These stanzas indicate a change of subject: height and width of the door are explained in 24.26cd-28ab, while the height of the storeys is not dealt with in SAS 24 at all; it is only implied in 26ab, where the height of the *pīṭha* is given (*upariṣṭād bhavet pīṭhaṃ talād ardhasamucchritam* – 'above that, there shall be a *pīṭha* half as tall as the [ground] floor'). I seems likely that one or more stanzas were lost between 24.25ab and cd – see note on 24.25 below. The width of the wall is mentioned in 24.22-24, *dārukalā* seems to refer to the description of the several mouldings contained in 28cd-34, and *ekaśālāvidhāna* to the rules regarding orientation and taxonomy of *ekaśālā*s as given in 35-42.

Although 24.18-20 give a fairly accurate description of the contents of the remaining stanzas of the 24th *adhyāya*, the order in which these topics are dealt with is rather different.

Notice should be taken of the feminine gender of *śālā* in *ekaśālāvidhāna* (24.20a); it seems to imply a single *śālā*, rather than a *vāstu* with a single *śālā* (*ekaśāla*, n.). But 24.25b has *hīnavāstu*, a term that usually refers to *eka-* to *triśāla*s (cf. 1.5.6). It is probably safe to emend **ekaśālavidhāna*; the descriptions given in 24.18-45 seem to apply to this class of dwelling exclusively.

24.21-22:
ṣoḍaśānāṃ samudayo viṃśater api cāparaḥ |
viṃśateḥ sacatuṣkāyās tathāṣṭāviṃśater api || 21 ||

a) *samudāyo* (Kha Da); c) *viṃśater api catuṣkāyāṃ* (Kha Da)
anuṣṭubh (na-vipulā)

dvātriṃśato 'paraś ceti pañca vargādhipā matāḥ |
śālācaturthabhāgena bhittivistāra iṣyate || 22 ||

anuṣṭubh (pathyā)

21. 'The aggregate of [the *vāstu* measuring] sixteen [cubits] and the other one [measuring] twenty [cubits], of [that measuring] twenty-four and of [that measuring] twenty-eight;

22. and of the other one [measuring] thirty-two [cubits] – these are known as the five *vargādhipas*. The thickness of the wall is known to be one quarter [of the width] of the *śālā*.'

This is a clear reference to BṛS 52.12 (cf. note on 19.19 above). The expression *pañca vargādhipāḥ* seems to be peculiar to SAS; BṛS and MP have *gṛhapañcaka* and *bhavana-pañcaka* instead.

Ka has the following *ṭippaṇa* on 24.22b with reference to *pañca vargādhipāḥ*: *pañcasamudāyāḥ viprādīnāṃ vyutkrameṇa yathā* [em. SASTRI/AGRAWALA for *yathaṃ*] *yojyāḥ* | *vyāsasyedaṃ ceṣṭamānam* – '[this is] the collection of five [house-plans] for brahmans etc. as they shall be applied in inverted order. And this is the prescribed measurement for their width;' *vyutkrameṇa* seems to refer to the fact that the five measurements are given in ascending order in 24.21-22, even though they should be applied to the four *varṇa*s in descending order.

The width of the *śālā*-wall as given in 24.22cd may seem unlikely; yet it is in perfect accord with BṛS 52.32 (if we take into account the rule given in 19.22 above, viz. that the width of the *śālā* should be one-fourth of the width of the entire plot):

vyāsāt ṣoḍaśabhāgaḥ sarveṣāṃ sadmanāṃ bhavati bhittiḥ |
pakveṣṭakākṛtānāṃ dārukṛtānāṃ tu na vikalpaḥ ||

'In all dwellings made of burnt bricks, the wall shall be one-sixteenth of the width [of the *vāstu*], but for those that are made of wood there is no rule.'

Cf. also MP 254.41:

> *pakveṣṭakā bhaved bhittiḥ ṣoḍaśāṃśena vistarāt* |
> *dāravair api kalpyāḥ syāt tathā mr̥nmayabhittikā* ||

'The wall shall be of burnt brick, one-sixteenth of the width [of the *vāstu* in thickness]; is shall also be made of wood, [and it may] likewise [be] a mud wall.'

Cf. also VP 02.161:

> *vyāsāc ca ṣoḍuśo bhāgaḥ sarveṣāṃ mitayaḥ smr̥tā*<*ḥ*> |
> *pakveṣṭakākr̥tānāṃ ca dārūṇāṃ na kadācana* ||

'And one-sixteenth of the width [of the *vāstu*] is known to be the measure [of the walls] made of burnt brick, and never of [those made of] wood.'

It is interesting to note that in contrast to the older treatises, wooden houses seem not to have been considered in SAS at all.

24.23-24:

***vargeṣu bhittilakṣmoktaṃ ṣoḍaśādiṣu pañcasu* |**
***marmapīḍā bhaved yatra bhittistambhatulādibhiḥ* || 23 ||**

anuṣṭubh (pathyā)

***kurvīta hrāsaṃ vṛddhiṃ vā tatra marmavyathāṃ tyajan* |**
***atisaṃvṛtavistāraṃ kāryam uddiśya buddhimān* || 24 ||**

a) *hrāsavr̥ddhiṃ* (Ka); b) *tyajet* (Ka); °*saṃvr̥tta*° (Ka)
anuṣṭubh (ma-vipulā)

23. 'The property of the wall has been declared with regard to the five *vargas*, [those measuring] sixteen [cubits] and so on. Where there may occur injuring of the *marman*s through walls, posts, beams etc.:

24. It shall be diminished or increased, thus avoiding injuring of the *marman*; it shall be made of completely safe width according to the recommendation of the expert.'

For *marman*, cf. KERN (1872:289sq.). In 24c, *atisaṃvr̥tavistāra* seems to imply that in determining the width of the wall, one should err on the side of caution in order to avoid injuring the *marman* at all cost. *Saṃvr̥ta* (< *saṃ-vr̥* 'to cover') here seems to mean 'safe, cautious' (cf. pd q.v. 1) *var*: '[...] *saṃvr̥ta* [...] *m) gedeckt,* so v.a. *auf der Hut seiend.*').

24.25:
śālāpraviṣṭaṃ kurvīta hīnavāstuṣv alindakam |
caturaśrīkr̥te kṣetre bhūmibhāge samīkr̥te ||
anuṣṭubh (ma-vipulā)

'In the smaller *vāstu*s, the *alindaka* shall be made in accordance with the *śālā*; in a square field, on a level piece of ground:'

As indicated in the note on 24.18-20 above, I believe that two half-stanzas have been lost here: as indicated by *upariṣṭād* in 26 ab, that half-stanza clearly seems to form a semantic and syntactic unit with 25cd; and 26ab presupposes some mention of the height of the ground floor – the point of reference, as it were, for the height of the *pīṭha*. Cf. also note on 24.18-20 above.

The precise meaning of the compound *śālāpraviṣṭa-* is not quite clear; *praviṣṭa-* could mean either 'situated in' or 'being in accordance with.' As the *alinda* is usually treated as distinct from the *śālā*, the latter seems more likely: the size of the *alinda* shall be adjusted according to the size of the *śālā*; cf. 19.22 above.

Ka inserts the following *ṭippaṇa* after a): *pañca– – – –hīnavāstupramāṇaṃ tad gr̥haṃ śālākhyaṃ tadantargataṃ ṣaḍdārukaṃ kuryāt* – '[That which has] the size of the five [...] small *vāstu*s – that house is called *śālā*; inside it, *ṣaḍdāruka* shall be made.' In the 23rd *adhyāya*, *ekaśāla*s are distinguished by the position of their *ṣaḍdāru*/-*ka*s, a rather cryptic term which apparently refers to some kind of wooden construction associated with the *alinda*.

The rule regarding the height of the storeys is given in 28.16-17:

> *vistārāt ṣoḍaśo bhāgaś caturhastasamanvitaḥ |*
> *talocchrayaḥ praśasto 'yaṃ bhaved viditaveśmanām || 16 ||*
> *saptahasto bhavej jyeṣṭhe madhyame ṣaṭkaronmitaḥ |*
> *pañcahastaḥ kaniṣṭhe tu vidhātavyas tathodayaḥ || 17 ||*

16. 'One-sixteenth of the width [of the *vāstu*] to which are added four cubits – that is the prescribed height of the [ground] floor for all dwellings.
17. Seven cubits shall be [the height of the ground floor] in the largest [dwelling], in the middle-sized one [it shall] measure six [cubits]; but in the smallest [dwelling], the height [of the ground floor] shall be made five cubits.'

This rule is amended in 28.47:

> *vedikājālasaṃpannaṃ talaṃ kāryaṃ manoramam |*
> *bhūmau bhūmau bhavet tac ca dvādaśāṃśavivarjitam ||*

'A pleasant [upper] storey shall be made, endowed with a balustrade and lattice-windows; and on each consecutive storey, that shall be dimished by one-twelfth.'

Cf. BṛS 52.22:

> *vistāraṣoḍaśāṃśaḥ sacaturhasto bhaved gṛhocchrāyaḥ |*
> *dvādaśabhāgenonono bhūmau bhūmau samastānām ||*

'The height of the house [i.e. ground floor] shall be one-sixteenth of the width plus four cubits; [this shall be] diminished by one-twelfth on each storey for all [dwellings].'

Cf. also MP 254.39cd-40:

> *vistarāt ṣoḍaśo bhāgas tathā hastacatuṣṭayam ||*
> *prathamo bhūmikocchrāya upariṣṭāt prahīyate |*
> *dvādaśāṃśena sarvāsu bhūmikāsu tathocchrāyaḥ ||*

'One-sixteenth of the width [of the house] plus four cubits – [that is] the height of the ground floor; it shall be diminished by one-twelfth [successively] on all storeys in ascending order.'

Virtually the same rule is given in VP 02.155cd-156, albeit rather incompletely:

vistāraṣoḍa(śośas)śāṃśas tu caturhastayutaś ca yaḥ ||
tadantarasyoccataraṃ pramāṇaṃ pravaded budhaḥ |
dvādaśabhāgenonaṃ ca samastānāṃ prakalpayet ||

'One-sixteenth of the width [of the building] augmented by four cubits – as approximating that the expert shall declare the maximum height; it shall be fixed as dimished by one-twelfth for all [successive storeys].'

24.26-27:

***upariṣṭād bhavet pīṭhaṃ talād ardhasamucchritam* |**
***niyukte tu tataḥ pīṭhe vāstuvistārato 'ṅgulam* || 26 ||**
anuṣṭubh (pathyā)

***pratihastaṃ samuddhṛtya saptatyā saha yojayet* |**
***dvārocchrāyāḥ samākhyātā vargeṣūkteṣu pañcasu* || 27 ||**
anuṣṭubh (pathyā)

26. 'Above [that], there shall be a *pīṭha* half as tall as the [ground] floor; but when the *pīṭha* is applied, then one digit with reference to the width of the *vāstu* –

27. for every cubit [which] shall be added to seventy – [that] high; [thus] have been explained the heights of the doors in the five groups [of buildings] mentioned [above].'

The contents of 24.26cd-27ab requires some explanation. Apparently, what is meant is that the height of the door in digits shall be the width of the *vāstu* in cubits plus seventy; cf. BṛS 53.24:

ekādaśabhāgayutaḥ sasaptatir nṛpabaleśayor vyasaḥ |
ucchrāyo 'ṅgulatulyo dvārasyārdhena viṣkambhaḥ ||

'The [width of] the dwelling of king and commander of the army [respectively], augmented by one-eleventh, increased by seventy – that shall be the height of the door in digits, half [of that shall be its] width.'

The most obvious differences between this stanza and ours is that (1) in the latter, the width of the *vāstu* is not to be augmented by one-eleventh, and (2) that the former claims to apply only for the houses of kings and commanders of the army (for the houses of the *varṇins*, an alternative rule is given in the consecutive stanza).

A different rule is given in MP 254.42cd-43ab:

> *gṛhavyāsasya pañcāśad aṣṭādaśabhir aṅgulaiḥ* ||
> *saṃyuto dvāraviṣkambho dviguṇaś cocchrayo bhavet* |

'50 [cubits?] of the width of the house [?] to which are added 18 digits – [that is] the width of the door, and the height shall be twice that.'

It is obvious that the text is corrupt; cf. also VP 02.162-163:

> *nṛpasenāpatigṛham aṣṭāśītiśatair yutāḥ* [sic!] |
> *aṅgulāni* [sic!] *dvāramānaṃ pravadanti manīṣiṇaḥ* || 162 ||
> *viprādīnāṃ tathā saptaviṃśatis tv aṅgulāni ca* |
> *dvārasya māna<ṃ> tat proktaṃ triguṇocchrāyam ucyate* || 163 ||

162. '[The width of] the house of king, commander [etc.], augmented by 188 – that is said to be the size of the door in digits by the experts. 163. Accordingly, the size of [i.e., the width of] the door is said to be 27 digits for brahmans etc., the height is said to be three times that.'

Again, the text seems to be incomplete. – The formula for the height of the door prescribed in SAS 24.26-27 can be stated as follows:

(width of *vāstu* + 70)/24 = height of door.

According to this rule, the door of a *vāstu* 32 cubits wide would be 4 1/4 cubits tall, that of a 28-cubits-*vāstu* 4 3/24 cubits, and the door of a *vāstu* 24, 20, and 16 cubits in width respectively would measure 3 11/12, 3 3/4, and 3 7/12 cubits respectively.

The same rule is given in SAS 28.02:

> *dvārasya gṛhavistārair hastatulyāṅgulair bhavet* |
> *ucchrāyaḥ *saptatyā yuktair vistṛtis tu tadardhataḥ* ||

'The height of the door shall be as many digits as the width of the house has cubits plus seventy, the width [of the door], thoug, shall be half of that.'

All mss as well as the printed edition and SHUKLA's publication read *saptabhir* in c), which cannot be correct. 28.03-07 give further rules regarding the dimensions of the door:

prakalpayed gr̥hadvāraṃ krameṇaiva kanīyasām |
trairāśikena madhyānāṃ dvādaśāṃśaṃ parityajet || 03 ||
ity ucchritis tadardhena sarveṣām api vistaraḥ |
ucchrāyam uttamānāṃ tu kuryād aṣṭāṃśavarjitam || 04 ||
vistārāṅgulasaṃyuktaṃ kuryād atikanīyasām |
catuḥṣaṣṭigr̥hadvāram udayenārdhavistr̥tam || 05 ||
vistārahastatulyāni ṣaṣṭyā pañ(ca)cāśatāthavā |
saṃyutāny aṅgulāni syād ucchrāyo 'rdhena vistr̥tiḥ || 06 ||
gr̥hotsedhena vā tryaṃśahīnena syāt samucchritiḥ |
tadardhena tu vistāro dvārasyety aparo vidhiḥ || 07 ||

03. 'The [size of the] front door shall be fixed gradually for the smallest [dwellings]; by [application of] the rule of three [?], it shall be diminished by one-twelfth for the middle-sized [dwellings].
04. This [is the rule regarding] the height, the width [shall be] half of that in all cases; the height [of the door] of the largest [dwellings] shall be diminished by one-eighth.
05. For the very smallest [dwellings, the height of the door] shall be augmented by the [number of cubits of the] width [of the *vāstu*] in digits; the front door of [a dwelling that is] 64 [cubits in width shall be] half the height in width.
06. Its height shall be one digit for every cubit of the width [of the *vāstu*] to which has been added 60 or 50 shall be the height, half [of that shall be] the width.
07. Or, the height of the door shall be the height of the house [i.e., storey] diminished by one-third, half of that [shall be its] height – Thus says a different rule.'

It is interesting to note that the only 'large' dwelling expressly mentioned in this passage is the *vāstu* with a width of 64 cubits – cf. the house of *senāpati* and *purodhasa* in 19.15, the only *karm-*

opajīvins besides the king mentioned in the 19th *adhyāya*. The formulae for the height of the doors given in these stanzas can be stated as follows:

> **(width of *vāstu* + 70)/24 = height of door of the smallest dwelling;**
>
> **(width of vāstu + 70)/24 - [(width of *vāstu* + 70)/24]/12 = height of door of the middle-sized dwelling(s);**
>
> **(width of *vāstu* + 70)/24 - [(width of *vāstu* + 70)/24]/12 = height of door of the largest dwelling;**
>
> **(width of *vāstu* + 70)/24 + width of *vāstu*/24 = height of door of the smallest dwelling(s);**
>
> **(width of *vāstu* + 60)/24 = height of door of a dwelling 64 cubits wide;**

or

> **(width of *vāstu* + 50)/24 = height of door of a dwelling 64 cubits wide;**
>
> **height of storey - (height of storey/3) = height of door.**

– The absolutive locative *niyukte [...] pīṭhe* in 26c seems to indicate that the addition of a *pīṭha* is optional; but if that were the case, one would expect an alternative rule for the height of the door. Alternatively, and more likely, it could be indicative of a temporal subordination: 'after the *pīṭha* has been added [...] .'

Ka has the following *ṭippaṇa* on 26a: *talaśabdena prathama-bhūmyucchrāyaḥ* – 'by the word *tala* [is meant] the height of the first [i.e., ground floor].'

The last quarter of 24.28 marks the transition to the next topic, viz. *dārukalā* 'the woodwork.' What precisely *paṭṭa* refers to in this context is not clear; its meaning is usually given as 'a kind of moulding' (cf. ACHARYA 1946a:289sq.).

24.28:

ucchrāyārdhena vaipulyam aṣṭāṃśena vivarjitam |
dvāravistārapādāṃśe paṭṭavistāra iṣyate ||

anuṣṭubh (pathyā)

'The width [of the door shall be] half [its] height minus one-eighth; the width of the *paṭṭa* shall be known [to measure] one quarter of the width of the door.'

24.29:

vistārārdhena bāhalyaṃ sārdhaṃ *vedyās talopari |
uttarottaravaipulyaṃ kuryāc chākhāvaśād budhaḥ ||

a) *vedyā* (Ka Ga Śā), ab) *vistarārdhena bāhalyaṃ sārdhapedyā-talombare* (Kha Da, Da: °*vedyā*°); c) *uttarombara*° (Da). See also note

anuṣṭubh (pathyā)

'[Its] thickness shall be half [its] width, one-and-a-half times [its width shall be that of] the *vedī* on top of the floor [or: storey]; the width of the uppermost [part of the *vedī*] the expert shall make in the manner of the pillar.'

I emend **vedyās* for *vedyā* (cf. also SHUKLA ^{2}2001:143) for the following reason: If *vedyā* were to be taken as an (unattested) nominative singular, the syntax of 24.30ab below would be impossible to construe, an instrumental being normally expected in the context; the nominative is thus more likely to be *vedī*. In 24.29ab, however, a second instrumental (besides *vistārārdhena*) would be hardly any help, while a genitive would make much better sense. A corruption of the text is all the more likely given the considerable degree of confusion among the mss. Just as *paṭṭa* in the preceding stanza, *vedī* here seems to refer to some kind of moulding.

24.30-33:

vedyā vistārabāhalye vidheye śākhayor api |
***dvāravistārapādena mūle stambhasya vistṛtiḥ* || 30 ||**

a) *vaidyā* (Śu)
anuṣṭubh (pathyā)

daśabhāgavihīnāgre paṭṭaḥ stambhena saṃmitaḥ |
***stambhāgrasya tribhāgena paṭṭakoṭir vidhīyate* || 31 ||**

c) *tribhāgonāṃ* (Kha Da)
anuṣṭubh (pathyā)

hīragrahaṇam āyāme stambhāgrāt tu caturguṇam |
***paṭṭān *nānyad bhavet tatra* vyāsabāhalyayos tathā* || 32 ||**

c) *paṭṭānyāny udbhavet* (Ka Ga Śa Śu), *padānnānyādbhávet* (Kha Da)
anuṣṭubh (pathyā)

paṭṭakoṭyardham utsedhād utsedhārdhena nirgatam |
***tantrakasya pramāṇaṃ syād iti śāstravido viduḥ* || 33 ||**

anuṣṭubh (pathyā)

30. 'Width and thickness of the two door-posts shall be fixed by [the proportions of] the *vedī*; the width of the pillar at the base [shall be] a quarter of the width of the door.

31. The *paṭṭa* [shall be] connected to the pillar at the top which is diminished by one-tenth; the *paṭṭakoṭi* shall measure one-third of the top of the pillar.

32. The *hīragrahaṇa* [shall be] four times [bigger] than the top of the pillar in width; and other than the *paṭṭa*, there shall be none of [the same] width [or] thickness there.

33. Half of the *paṭṭakoṭi* protrudes by half [its] height against [its] height; that shall be the size of the *tantraka* – thus it is known by those conversant with the *śāstra*.'

In 24.30, *śākhā* 'door-post' and *stambha* 'pillar' actually seem to refer to two different objects; this is suggested by the fact that two different measurements are given, and also by the taper of the pillar implied by 24.31a, which would be quite unpractical in a door-post.

For the term *hīragrahaṇa* in 24.32a, cf. MM *hīraka* (15.33, 34; 21.23).

24.34:

dravyāṇy uparyuparyasya parāparavibhāgataḥ |
paṭṭakoṭyāś caturthena pravibhāgena hrāsayet ||

anuṣṭubh (pathyā)

'One shall diminish the building elements by one-fourth of the *paṭṭakoṭi* according to the higher or lower parts in ascending order. [?]'

This stanza is rather obscure at first sight; its meaning becomes apparent when one relates it to BṛS 52.30:

> *stambhasamaṃ bāhulyaṃ bhāratulānām uparyuparyāsām |*
> *bhavati tulopatulānām ūnaṃ pādena pādena ||*

'The thickness of the *bhāratulā*s [is] equal to the [width of the] pillar; [the respective thickness] of the *tulā*s and *upatulā*s in ascending order is diminished by one quarter respectively.'

Utpala mentions four different beams which together make up the architrave: *bharatulā, upatulā, tulā,* and another *upatulā*. Each of these shall be diminished in width by one quarter successively in ascending order; it can be doubted that *bhāratulātaḥ pādena pādenonaṃ* in the commentary really implies that the width of each consecutive beam should be diminished by one quarter of the width of the *bhāratulā*, rather than diminished by one quarter as against the width of the directly preceding beam. This and the following stanza are quoted verbatim in VP 02.169-170; as they are the only stanzas in the *āryā* metre in VP, they are obviously interpolated – cf. KERN (1872:285 fn.2).

Cf. also MP 255.05cd-06:

> [...] *stambhatulyā tulā proktā hīnā copatulā tataḥ* || 05 ||
> *tribhāgeneha sarvatra caturbhāgena vā punaḥ* |
> *hīnaṃ hīnaṃ caturthāṃśāt tathā sarvāsu bhūmiṣu* || 06 ||

05. '[...] The *tulā* is said to be equal to the pillar, and the *upatulā* [shall be] diminished:
06. by one-third in all instances, or by one-fourth; [each building element ?] shall be diminished by one-fourth on all [consecutive] storeys.'

The last line seems to be unrelated to the preceding statement.

24.35-43:

***pūrvāmukhaṃ gṛhaṃ yat tu dvāraṃ māhendrasaṃyutam* |**
***hastinī ca bhavec chālā tad gṛhaṃ bhadrasaṃjñitam* || 35 ||**

b) *māhendrasaṃmukham* (Kha Da)

anuṣṭubh (pathyā)

***bhadraṃ bhadrakaraṃ bhartur yaśobalavivardhanam* |**
***sidhyanti cāsya kāryāṇi bhadrākhye vasato gṛhe* || 36 ||**

anuṣṭubh (pathyā)

***dakṣiṇābhimukhaṃ veśma dvāraṃ cāsya gṛhakṣatam* |**
***mahiṣī ca bhavec chālā tad gṛhaṃ nandapīṭhakam* || 37 ||**

anuṣṭubh (pathyā)

***nandapīṭhagṛhaṃ puṃsā nityānandakaraṃ smṛtam* |**
***sarvasaṃpadguṇopetaṃ dhanadhānyavivardhanam* || 38 ||**

anuṣṭubh (pathyā)

***vāruṇyabhimukhaṃ sadma dvāraṃ ca kusumāhvayam* |**
***gāvī caiva bhavec chālā saurabhaṃ tad vidur budhāḥ* || 39 ||**

anuṣṭubh (pathyā)

***saurabhe nityahṛṣṭatvaṃ vasatāṃ gṛhamedhinām* |**
***saphalaṃ kṛṣivāṇijyaṃ putrāṃś ca vaśavartinaḥ* || 40 ||**

anuṣṭubh (pathyā)

uttarābhimukhaṃ dhiṣṇyaṃ dvāraṃ bhallāṭasaṃyutam |
***chagalī ca bhavec chālā puṣkarākhyaṃ tad ucyate* || 41 ||**

anuṣṭubh (pathyā)

śīlavān nityasaṃtuṣṭaḥ suhṛtsujanavatsalaḥ |
***subhagaḥ puṣkarākhye ca bahuputradhanānvitaḥ* || 42 ||**

ab) °*saṃhṛṣṭasuhṛtsvajana*° (Kha), °*saṃruṣṭasuhṛtsvajana*° (Da)
anuṣṭubh (pathyā)

bhadraṃ ca nandapīṭhaṃ ca saurabhaṃ puṣkaraṃ tathā |
***prathamārdhe tu vargasya prathamasya prayojayet* || 43 ||**

anuṣṭubh (pathyā)

35. 'That building, though, that faces east [and whose] door is connected with [the *pada* of the *vāstupuruṣamaṇḍala*] belonging to Mahendra – that house is called *bhadra*, and the *śālā* shall be [called] *hastinī*.

36. [The house called] *bhadra* causes happiness for the master [of the house, and] increases [his] fame and power; and the works of him who lives in the house called *bhadra* are realized.

37. The dwelling faces south, and its door [is situated in the field associated with] Gṛhakṣata – that house [is called] *nandapīṭhaka*, and the *śālā* shall be [called] *mahiṣī*.

38. One knows the house of the type of *nandapīṭha* to cause bliss at all times; [it is] endowed with all qualities of prosperity, [and] causes increase of wealth and grains.

39. The dwelling faces [the direction] of Varuṇa, and its door [is situated in the *pada* associated with] Kusumāhvaya – that [building] the wise shall know as *saurabha*, and the *śālā* shall be [called] *gāvī*.

40. The masters of the house residing in [a house of the type of] *saurabha* experience joy at all times, fruitful plowing and commerce, and [they shall have] obedient sons.

41. The dwelling faces north, the door is connected with [the *pada* belonging to] Bhallāṭa – that [house] is called *puṣkara*, and the *śālā* shall be [called] *chagalī*.

42. [Residing] in [a house of the type of] *puṣkara*, [the master shall be] virtuous, content at all times, a friend to [his] friends and [all] good people, of good fortune, and endowed with many sons and wealth.

43. *Bhadra* and *nandapīṭha*, *saurabha*, and *puṣkara* – [each of these] shall be used in the first half of the first *varga*.'

As indicated above (1.5.5), *gṛha* usually refers to the compound as a whole, the meaning generally covered by the term *vāstu*. Stanzas 24.35-42 give a classification of edifice and *śālā* according to their orientation with reference to the cardinal directions and, in the former case, according to the position of the front door.

The treatment of the *śālā* in this passage is not without difficulties; from the passage alone, it is not clear whether the names given here – *hastinī*, *mahiṣī*, *gāvī* and *chagalī* – refer (1) to the *śālā* in an edifice called *bhadra*, *naṇḍapīṭha*, *saurabha*, or *puṣkara*; (2) to a *śālā* that faces east, south, west, or north respectively; or (3) to a *śālā* that is situated on the eastern, southern, western, or northern side of the courtyard. While this third possibility appears to be the least likely on the face of it – the orientation of a *śālā* is usually given with reference to its entrance, not with reference to its position in the compound, cf. 39.06-09 –, it is nonetheless confirmed by AP 92.09-10:

> *hastinī mahiṣī caiva gāvī ca chāgalī tathā* |
> *padānāṃ tu diśābhedaiḥ prācyādiṣu pradakṣiṇam* || 09 ||
> *hastinī cendrasaṃsthāne mahiṣī ca yamasthale* |
> *gāvī ca varuṇasthāne saumyasthāne tu chāgalī* || 10 ||

09. '*Hastinī* and *mahiṣī*, *gāvī* and *chāgalī*: because of the division of the *padas* according to orientation, [these are situated] in [the cardinal directions] beginning with the east [and proceeding] in clockwise direction.

10. And *hastinī* [is situated] in the place of Indra, and *mahiṣī* in the place of Yama; and *gāvī* in the place of Varuṇa, but in the place belonging to Soma [is] *chāgalī.*'

What is puzzling about this is that *hastinī* is said to be situated in the *pada* of Indra, i.e. the northeastern *pada* in the eastern section of the *vāstupuruṣamaṇḍala*, whereas the other three are said to occupy the outer central *padas* (cf. fig.1); AP 92.09 seems to go back to SAS 23.38:

> *kathitaṃ tac ca saṃsthānair nāmabhiś ca yathākramam* |
> *hastinī mahiṣī gāvī chāgalī ca yathākramam* ||

'And that [the total number of *ekaśālas*, 23.37] has been declared in due order, according to their positions and names: *hastinī, mahiṣī, gāvī,* and *chāgalī* in due order.'

Cf. also 1.7.1 above. – It is perhaps no coincidence that according to 24.40, a house of the type of *saurabha* should be conducive to agricultural and commercial activity, given that in 39.08, a *vāstu* facing west (the direction commonly associated with Varuṇa) is expressly recommended for members of the *vaiśya*-class; the same might be the case with 24.42. – Note the variant reading recorded for the latter stanza in Da.

The contents of 24.43cd is not clear; *varga* can be taken as a reference to *pañca-vargādhipāḥ*, i.e. the set of five different-sized ground plans – cf. note on 24.22 above. But what precisely should the first half of the first *varga* be? The list given in 24.21-22 is remarkable insofar as it starts with the smallest *vāstu*, contrary to the usage of BṛS 52 and MP 254; as each *varga* consists of one to four *vāstus* depending on the *varṇa* of the owner, 24.43cd could refer to the two *vāstus* of 16 cubits reserved for a brahman and a *kṣatriya*. However, such limited applicability is rather unlikely for a rule referred to above (24.20) as *eka***śālavidhāna*.

24.44:

sarvabhadrādikāḥ sarve niveśā ye prakīrtitāḥ |
utpannās te vimānebhyaḥ pañcabhyaḥ pañcapañcake ||
anuṣṭubh (pathyā)

'All dwellings that are known as *sarvabhadra* and so on have originated from the five *vimānas*, five each.'

The first half of this stanza refers to the five varieties of *catuḥśāla – sarvatobhadra, nandyāvarta, vardhamāna, svastika, rucaka* – described in BṛS 52.31-35, and also appearing in SAS 19.75-79; the five *vimānas* are mentioned in SAS 49.02-03:

purā brahmāsṛjat pañca vimānāny asuradviṣām |
viyadvartmavicārīṇi śrīmanti ca mahānti ca || 02 ||
tāni vairājakailāse puṣpakaṃ maṇikābhidham |
haimāni maṇicitrāṇi pañcamaṃ ca triviṣṭapam || 03 ||

02. 'Once upon a time, Brahman made five *vimānas* for the gods, moving in the air, glorious, [and] great;
03. of golden colour, studded with gems: *vairāja, kailāsa, puṣpaka,* [and] *maṇika* by name, and the fifth [was called] *triviṣṭapa.*'

These are supposed to have been the models for the first temples; it is interesting to note that in 24.44, they are also said to be connected with the origin of residential buildings.

Pañcapañcake seems to indicate a combination of *pañcavargādhipāḥ* and the five types of *catuḥśāla.*

24.45:

dvārasya pīṭhasya ca mandireṣu
bhitteś ca mānaṃ kathitaṃ krameṇa |
tathoditā dārukalās tu samyak
prahīnavāstoḥ sakalaṃ ca lakṣma ||
upajāti

'The measurement of door and *pīṭha*, and of the walls in a dwelling have been pronounced in due order; then the wood-carvings have been declared in their entirety, and all characteristics of the small [or: diminished] *vāstu*s.'

Note that contrary to 24.18, the height of the storeys is not mentioned in this stanza. This might point to the fact that the concluding stanzas are not original, but were added in the course of textual transmission perhaps together with the colophons – in this particular instance, only after the stanza(s) giving the rules for the height of the storeys were lost.

iti mahārājādhirājaśrībhojadevaviracite samarāṅgaṇa-sūtradhārāparanāmni vāstuśāstre dvārapīṭhabhittimāna-dārukalāhīnavāstulakṣaṇaṃ nāma caturviṃśo 'dhyāyaḥ |

Thus ends the twenty-fourth chapter in the *vāstuśāstra* composed by Mahārājādhirāja Śrībhojadeva also called *Samarāṅgaṇasūtradhāra*, called 'The measurements of door, *pīṭha*, and wall, [and] the woodwork, [and] the properties of the *hīna-vāstu*s.'

2.5 *adhyāya* 39.01-34

39.01:
gr̥hāṇy uktāni sarveṣām evaṃ karmopajīvinām |
varṇināṃ ca gr̥hasthānāṃ kathyante 'taḥ paraṃ yathā ||

b) *iva* (Da)

anuṣṭubh (pathyā)

'The houses for [the use of] all *karmopajīvin*s have been thus declared; and the houses for [those] *gr̥hastha*s [who are] *varṇin*s are now declared as follows.'

The first half of this stanza refers to the context of the preceding 38th *adhyāya* (*vāstusaṃsthānalakṣaṇam*); for the difference between *karmopajīvin*s and *varṇin*s, cf. KERN (1872:281 fn. 1). The following stanzas (39.02-10) give the relative position of living area and front door within the *vāstu* with reference to the *varṇa* of the owner; cf. Br̥S 52.68 quoted on p. 40 above; this has a parallel in MP 254.07ab:

vāsagehāni sarveṣāṃ praveśe dakṣiṇena tu |

'In all [dwellings], the main living areas [shall be] to the right of the [main] entrance [...].'

VP 07.12, however, assigns the front doors to different directions:

pratyaṅmukhaṃ brāhmaṇānāṃ kṣatriyāṇāṃ tathottare |
vaiśyānāṃ pūrvadigdvāraṃ śūdrāṇāṃ dakṣiṇe śubham ||

'Facing west [is the door] for brahmans, and for *kṣatriya*s, [it is] in the west; for *vaiśya*s, the door is in easterly direction, for *śūdra*s, it is auspicious in the south.'

The same positions of the front doors as in SAS 39.02-10 are given in 24.35-42 (cf. 1.3.3 above); they tally with the account of Br̥S 52.69cd-73, where some of the neighbouring *pada*s are also quoted as being auspicious (cf. fig. 4; in the translation, the *phala*s pertaining to those quarters mentioned in SAS 39.02-10 are given in bold print):

dvārāṇi yāni teṣām analādīnāṃ phalopanayaḥ || 69 ||
anilabhayaṃ strījananaṃ prabhūtadhanatā
narendravāllabhyam |
krodhaparatānr̥tatvaṃ krauryaṃ cauryaṃ ca pūrveṇa || 70 ||
alpasutatvaṃ praiṣyaṃ nīcatvaṃ bhakṣyapānasutavr̥ddhiḥ |
raudraṃ kr̥taghnam adhanaṃ sutavīryaghnaṃ ca yāmyena || 71 ||
sutapīḍā ripuvr̥ddhir na sutadhanāptiḥ sutārthaphalasampat |
dhanasampan nr̥patibhayaṃ dhanakṣayo roga ity apare || 72 ||
vadhabandho ripuvr̥ddhiḥ sutadhanalābhaḥ
samastaguṇasampat |
putradhanāptivairyaṃ sutena doṣāḥ striyā naiḥsvam || 73 ||

69. '[... now follows] an introduction to the *phala*s of the doors, beginning with [the one situated in the *pada* of] Agni:
70. Danger from storm; birth of a daughter; abundance of wealth; **the king's favour**; a choleric nature; falsehood; cruelty; theft in the east.
71. Dearth of sons; servitude; lowliness; **abundance of food, drink, and sons**; demons; destruction of what has been accomplished; absence of wealth; loss of sons and power in the south.
72. Harming of sons; increase of enemies; no gain of sons and wealth; **abundance of sons and success**; abundance of wealth; danger from the king; loss of wealth; disease in the west.
73. Death and captivity [?]; increase of enemies; gain of sons and wealth; **acquisition of all virtues**; gain of sons and wealth; quarrel with one's sons; faults of the wife; poverty in the north.'

Cf., with some surprising correspondences, VP 07.56-65ab:

īśānam āditaḥ pūrve āgneyād dakṣiṇe sthitāḥ |
nairr̥tyāt paścime jñeyā vāyavyāt saumyadiksthitāḥ || 56 ||
pūrvādikramayogena hutāśe 'gnibhayaṃ bhavet |
parjanye pracurā nāryo jāyante bahuvittadāḥ [sic!] || 57 ||
māhendre nr̥pavātsalyaṃ sūrye 'tikrodhatā bhavet |
satye 'nr̥tatvaṃ vijñeyaṃ krūratva<*ṃ*> *ca bhr̥(śaṃ)śe bhavet* || 58 ||
antarikṣe ca vijñeyo nityaṃ corasamāga(taḥ)maḥ |
dakṣiṇe [?] *syāt putranāśo vāyavye* [?] *preṣyam eva ca* || 59 ||
nīcatvaṃ vitathe jñeyaṃ gr̥he tiṣṭhati santatiḥ |
śūdrakarmā bhavet pauṣṇe [?] *nairr̥tye* [?] *kartr̥nāśanam* || 60 ||
adhanaṃ bh<*r̥ṅ*>*garājākhye mr̥ge putravināśanam* |
paścime pitrye svalpāyur adhanaṃ ca (mahadbhayam)
**dauvārike?* || 61 ||

sugrīve putranāśaḥ syāt puṣpadante tu vardhanam |
varuṇe krodhabhogitvaṃ nṛpabhaṅgas tathā {'}sure || 62 ||
nityātiśo(ṣi)ṣatā śo(ke)ṣe pāpākhye pāpasaṃcayaḥ |
uttare [?] *rogavadhau nitya<ṃ> nāge ripubhaya<ṃ> mahat* || 63 ||
mukhye dhanasutotpattir bhallāṭe vipulāḥ śriyaḥ |
some tu dharmaśīlatvaṃ bhujaṅge bahuvairatā || 64 ||
kanyādoṣāḥ sadāditye [sic!] *aditau* [?] *dhanasaṃcayaḥ* |

56. '[Those doors that are situated] in the east, [beginning with] Īśāna, those that stand in the south [beginning in] the south-east; in the west, they are to be known [starting] from the south-west, those standing in the north, [beginning in] the north-west:
57. Progressing from the east [in clockwise direction], there shall be danger of fire [if the door is situated] in [the *pada* of] Agni; in Parjanya, there is abundant female [progeny], in Jāyanta, there is abundance of wealth.
58. In [the *pada*] of Mahendra, there is friendliness of the king, in Sūrya, there shall be excessive anger; in Satya, falsehood shall be known, there shall be cruelty in Bhṛśa.
59. In Antarikṣa, there shall always be known to be encounter with thieves; in the south (? Anila), there shall be loss of sons, and in the south-east (? Pūṣan), servitude.
60. Lowliness is to be known [as the reslut of a door] in Vitatha, in Gṛha[kṣata], there dwells continuation of the line; the work of Śūdras shall be [the result] in [the *pada*] of Pūṣan (? Yama), in the south-west (? Gandharva), the builder will perish.
61. Absence of wealth in the one called Bhṛṅgarāja, in Mṛga, loss of sons; in the west, [the results are as follows:] in [the *pada* called] Pitrya, a short lifespan, and absence of wealth *in Dauvārika.
62. In Sugrīva, there shall be loss of sons, but in Puṣpadanta, [their] increase; in Varuṇa, one shall reap anger [?], and breaking of the king [?] in Asura.
63. Excessive draught [?] [shall] always [be the result of a door] in Śoṣa, in the one called Pāpa[yakṣman], an accumulation of what is wicked; in the north (? Roga), there shall always be disease and murder, in Nāga, great danger from enemies.
64. In Mukhya, gain of wealth and sons, in Bhallāṭa, abundant riches; and in Soma, goodliness and righteousness, in Caraka, great enmity.
65. Faults in the daughter at all times in [the *pada*] belonging to Aditi, in Aditi (? Diti), accumulation of wealth [...].'

MP 254.07cd-09, on the other hand, contents itself with enumerating those *padas* it regards as auspicious:

> *dvārāṇi tu pravakṣyāmi praśastānīha yāni tu* || 07 ||
> *pūrveṇendraṃ jayantaṃ ca dvāraṃ sarvatra śasyate* |
> *yāmyaṃ ca vitathaṃ caiva dakṣiṇena vidurbudhāḥ* || 08 ||
> *paścime puṣpadantaṃ ca vāruṇaṃ ca praśasyate* |
> *uttareṇa tu bhallāṭaṃ saumyaṃ tu śubhadaṃ bhavet* || 09 ||

07. '[...]I shall declare those doors which are considered auspicious here:
08. in the east, a door [situated on the *pada* of] Indra and Jayanta is recommended in all instances; the experts [declare a door situeated on the *pada*] of Yama and Vitatha [to be auspicious] in the south.
09. In the west, [a door in] Puṣpadanta and [the *pada*] of Varuṇa is recommended; but in the north, [a door in] Bhallāṭa [and on the *pada*] of Soma shall be auspicious.'

It is remarkable that the pada of Yama should be regarded as auspicious, and that Gṛhakṣata should be omitted.

39.02:
bhallāṭe dhanade yad vā carake pṛthivīdhare |
brāhmaṇasya bhaved veśma māhendradvāram uttamam ||
anuṣṭubh (pathyā)

'The best dwelling for a brahman shall be [located] in [the quarters of the *vāstupuruṣamaṇḍala* associated with] Bhallāṭa, Dhanada, Caraka, or Pṛthivīdhara, with its door in [the quarter] bclonging to Mahendra.'

Bhallāṭa, Dhanada, Caraka, and Pṛthivīdhara are four deities of the *vāstupuruṣamaṇḍala*; together they occupy the northern part of the square, while Indra is located in the northeastern *pada* in the eastern part (fig. 2). The relative position of living quarters and the main entrance within the compound are the same for all castes; it is merely their position with reference to the cardinal directions that changes. Cf. note on SAS 24.35.

39.03:
māhendre 'rke 'tha satye vā āryake vā niketanam |
kāryaṃ gr̥hakṣatadvāraṃ kṣatriyasya śubhāvaham ||
b) *āryaste* (Kha Da); *niveśanaṃ* (Da)
anuṣṭubh (pathyā)

'The abode that is auspicious for a *kṣatriya* shall be made in [the quarter of] Mahendra, Arka, Satya, or Āryaka with its door in [the field of] Gr̥hakṣata.'

This stanza refers the living quarters of a *kṣatriya* to the eastern part of the ground plan, occupied by Indra, Sūrya, Satya, and Āryaman, and the entrance to the *pada* of Gr̥hakṣata in the southeastern corner of the southern section of the *vāstupuruṣamaṇḍala* (fig. 3). For the elision of *sandhi* at the caesura in the first line, cf. p. 9. Cf. also the note on 24.37.

39.04:
yāmye vaivasvate vāpi gāndharve 'tha gr̥hakṣate |
vaiśyasya bhavanaṃ kāryaṃ dvāraṃ puṣpāhvahe śubham ||
anuṣṭubh (pathyā)

'The abode of a *vaiśya* shall be made in [the quarter] belonging to Yama, Vivasvant, or Gandharva, [or in the field associated with] Gr̥hakṣata; the door is auspicious in [the field of] Puṣpāhvaha.'

The living quarters of a *vaiśya* are thus relegated to the southern part of the compound. Puṣpadanta occupies the southwestern *pada* in the western section (fig. 2). Cf. note on 24.39.

39.05:
vāruṇe pauṣpadante vā yad vā maitre 'thavāsure |
śudrasya sadanaṃ kāryaṃ bhallāṭadvāram uttamam ||
anuṣṭubh (pathyā)

'The best dwelling for a *śūdra* shall be made in [the quarter] belonging to Varuṇa or Puṣpadanta, or Mitra, or Asura with its door in [the quarter associated with] Bhallāṭa.'

The living area of a *śūdra* should thus be situated in the western section of the compound, and the entrance in the northwestern part of the northern section (fig. 2). Cf. Note on 24.41.

39.06:
viprāṇāṃ prāṅmukhaṃ vāstu gṛhaṃ syād dakṣiṇāmukham |
vardhate dhanadhānyena putrapautraiś ca nityaśaḥ ||
anuṣṭubh (pathyā)

'The *vāstu* of the brahmans faces east, the house shall be facing south; at all times he prospers with wealth and grains, and with sons and grandsons.'

For the difference between *vāstu* and *gṛha*, cf. 1.5.5 above. As we have seen, the main entrance of a brahman's *vāstu* is situated on its eastern side; the living quarters are found on the northern side facing the compound. As stated above, the same internal arrangement applies to the houses of the other castes as well. This setup corresponds to the *pūrṇabāhu*-groundplan described below (39.15,16). Cf. also note on 24.36.

39.07:
dakṣiṇābhimukhaṃ vāstu bhavanaṃ paścimāmukham |
kṣatriyasya dhanaṃ dhānyaṃ vikramaś ceha vardhate ||
anuṣṭubh (pathyā)

'The *vāstu* faces south, the abode faces west; a *kṣatriya's* wealth, grain, and valour increase here.'

39.08:

vāstunaḥ paścimaṃ dvāraṃ bhavanasyottarāmukham |
tatraidhate dhanair dhānyaiḥ putrapaśvādibhiś ca viṭ ||

a) *paścimadvāraṃ* (Da)
anuṣṭubh (pathyā)

'The door of the *vāstu* faces west, [that] of the abode faces north; there thrives the *vaiśya* with wealth, grains, sons, cattle and so on.'

39.09:

vāstu syād uttaradvāraṃ gṛhaṃ pūrvāmukhaṃ tathā |
śūdrasya karmavṛttis tu dhanadhānyair vivardhate ||

a) *vāstuḥ* (Da); b) *yathā* (Da); c) °*vṛttis tad*° (Da); d) *vivardhyate* (Da)
anuṣṭubh (pathyā)

'The *vāstu* shall have its door in the north, and the house is facing east; and [there] the livelihood of a *śūdra* prospers with wealth and grains.'

39.10:

ekasyām api śālāyāṃ catvāraḥ saṃprakīrtitāḥ |
niveśyadvārabhāgāś ca kathyante ca śubhāśubhāḥ ||

c) *niveśyagadvārāś ca* (Da), *niveśyagṛhadvārāś ca* (Kha)
anuṣṭubh (pathyā)

'Of the single *śālās*, [these] four have been proclaimed; and both the auspicious and the inauspicious quarters for dwelling and door are [now] explained.'

The vll. in Kha and Da seems to suggest that Da depended on Kha, and not vice versa; °*ga*° is obviously a secondary scribal error for °*gṛha*°.

39.11:
utsaṅgo hīnabāhuś ca pūrṇabāhus tathāparaḥ |
pratyakṣāyaś caturthaś ca niveśaḥ parikīrtitaḥ ||
c) *pratyakṣoyaś* (Da)
anuṣṭubh (pathyā)

'*Utsaṅga* and *hīnabāhu*, next *pūrṇabāhu*; and *pratyakṣāya* has been proclaimed as the fourth [type of] dwelling.'

For the parallel of 39.11-17 in SAS 48.25-31, cf. pp. 1.3.3; for 39.11, cf. 48.25:

> *utsaṅgaḥ pūrṇabāhuś ca hīnabāhus tathāparaḥ |*
> *pratyakṣāya iti proktaṃ praveśanaṃ catuṣṭayam ||*

'*Utsaṅga* and *pūrṇabāhu*, next *hīnabāhu*; [and] *pratyakṣāya* – thus are proclaimed the four [types of] entrance.'

AP 83.10-12 applies the four terms introduced in this stanza to the city gates:

> *utsaṅgaḥ pūrṇabāhuś ca hīnabāhus tathāparaḥ |*
> *pratikāya* [!] *iti proktaṃ pratolīnāṃ catuṣṭayam* || 10 ||
> *uttarāmukha utsaṅgaḥ pūrṇabāhuś ca pūrvataḥ |*
> *apare hīnabāhuś ca pratikāyas tu dakṣiṇe* || 11 ||
> *sr̥ṣṭipraveśa utsaṅgaḥ pratikāyo 'pasavyataḥ |*
> *pūrṇabāhuḥ pūrvavaktro vāmā*stho hīnabāhukaḥ* || 12 || (ed.: *vāmāsyo*)

10. '*Utsaṅga* and *pūrṇabāhu*, then *hīnabāhu* [and] *pratikāya* – thus are declared the four types of *pratolī*.
11. The *utsaṅga* faces north, and the *pūrṇabāhu* east; and the *hīnabāhu* west, the *pratikāya*, though, [faces] south.
12. An entrance for offspring is the *utsaṅga*, the *pratikāya* the opposite; the *pūrṇabāhu* faces east, the *hīnabāhu* is on the left.'

The difference becomes apparent at once: besides the obvious deviation *pratikāya* for *pratyakṣāya*, and the apparently corrupt second half of 83.12, the application of the four terms in AP betrays a much lesser degree of sophistication; it does not take into account the relative direction in which entrance takes place – straight, clockwise, counter-clockwise, or in an about-turn –, but simply applies SAS' terminology to the four cardinal directions. AP 72.12 also mentions the four different types of entrance in the context of the royal fort (*mahārājādhirājapura*):

> *utsaṅgaḥ pūrṇabāhuś ca hīnabāhus tathāparaḥ* |
> *pratikāyam iti proktaṃ praveśāṇāṃ catuṣṭayam* ||

'*Utsaṅga* and *pūrṇabāhu*, then *hīnabāhu* [and] *pratikāya* – thus are declared the four types of entrances.'

As the topic is not taken up again in the following stanzas, it may well be an interpolation.

39.12:
***utsaṅga ekadikkābhyāṃ dvārābhyāṃ vāstuveśmanoḥ* |**
***sa saubhāgyaprajāvṛddhidhanadhānya*kṣaya*pradaḥ* ||**

ab) *evadīkṣābhyāṃ dvārāṇāṃ* (Ka Kha Ga Da); d) °*jaya*° (Ka Kha Ga Śa Śu), °*bhaya*° (Da)
anuṣṭubh (pathyā)

'[It is called] *utsaṅga* because the two doors of *vāstu* and abode [respectively] face one [and the same] direction; it brings about destruction of the good fortune and of the increase of progeny, wealth, and grain.'

Cf. SAS 48.26,28:

> *gṛhasya saṃmukhaṃ yatra dvāraṃ bhavati vāstunaḥ* |
> *utsaṅga iti sa proktaḥ pūrṇabāhuḥ pradakṣiṇaḥ* || 26 ||
> *utsaṅgākhye praveśe syāt prajāhāniḥ kuṭumbinaḥ* |
> *dhanadhānyakṣayo vāsya maraṇaṃ vā dhruvaṃ bhavet* || 27 ||

26. 'Where the door of the house is facing [that] of the *vāstu* – that is called *utsaṅga*, *pūrṇabāhu* [if it is situated] in clockwise direction [from the entrance of the *vāstu*].
27. In the case of an entrance called *utsaṅga*, there may be loss of progeny for the master of the house; or he may experience loss of wealth and grain, or his death shall certainly occur.'

The emendation of SASTRI/AGRAWALA in the first line – *eka-dikkābhyāṃ dvārābhyāṃ* for *evadīkṣābhyāṃ dvārāṇāṃ* – is made plausible by the parallel in 48.26. As for my emendation in the last quarter (for which I am indebted to Roland Steiner), the parallel in 48.28 clearly shows that the reading of Ka Kha Ga cannot be correct; the reading of Da: °*bhaya*°, on the other hand, while pointing in the correct general direction, is still too weak in its implications. Since *kṣaya* also occurs in 48.27, it has been emended for *jaya*; the reading in Da seems to represent an earlier attempt at restoring the text of the original.

39.13:

yatra praveśato vāstugṛhaṃ bhavati vāmataḥ |
tad dhīnabāhukaṃ vāstu ninditaṃ vāstucintakaiḥ ||

c) °*dhīnaṃ bāhukaṃ* (Da)
anuṣṭubh (pathyā)

'Where the house of the *vāstu* is [situated] on the left of the door – that *vāstu* is called *hīnabāhuka* by the experts on *vāstu*.'

Cf. 48.27ab:

vāmato hīnabāhuḥ syāt pratyakṣo yas tu pṛṣṭhataḥ |

'[Where the entrance to the house is situated] to the left [of the entrance to the compound] – that shall be [called] *hīnabāhuḥ*, *pratyakṣa* [shall be called that] which is in the back [of the house].'

Note the caesura within the compound in ab); if *vāstu* and *gṛha* were to be read separately the stanza would be difficult to construe.

39.14:

tasmin vasann alpavittaḥ svalpamitro 'lpabāndhavaḥ |
strījitaś ca bhaven nityaṃ vividhavyādhipīḍitaḥ ||

anuṣṭubh (ra-vipulā)

'He who dwells there has few possessions, very few friends, [and] few relatives; he shall always be in the power of women, and tormented by various diseases.'

This stanza has an almost verbatim correspondence with 48.30:

> *alpamitro gṛhī hīnabāhāv atyalpabāndhavaḥ |*
> *syād alpavitto jīyeta strībhiḥ pīḍyeta vāmayaiḥ ||*

'In the case of [an entrance of the type of] *hīnabāhu*, the master of the house has got few friends [and] very few relatives; he shall be of few possessions, overpowered by women, or tormented by diseases.'

39.15:
vāstupraveśato yat tu gṛhaṃ dakṣiṇato bhavet |
pradakṣiṇapraveśatvāt tad vidyāt pūrṇabāhukam ||

> a) *vāstupravesito yaṃ tu* (Da), *vāstupraveśito yaṃ tu* (Kha Ga)
> anuṣṭubh (pathyā)

'That house which may be [situated] to the right of the entry of the *vāstu* – that shall be known as *pūrṇabāhuka* on account of the fact that entry takes place in clockwise direction.'

Cf. 48.26 quoted in the note on 39.12 above.

39:16:
tatra putrāṃś ca pautrāṃś ca dhanadhānyasukhāni ca |
prāpnuvanti narā nityaṃ vasanto vāstuni dhruvam ||

> anuṣṭubh (pathyā)

'Certainly there the men who reside in that *vāstu* always aquire sons and grandsons, and the happiness of wealth and grains.'

Cf. 48.29.

> *pūrṇabāhau putrapautrā dhanadhānyasukhāni ca |*
> *bhavanti vasato nityaṃ gṛhiṇas tatra vāstuni ||*

'In the case of [an entrance of the type of] *pūrṇabāhu*, there are always sons and grandsons, and the happiness of wealth and grain for the householder residing in that *vāstu*.'

39.17:

gṛhapṛṣṭhaṃ samāśritya vāstudvāraṃ yadā bhavet |
pratyakṣāyas tv asau nindyo vāmāvartapraveśavat ||

anuṣṭubh (pathyā)

'If the door of the *vāstu* is situated at the back of the house – that is the ill-reputed *pratyakṣāya* with its entrance in counter-clockwise direction.'

The expression *vāmāvartapraveśavat* in this context is noteworthy, as it refers to a full 'u-turn,' rather than just a turn to the left by 90 degrees; one might have expected it in the context of the *hīnabāhuka* just as well.

39.18-19:

brāhmaṇo nivasen mukhye dvināmni kṣatriyo vaset |
vitathe nivased vaiśyaḥ śūdraḥ sugrīvanāmani || 18 ||

d) *śūdraṃ* (Da)

anuṣṭubh (pathyā)

ete vaiśeṣikāḥ sarve varṇānām anupūrvaśaḥ |
vāstudvāraniveśaś ca vāsaiḥ saha nirūpitāḥ || 19 ||

anuṣṭubh (pathyā)

18. 'A brahman shall settle down [for the night] in [the *pada* of the *vāstupuruṣamaṇḍala* associated with] Mukhya, a *kṣatriya* shall stay in [that of] Dvināman; a *vaiśya* shall settle down [for the night] in [the *pada* of] Vitatha, a *śūdra* in [the *pada* of the one] called Sugrīva.

19. All these particular *vāstu*-doors and abodes together with the sleeping chambers for the caste members have been described as before.'

The *padas* mentioned here are just outside the area prescribed for the main living area in 39.01-10; obviously, *(ni-)vas* is used here in its more original meaning 'to settle down for the night'. The sleeping area of the master of the house would thus be situated to the left of the main living area; the rendering of *vāsa* as 'sleeping chamber' is made necessary by the fact that in 39.19, *niveśa* and *vāsa* would otherwise be synonymous. This is probably also the meaning intended in KS I.4.03, where *dvivāsagṛha* obviously refers to a house with two separate beds or bedrooms for sleeping and sexual congress respectively, rather than a house with two separate living areas as SCHLINGLOFF seems to believe (1969:25 fn.5).

39.20:
yathottaram athocyante varṇānāṃ gṛhakalpanāḥ |
śūdraviṭkṣatrivipraṇāṃ rājñāṃ ca jayakāṅkṣiṇām ||

c) *śūdraviṭkṣatravipraṇāṃ* (Ka Kha Ga Da)
anuṣṭubh (pathyā)

'In due order, the prescriptions for the houses of *varṇins* are now declared: for *śūdras*, *vaiśyas*, *kṣatriyas*, [and] brahmans, as well as for kings who are desirous of victory.'

It is interesting to note that the king should be included with the *varṇins* in this stanza, as he is usually grouped with the *karmopajīvins*. The remaining stanzas of this section are devoted to the permissible overall height of the buildings; 39.21-28 give the maximum number of storeys, 39.29-32ab the maximum overall height in cubits, and 39.32cd-39.34(1) the minimum number of storeys.

It should be noted that these stanzas have no direct parallel in BṛS 52; the height of a building is only mentioned in passing in BṛS 52.11:

> *vāstuni yo vistāraḥ sa eva cocchrāyaniścayaḥ śubhadaḥ |*
> *śālaikeṣu gṛheṣv api vistārād dviguṇitaṃ dairghyam ||*

'It is auspicious for a building if the height is fixed as equal to its width. And in the case of houses of the *ekaśāla*-type, the length is double the width.'

and again in 52.16:

> *paśvāśramiṇām amitaṃ dhānyāyudhavahniratigṛhāṇāṃ ca* |
> *necchanti śāstrakārā hastaśatād ucchritaṃ parataḥ* ||

'For cattle, hermits, granaries, arsenals, *agniśālās*, and pleasure-houses there is no [prescribed] measure; the authors of the *śāstras* do not approve of a height exceeding 100 cubits.'

No corresponding stanzas were found in MP; cf. VP 02.157-159ab:

> *yajante rājasūyādyaiḥ kratubhir hy avanīśvarāḥ* |
> *(na)talair ardhāṣṭamais teṣāṃ kārayed bhavanottamam* || 157 ||
> *tathā ca saptamair* [sic!] *eva viprāṇāṃ kārayed gṛham* |
> *ardhaṣaṣṭhaiḥ kṣatriyāṇāṃ vaiśyānām ardhapañcamaiḥ* || 158 ||
> *tribhiḥ sārdhaiś ca śūdrāṇāṃ bhavanaṃ śubhadaṃ smṛtam* |

157. 'Kings [who] perform sacrifices like the *rājasūya* etc. – for them the best dwelling shall be built with seven-and-a-half storeys.
158. Accordingly, the house of brahmans shall be built with seven, that of *kṣatriyas* with five-and-a-half, that of *vaiśyas* with four-and-a-half.
159. The dwelling of *śūdras* is known to be auspicious [if it has] three-and-a-half [storeys ...].'

Note that the ordinal numbers are used in two instances *metri causa*; one might be tempted to emend **tathārdhasaptamair* in 158a. The edition reads *nala* instead of **tala*, obviously a printing error. It is quite likely that VP 02.157-159ab was the model for SAS 39.21-28.

39.21-28:

***sārdhaṃ tribhūmi śūdrāṇāṃ* veśma kuryād vibhūtaye |**
***ato 'dhikataraṃ yat syāt tat karoti kulakṣayam* || 21 ||**

a) *sārdhatribhūmi śūdrāṇāṃ* (Ka Śa Śu), *sārdhaṃ tribhūmi-śūdreṇa* (Kha Ga Da)
anuṣṭubh (pathyā)

***vaiśyasya vardhayed geham ardhapañcamabhūmikam* |**
***atipramāṇe tatrāsya dhanabandhuparikṣayaḥ* || 22 ||**

anuṣṭubh (ma-vipulā)

***kṣatriyasya gṛhaṃ kuryād ardhaṣaṣṭhatalaṃ param* |**
***sampadbalasamṛddhyai tadatiriktaṃ tu tacchide* || 23 ||**

c) °*samṛddhau* (Da)
anuṣṭubh (pathyā)

***paraṃ viprasya bhavanam ardhasaptamabhūmikam* |**
***svādhyāyācārabhogārtham atyuccaṃ tu bhayāvaham* || 24 ||**

anuṣṭubh (na-vipulā)

***yajante rājasūyādyaiḥ kratubhir ye 'vanīśvarāḥ* |**
***talair ardhāṣṭamais teṣāṃ kārayed bhavanottamam* || 25 ||**

a) *jayante* (Da); b) *ṛtubhir* (Da); c) *tailair ardhāṣṭameteṣāṃ* (Da)
anuṣṭubh (pathyā)

***āhartānekayajñānāṃ rājā rājādhipaś ca yaḥ* |**
***tasyāpy ardhāṣṭamatalaṃ bhavanaṃ saṃniveśayet* || 26 ||**

anuṣṭubh (na-vipulā)

***vājapeyena vā yaṣṭā yo dvijaḥ syāt samāhitaḥ* |**
***gavāṃ koṭiprado yo vā so 'pi tasmin bhaved abhīḥ* || 27 ||**

c) *koṭiḥ pradeyā vā* (Da), *koṭiḥ pradeyā vāso* (Kha Ga); d) *bhaved ubhī* (Kha Ga Da)
anuṣṭubh (pathyā)

***yathāpramāṇanirdiṣṭe vasantas te nṛpādayaḥ* |**
***prāpnuvanti parām ṛddhim avṛddhiṃ tu viparyaye* || 28 ||**

anuṣṭubh (pathyā)

21. 'For *śūdras*, the dwelling shall be made three-and-a-half storeys for [their] welfare; that which may be in excess [of this] causes destruction of the household.

22. The house of a *vaiśya* shall make [him] prosper that has got four-and-a-half storeys; if its height is excessive, he [shall experience] loss of wealth and relatives.

23. The ideal house of a *kṣatriya* shall be made five-and-a-half storeys [high]; [it leads] to increase of prosperity and power, but [if it is] excessive, [it leads] to their destruction.

24. The ideal abode of a brahman is six-and-a-half storeys [high]; it has the revenue from recitation and observance as its aim, but [if it is] too tall, it brings about danger.

25. The kings who perform sacrifices by means of the ceremonies as the *rājasūya* etc. – for them shall be made the ideal abode with seven-and-a-half storeys.

26. The king and king of kings who is the performer of multiple sacrifices – for him, an abode of seven-and-a-half storeys shall be built.

27. The brahman who may perfom the *vājapeya*-rite of collected spirit, or who has donated ten million cows – he, too shall be fearless in [such a building].

28. If [the buildings] have the prescribed size, the inhabitants, kings and so on, attain the highest [degree of] prosperity, but ruin in the opposite case.'

The wording of 39.21a as it appears in the printed edition is awkward; from the context of the following stanzas, as well as from the parallel in VP 02.157-159ab quoted in the preceding note it is clear that the height of a *śūdra*'s house should not exceed three-and-a-half storeys. Since *sārdhatribhūmi* really means 'two-and-a-half,' and **ardhacaturbhūmi* would have disturbed the metre, I have suggested my emendation on the basis of the v.l. in Kha Ga Da.

The half storey mentioned in these stanzas seems to refer to the *pīṭha*, which according to SAS 24.26 should be half as tall as the ground floor.

It is interesting to note that the royalty is distinguished not by titles (cf. MS 40; ACHARYA 1946a:437), but by the rituals they have performed.

39.29-30:
sapīṭhatalakaṃ veśma mānataḥ saṃprakīrtitam |
sādhāraṇena hastena paraṃ śūdrasya viṃśatiḥ || 29 ||
anuṣṭubh (pathyā)

catvāriṃśad viśaḥ ṣaṣṭiḥ kṣatriyasya praśasyate |
aśītir dvijamukhyasya śatahastā mahīpateḥ || 30 ||
c) *dvayamukhyasya* (Kha Ga Da)
anuṣṭubh (pathyā)

29. 'Regarding its size, the abode of a *śūdra* has been declared to be twenty medium cubits at most, including the basement level.

30. Forty [cubits] has been declared [to be the proper height of the house] of a *vaiśya*, sixty for a *kṣatriya*; eighty for a brahman, one hundred cubits for a king.'

The measurements given here seem to be unrelated to the number of storeys given in the preceding stanzas; if we take into account the rules given in SAS 28.16-17 (disregarding, for the moment, the rule about the gradual diminution of the storeys given in 28.47), the largest dwelling of a *śūdra* 20 cubits in width would have a ground floor 5 1/4 cubits in height, and thus an overall height of 18 3/8 cubits – close enough to the 20 cubits fixed as the maximum permissible height. But the largest dwelling of a *vaiśya* with a width of 24 cubits by applying the same formula would have an overall height of 24 3/4 cubits – quite removed from the 40 cubits given in 39.30. The figures for *kṣatriya*, brahman, and king are 31 5/8, 39, and 52 1/2 (rather than 60, 80, and 100) cubits respectively.

For *sādhāraṇena hastena* in 39.29, cf. SAS 09.05; cf. also PARAMAHANS (1984:27sq.).

39.31-32:
nātaḥ paraṃ nṛṇām ūrdhvapramāṇaṃ śastam ucyate |
devadānavadaityānāṃ piśācoragarakṣasām || 31 ||
anuṣṭubh (pathyā)

siddhagandharvayakṣāṇāṃ vidhātavyam ato 'dhikam |
ekabhaumād adho naiva gṛhaṃ śūdrasya vidyate || 32 ||
anuṣṭubh (pathyā)

31. 'And a taller size has been declared to be unfit for [the abodes of] men; [the abodes] of *devas*, *dānavas*, *daityas*, *piśācas*, *uragas*, [or] *rakṣas*';

32. of *siddhas*, *gandharvas*, and *yakṣas* shall be built higher. – The house of a *śūdra* is known not to be lower than one storey.'

39.33:
vaiśyasya bhavanaṃ kāryam adho nādhyardhabhūmikāt |
dvibhūmikād adhaḥ kāryaṃ kṣatriyasya na mandiram ||
b) *nānyardha°* (Ka Kha Ga Da)
anuṣṭubh (pathyā)

'The abode of a *vaiśya* shall not be made lower than one-and-a-half storeys, the abode of a *kṣatriya* shall not be made lower than two storeys.'

39.34(1):

sārdhadvibhaumād viprasya tritalād api bhūpateḥ **|**

a) °*bhūmād* (Da)

1/2 anuṣṭubh (ma-vipulā)

'[The abode] of a *brāhmaṇa* [shall not be built lower] than two-and-a-half storeys, and [that] of a king [not] lower than three storeys.'

39.34(2):

hīnapramāṇād amuto gṛhaṃ yat
kuśilpinā syād vihitaṃ kathaṃcit **|**
bhartur bhiye siddhivināśanaṃ tat
praśastaśīlādiviparyayāya **||**

c) *dvitrivināśanaṃ*? (Ga Kha), *bhiyai dvitrivināśanaṃ* (Da); d) °*līlā ca viparyayāya* (Da)

upajāti

'If the house should somehow be built [lower than] this minimum size by an incompetent builder, it will cause danger for the master [of the house], desctruction of success, and perversion of the sanctioned customs etc.'

3. Glossary of Technical Terms

NB. This glossary contains the technical terms of SAS 18-24, 28, 39, and 48. Only words referring to buildings, settlements, and their component parts were entered; words denoting abstract concepts such as *vistṛti*, *prastāra* etc. have been left out. Wherever the names of certain buildings have been found to differ slightly in different places, they have been treated as one entry separated by a slash, e.g. *kāca/kānta*. Optional final syllables with no semantic function (usually *-ka*, or *-na*) have been separated by a comma (e.g. *alinda, -ka*); diminutives have been treated as a separate entry (e.g. *avalokana*, *avalokanaka*). Generic terms have been given in small capitals (e.g. ABODE).

It should be emphasized that this glossary was not compiled with the aim of defining each entry as precisely as possible; rather, it serves as a kind of annotated index whose purpose it is to facilitate (1) the identification of certain rare words, and (2) a comparison of the technical vocabulary related to residential architecture of SAS with that of other treatises.

A

agāra n. ABODE. 18.09a

aṅgaṇa n. courtyard. 18.29a; 18.42b

> *gṛhāṅgaṇa*

ajā f. syn. for > *chagalī*. 22.09c

ajira n. courtyard. 24.01c

> *āśramājira, bhavanājira, vanājira*

aṭṭa m. watchtower. 18.45b

aṭṭālakā f. small watchtower. 18.45d; 18.53d

aṭṭālī f. very small watchtower. 18.46b

aṭṭālikā f. exceedingly small watchtower. 18.46d

adhirohaṇa n. ascent. 18.11b

anala n. a type of > *cullī*$_2$. 22.20a; 22.47c

anila n. a type of > *vāta*$_1$. 22.18d; 22.42d

anupallava m. *a kind of moulding. 28.29b

anupāla m. a kind of battlement. 18.54c

antika n. a type of > *tribhadra*. 19.48b; 19.94b

apara n. a particular type of > *saptaśāla*. 20.34c

apavaraka m. chamber; bedroom. 18.24b; 18.26b

abhigupti f. covered portion of the rooftop terrace. 18.13c

amūṣa n. a house without > *mūṣā*. 22.10c

amedhyā f. latrine. 18.44a

ambudavidhvaṃsa/roga n. a type of > *vāta*$_1$. 22.19a; 22.44b

ayogama n. a type of > *dvibhadra*. 19.46d; 19.88d

argalā f. door-bolt. 18.32d; 48.134c

argalasūcī f. a type of door-bolt. 18.33a

arcāgṛha n. temple. 18.57b

arcāyana n. a type of > *caturbhadra*. 19.54a; 19.124d

ardhacandra m. *a kind of decoration. 28.37c

ardharca n. a type of > *dvibhadra*. 19.45c; 19.84c

alinda, -ka m. verandah; gallery; corridor. 19.22c; 19.26c; 19.27a; 19.29c; 19.32c; 19.38c; 19.40d; 20.10c; 20.11a; 20.12b; 20.13a; 20.14a; 20.19.c; 20.27a; 20.27b; 20.36b; 21.05c; 22.04b; 24.25b; 28.19d; 48.18b; 48.79b; 48.137a

alindā f. front porch, verandah. 18.23b

avakosimā f. corner-room. 19.27b; 19.29b; 19.75d; 19.77d; 19.78d

avadhāraṇa n. a type of roof. 28.54d

avalokana n. window. 18.14b

avalokanaka n. small window. 18.14d

avaskara m. latrine. 18.44b

avyaya$_1$ n. a type of > *caturbhadra*. 19.57d; 19.159d

avyaya$_2$ n. a type of > *pañcabhadra*. 19.65b; 19.204b

aśoka n. a type of > *ṣaḍbhadra*. 19.67c; 19.213c

aṣṭabhadra n. a house with five > *mūṣās*. 19.224(2)b

aṣṭaśāla n. a building consisting of eight wings. 19.09a

askhala

v. *ākhila*

asthira n. a type of > *ṣaḍbhadra*. 19.66d; 19.209b

Ā

ākrīḍa, -ṇa n. a type of > *caturbhadra*. 19.57c19.157b

ākrīḍabhūmi f. sporting ground. 18.56cd

ākhila/askhala n. a type of > *caturbhadra*. 19.58d; 19.167b

āgastya n. a type of > *caturbhadra*. 19.58a; 19.162d

āgāra n. a type of > *tribhadra*. 19.51d; 19.116c

āgneya n. a type of > *dvibhadra*. 19.45a

ānīra n. a type of > *dvibhadra*. 19.46a; 19.86c

āpya$_1$ n. a type of > *dvibhadra*. 19.45b; 19.84a

āpya$_2$ n. a type of > *tribhadra*. 19.50a; 19.105b

āyata n. a type of > *tribhadra*.

19.51b; 19.114b

āyasta n. a type of > *tribhadra*. 19.48c; 19.95d

āyāta n. a type of > *tribhadra*. 19.49a; 19.99d

āyāma n. a type of > *tribhadra*. 19.48a; 19.92d

āyāsya n. a type of > *caturbhadra*. 19.55a; 19.137d

āyuta n. a type of > *tribhadra*. 19.52a; 19.118b

ārāma m. grove, garden. 18.55a

ālaya m. ABODE. 18.09b; 22.31a; 22.33b

ālīna n. a type of > *pañcabhadra*. 19.63c; 19.193b

ālokana n. a type of window. 48.43b; 48.121b; 48.133c

āvāsa m. ABODE. 18.08a; 24.13a

āśrama m. hermitage. 18.29d

āśramājira n. the courtyard of a hermitage. 18.29d

āsthalaka n. brick-paved section of floor near the door. 18.43d

I

indra n. a type of > *sukṣetra*$_1$. 21.10b; 21.31b

indrakīla m. a type of door-bolt. 48.107a

iṣṭakā f. brick. 18.43a

Ī

īra n. a type of > *dvibhadra*. 19.45a; 19.82d

īrita n. a type of > *tribhadra*. 19.50b

īśāna n. a type of > *caturbhadra*. 19.57d; 19.158a

īśvara n. a type of > *halaka*. 24.02a; 24.05c

īhāmṛga m. decoration in the shape of a composite figure. 18.16d

U

utkālaka m./n. *a kind of moulding. 28.24a; 28.24c

uttarodumbara m. lintel. 18.30a

utsaṅga m. a constellation of the doors. 39.11a; 39.12a; 48.25a; 48.26c; 48.28a

utsuka n. a type of > *caturbhadra*. 19.54b; 19.128d

udakabhrama m. drain. 18.28d

udumbara m. threshold; lintel. 28.10b; 28.10d; 28.19a; 48.98a

uddaṇḍa$_1$ n. a type of > *caturbhadra*. 19.58c; 19.165d

uddaṇḍa$_2$ n. a type of > *daṇḍa*$_1$. 22.17b; 22.36c

udyanta n. a type of > *caturbhadra*. 19.59a; 19.168d

udyāna n. garden-pavilion. 18.55b

udvejana n. a type of > *cullī*$_1$. 21.14a; 21.42d

upakārya m.? a kind of battlement. 18.53c

upatulā f. a kind of beam. 48.96a

upaniṣkala m./f.? a road on the inside of the city wall. 18.54d

uparibhūmi f. upper storey; top

level. 18.10a

upasthāna n. 18.05a; reception room, audience chamber. 18.21c

upasthānaka n. a small reception room. 18.21d; 18.26a

**ulloka* m. opening in the middle of the flat roof. 18.15b

R̥

r̥ṣa n. a type of > *caturbhadra*. 19.56d; 19.149d

E

ekabhadra n. a house with one > *mūṣā*. 19.41a; 19.42a; 19.43c; 19.71c; 19.224(2)a

ekamūṣa n. a house with one > *mūṣā*. 22.10c

ekaśāla, -ka n. a house consisting of a single cottage with an adjoining courtyard. 18.19a; 19.02a; 19.05a; 22.52(2)c; 24.20a

ekākṣa n. a type of > *tribhadra*. 19.48b; 19.93d

ekoja n. a type of > *caturbhadra*. 19.58b; 19.163b

AI

aindra n. a type of > *tribhadra*. 19.48a; 19.90d

aibha n. a type of > *dvibhadra*. 19.45c; 19.84d

O

okas n. ABODE. 18.09d; 19.90b

KA

kakuda n. a type of > *cullī*$_1$. 21.14d; 21.46b

kakṣā f. interior courtyard. 18.25c; 48.39b; 48.40b

> *sakakṣa*.

kaṭa n. a type of > *saptabhadra*. 19.68d; 19.223a

kaṇṭha$_1$ m. wall (cf. > *kaṇṭhā*). 18.42b

kaṇṭha$_2$, *-ka* m. a kind of moulding. 28.26d; 28.39b; 28.44c

kaṇṭhā f. parapet; outwall. 18.15d; 18.26c; 48.138?

katha n. a type of > *tribhadra*. 19.53b; 19.122b

kanaka n. a type of > *hiraṇyanābha*$_1$. 21.07a; 21.21b

kandakūṭa m./n.? a type of roof? 48.133d

kandara n. a type of > *cullī*$_1$. 21.14d; 21.46c

kapāṭa n. door-leaf. 18.31a; 18.32a

kapāṭapuṭa n. door-leaf. 18.31b

kapāṭayugala n. pair of leaves in a double door. 18.32b

kapāṭāśraya m. threshold. 18.30d

kapotālī f. a kind of moulding (cf. *marālapālī*). 28.55a; 48.106c

kapha n. a type of > *tribhadra*. 19.50c; 19.109b

kabandha n. a type of > *yamasūrya*$_1$. 22.16b; 22.32d

karāla n. a type of > *yamasūrya*$_1$. 22.16a; 22.31c

karuṇānana n. a type of > *cullī*$_1$. 21.14b; 21.44b

kareṇu f. syn. for > *hastinī*. 22.09a; 22.10a

karṇa n. a type of > *tribhadra*. 19.50c; 19.110a

karṇasāmi m./f.? *synonym for > *avakosimā*. 19.28d

karṇasūtra n. a kind of demarcation? 19.21a

karṇaśālā f. corner-room. 19.29a; 24.01a

kardama n. a type of > *sukṣetra*$_1$. 21.11c; 21.35c

karvāṭa n. market town. 18.03b; 18.03c

kala n. a type of > *caturbhadra*. 19.60a; 19.175d

kalaha/-bha$_1$ n. a type of > *caturbhadra*. 19.55a; 19.135d

kalaha$_2$ n. a type of > *vāta*$_1$. 22.19b; 22.45b

kalahottara n. a type of > *ekabhadra*. 19.43a

kali m. a type of > *vāta*$_1$. 22.19b; 22.45d

kalicullī f. a type of > *vāta*$_1$. 22.19c; 22.46b

kalikā f. door-knob. 18.32c

kalyāṇa n. a type of > *hiraṇyanābha*$_1$. 21.08c; 21.26c

kalyāṇa, -ka n. a type of > *siddhārtha*. 22.14a; 22.24b

kāca$_1$ n. a type of > *dviśāla*. 20.31b; 22.02c; 22.10a; 22.11a; 22.20c; 22.48d

kāca$_2$*/kāñca* n. a type of > *kāca*$_1$. 22.20c; 22.50a

kāñcana n. a type of > *hiraṇyanābha*$_1$. 21.07a; 21.21d

kāṇḍa n. a type of > *daṇḍa*$_1$. 22.17b; 22.37a

kānala n. a type of > *pañcabhadra*. 19.61a; 19.176d

kānta$_1$ n. a type of > *dvibhadra*. 19.46b; 19.86d

kānta$_2$ n. a type of > *tribhadra*. 19.49b; 19.100a

kānta$_3$ m./n. *a kind of moulding. 28.38c

kāma(pra)da n. a type of > *siddhārtha*. 22.14b; 22.25c

kāla n. a type of > *yamasūrya*$_1$. 22.15d; 22.30a

kāvya n. a type of > *dvibhadra*. 19.46a; 19.86a

kāṣṭha n. plank; timber. 18.12b; 18.16a; 18.17b; 18.17d; 18.48b

kāṣṭhaka n. plank; timber. 18.11a

kāṣṭhanāḍī f. wooden pipe. 18.48d

kāṣṭhanāla n. wooden pipe. 18.47b

kāṣṭhapraṇālī f. wooden pipe. 18.47c

kāṣṭhaviṭaṅka m. a house with a wooden gable. 18.12a

kinnara n. a type of > *ṣaḍbhadra*. 19.66a; 19.204d

kuñjara n. a type of > *sukṣetra*$_1$. 21.10d; 21.33b

kuṭikā f. small hut. 18.06a

kuṭṭima n. house with a rooftop terrace or the terrace itself. 18.12d

kuḍya n. wall. 18.21b; 18.24a; 18.26d; 18.30b; 19.74c; 48.45a; 48.46a

kubera$_1$ n. a type of > *siddhārtha*. 22.14d; 22.28b

kubera$_2$ m. a particular type of pillar. 28.32a; 28.33b

kumuda n. a type of roof. 28.49b; 28.53b

kumbhika m./n.? *a kind of moulding. 28.24c

kulaghna/*-ha* n. a type of > *kāca*$_1$. 22.20d; 22.50d

kṛta n. a type of > *caturbhadra*. 19.54a; 19.123d

kṛtrima n. a type of > *tribhadra*. 19.52d; 19.120b

kesarī f. a type of > *sukṣetra*$_1$. 21.10a; 21.30b

koṭara n. a type of > *daṇḍa*$_1$. 22.17b; 22.37c

kopa n. a type of > *cullī*$_1$. 21.13d; 21.41d

koṣṭhaka m. room. 18.26c

kaustubha n. a type of > *ṣaḍbhadra*. 19.66a; 19.205b

kramāgata n. a type of > *tribhadra*. 19.50d; 19.111d

kramiṇa n. a type of > *ṣaḍbhadra*. 19.66d; 19.209c

krānta$_1$ n. a type of > *dvibhadra*. 19.47a; 19.89c

krānta$_2$ n. a type of > *tribhadra*. 19.50d; 19.111b

krīḍāgāra n.pleasure house. 18.56b

krīḍāgṛha n. pleasure house. 18.55a; 18.56a

kruṣṭa n. a type of > *tribhadra*. 19.50d

kṣapa/*-ya* n. a type of > *caturbhadra*. 19.57b; 19.156b

kṣama n. a type of > *tribhadra*. 19.49a; 19.98b

kṣamiṇa n. a type of > *pañcabhadra*. 19.62c; 19.187b

kṣaya$_1$ m. ABODE. 18.01d; 18.08d

kṣaya$_2$ n. a type of > *halaka*. 24.02d; 24.15a

kṣaya$_3$

v. *kṣapa*

kṣitilaya m. ABODE. 18.01d

kṣipra n. a type of > *caturbhadra*. 19.58a; 19.162a

kṣema m. a kind of battlement. 18.53d

kṣobha n. a type of > *tribhadra*. 19.52c; 19.119d

kṣobhaṇa n. a type of > *tribhadra*. 19.52d; 19.120d

KHA

khara n. a type of > *pañcabhadra*. 19.63d; 19.194d

kharva n. a type of > *caturbhadra*. 19.59a; 19.167c

khala n. a type of > *ṣaḍbhadra*. 19.66d; 19.210a

khalva m. *a kind of moulding. 28.38a

khalvaśakhā f. a part of the door

frame. 28.12b

khādaka n. a type of > *halaka*. 24.02c; 24.11b

GA

gajavāraṇa n. a horizontal beam for locking the city gate. 18.33d

gaṇa n. a type of > *dvibhadra*. 19.46d; 19.88b

garbha m. central section of the house. 48.38b; 48.136a

garbhagr̥ha$_1$ n. central (covered) section of the house. 18.20d

garbhagr̥ha$_2$ n. central courtyard. 19.27b

gavaya n. a type of > *dvibhadra*. 19.46c; 19.87c

gavākṣa, -ka m. (lattice) window. 18.34a; 18.34c; 19.38d; 48.38d; 48.43b; 48.70b; 48.121b

gāvī f. a type of > *śālā*. 22.08ab; 22.08c; 22.10a; 24.39c

gr̥ha$_1$ m. ABODE. 18.04b

gr̥ha$_2$ n. ABODE. 18.09d; 18.10a; 18.12b; 18.13d; 18.19b; 18.19c; 18.21a; 18.24c; 18.25d; 18.40c; 18.44c; 19.09a; 19.10a; 19.18a; 19.39a; 19.78a; 19.79d; 19.83b; 19.94b; 19.108d; 19.117d; 19.120b; 19.125b; 131c; 19.132b; 19.134d; 19.138d; 19.142b; 19.144d; 19.147a; 19.151a; 19.151d; 19.152b; 19.163d; 19.165b; 19.169b; 19.204d; 19.220b; 19.220d; 19.224(2)b; 20.01b; 20.06d; 20.08d; 20.13b; 20.36a; 21.15d; 21.18d; 21.20b; 21.24b; 21.25d; 21.33d; 21.34d; 21.37c; 21.40d; 21.46d; 21.56d; 22.22d; 22.24d; 22.29c; 22.35a; 24.05d; 24.07b; 24.08d; 24.10b; 24.11b; 24.14b; 24.19d; 24.35a; 24.35d; 24.36d; 24.37d; 28.01c; 28.02a; 28.07a; 28.33c; 28.48c; 28.49c; 28.52d; 39.01a; 39.01c; 39.06b; 39.09b; 39.13b; 39.15b; 39.17a; 39.20b; 39.23a; 39.32d; 39.34a; 48.01a; 48.18c; 48.23a; 48.24b; 48.26a; 48.36b; 48.37b; 48.53a; 48.57b; 48.62a; 48.63d; 48.67d; 48.71c; 48.106d; 48.108d; 48.120a; 48.126a; 48.128d; 48.131c; 48.131d; 48.139a; 48.139d; 48.140a

gr̥hadvār f. front door. 28.15d

gr̥hadvāra m. front door. 18.35a; 28.03a; 28.05c

gr̥hanābhi m. *syn. for > *gr̥hāṅgaṇa*. 19.13b

gr̥hamālā f. an uninterrupted row of > *śālā*s surrounding the interior courtyard. 19.13a

gr̥hasaṅghaṭṭa m. two > *śālā*s sharing one wall. 20.35b

gr̥hasaṃcarabhūmi f. *footpath along the estate boundary. 18.40b

gr̥hāṅgaṇa n. interior courtyard of a dwelling. 19.13b

geha n. ABODE. 18.09b; 19.41a; 24.03d; 39.22a

gopura n. city gate. 18.52d

goṣṭha n. herders' village; corral. 18.04c; 18.58d

goṣṭhaka n. small herders' village. 18.04d

gaura n. a type of > *ṣaḍbhadra*. 19.66c; 19.208d

grāma m. village. 18.04a; 18.04b

GHA

ghaṭapallavaka m. a particular type of pillar. 28.31a

ghaṭikā f. *a kind of moulding. 28.30a

ghana n. a type of > *tribhadra*. 19.50b; 19.108b

ghanāri n. a type of > *vāta*$_1$. 22.19a; 22.43d

ghoṣa n. a type of > *ṣaḍbhadra*. 19.68a; 19.218a

ghoṣaṇa n. a type of > *pakṣaghna*$_1$. 21.16c; 21.49d

CA

cakra$_1$ n. a type of > *tribhadra*. 19.51b; 19.113b

cakra$_2$ n. a type of > *pañcabhadra*. 19.65a; 19.201a

caṇḍa n. a type of > *daṇḍa*$_1$. 22.17a; 22.35c

catura n. a type of > *pañcabhadra*. 19.64c; 19.198d

caturbhadra n. a house with four > *mūṣās*. 19.53d; 19.60b; 19.73a

catuḥśāla n. edifice with four wings arranged around an open courtyard. 18.18b; 19.03a; 19.06d; 19.15a; 19.38a; 19.70a; 19.74b; 19.74d; 19.224(2)c; 20.33a; 48.17b

candra n. a type of > *halaka*. 24.02a; 24.07c

candrarekhā f. a kind of ornamentation. 28.53d

candrāvalokitā f. a kind of window. 48.38b

caya$_1$ m. wall. 18.26d; 18.45a

caya$_2$, *-na* n. a type of > *caturbhadra*. 19.60a; 19.174d

cara n. a type of > *pañcabhadra*. 19.62a; 19.184a

cala n. a type of > *dvibhadra*. 19.47a; 19.89b

cāmīkara n. a type of > *hiraṇyanābha*$_1$. 21.07d; 21.24a

cārurucya n. a type of > *tribhadra*. 19.53a; 19.121a

citra$_1$ n. a type of > *tribhadra*. 19.49b; 19.100c

citra$_2$ n. a type of > *caturbhadra*. 19.56b; 19.145a;

cullī$_1$ f. a type of > *triśāla*. 20.26d; 21.02d; 21.04c; 21.12c; 21.14c; 21.15a; 21.45c

cullī$_2$ f. a type of > *dviśāla*. 20.32b; 22.02c; 22.09d; 22.11a; 22.20a; 22.20b; 22.46d

cullī$_3$ f. a type of > *cullī*$_1$. 21.14c; 21.45c

cullī$_4$ f. a type of > *cullī*$_2$. 22.20a; 22.47b

caitya n. temple. 18.57b

caitra n. a type of > *pañcabhadra*. 19.64a; 19.196a

cauṣya n. a type of > *ṣaḍbhadra*. 19.67c; 19.214d

CHA

chagalī f. a type of > *śālā*. 22.08c; 22.09a; 24.41c

chada m. ceiling; roof. 18.16b; 18.47d

chala₁ n. a type of > *caturbhadra*. 19.55a; 19.136d

chala₂ n. a type of > *kāca₁*. 22.20c; 22.49a

chādya, -ka n. roof. 28.48c; 28.49c; 28.50b; 28.51c; 28.54c; 48.133d; 48.136a

cheda m. *roof. 18.17d; 28.29a?; 28.30c

JA

jaṅghā f. *a kind of moulding. 28.27b; 28.32d

janapada m. the countryside. 18.07b

japa n. a type of > *pañcabhadra*. 19.61d; 19.182b

jama n. a type of > *pañcabhadra*. 19.62a; 19.183b

jaya₁ n. a type of > *ekabhadra*. 19.42d; 19.80d

jaya₂ n. a type of > *pañcabhadra*. 19.61d; 19.181b

jayantī/-ikā f. *a kind of moulding. 28.42a; 28.43d

jalaveśman n. a type of water-pavilion. 18.55d

jalodyāna n. water-pavilion 18.55c

jāta

v. *jñāta*

jāmbūnada n. a type of > *hiraṇyanābha₁*. 21.06c; 21.18d

jāla n. lattice window. 18.34d; 28.45a; 28.47a; 48.134d

jina n. a type of > *pañcabhadra*. 19.61b; 19.179b

jihma n. a type of > *pañcabhadra*. 19.61a; 19.177d

jñāta/jāta n. a type of > *pañcabhadra*. 19.61d; 19.181d

ṬHA

ṭhakāra m. ornamentation in the shape of the letter *ṭha*. 18.39c

TA

tata n. a type of > *pañcabhadra*. 19.63b; 19.191d

tantraka n. a kind of moulding. 24.33c

tapa n. a type of > *pañcabhadra*. 19.61d; 19.182d

tapana n. a type of > *hiraṇyanābha₁*. 21.08a; 21.24d

tala m./n. level; floor, storey. 18.12c; 24.18d; 24.26b; 24.29b; 28.16c; 28.19b; 28.19c; 28.47b; 39.23b; 39.25c; 39.26c; 39.29a; 39.34(1)b; 48.137b

talapaṭṭa n. *a kind of moulding. *28.34b; 28.40c

tāpanīya n. a type of > *hiraṇyanābha₁*. 21.08a; 21.25b

tilaka n. a type of roof. 28.49a; 28.52c

tīrṇa n. a type of > *caturbhadra*.

19.60a; 19.176a

tumbikā f. *a kind of moulding. 28.38d; 28.39c

tulā f. beam. 24.23d; 28.44a; 48.48c; 48.70a; 48.96a; 48.99c; 48.102b; 48.118b; 48.122b; 48.134b; 48.137b

tulāpaṭṭa m. *a kind of moulding. 28.43c

tulāpiṇḍa m. *a kind of moulding. 28.46; 48.100a

toyada n. a type of > *sukṣetra*$_1$. 21.10d; 21.33d

toraṇa n. arch; tympanon. 18.38a; 18.39c; 48.133c

trikaṇṭa, -ka n. *a kind of moulding. 28.37a; 28.38c

trinābha n. a type of > *caturbhadra*. 19.55b; 19.139a

tripuṣṭa n. a type of > *ṣaḍbhadra*. 19.67b; 19.212a

tribhadra n. a house with three > *mūṣā*s. 19.47d; 19.53c; 19.72c; 19.90c; 19.122c

trisama n. a type of > *caturbhadra*. 19.57a; 19.152d

triśāla n. edifice with three wings arranged around an open courtyard. 18.18c; 19.02d; 19.06b; 20.24b; 20.33a; 20.36c; 21.01b; 21.57a; 21.57d; 21.57f; 48.17a

triśikha n. a type of > *pañcabhadra*. 19.64c; 19.198b

traita n. a type of > *pañcabhadra*. 19.62d; 19.188d

tryaṃśa n. a type of > *caturbhadra*. 19.56c; 19.149b

DA

daṇḍa$_1$ n. a type of > *dviśāla*. 20.30a; 22.02b; 22.08c; 22.27a; 22.28a; 22.34c

daṇḍa$_2$ n. a type of > *daṇḍa*$_1$. 22.17a; 22.36a

daṇḍa$_3$, *-ka* n. a type of roof. 28.48c; 28.50b; 28.50d

dantidāruṇa n. a type of > *daṇḍa*$_1$. 22.17d; 22.40b

darpaṇagṛha n. a room full of mirrors. 18.51d

daśaśāla n. a building consisting of ten wings. 19.11a

dāraṇa n. a type of > *cullī*$_1$. 21.14c; 21.45b

dāru n. plank, board; timber. 18.41a; 48.111b

dārukalā f. woodwork, carving. 24.19c; 24.45c

durga n. fortified city. 18.01a

durgama n. a type of > *tribhadra*. 19.52c; 19.119b

duḥsthita n. a type of > *pañcabhadra*. 19.64d; 19.200a

devatāyatana n. temple. 18.57c

devadāruṇa > *suradāruṇu*.

devadhiṣṇya n. temple. 18.57a

devāgāra n. temple. 48.18d

devāri n. a type of > *pakṣaghna*$_1$. 21.16b; 21.48d

devī f. a part of the door frame. 28.14a

deśa m. country; realm. 18.07d

dehalī f. threshold. 18.30c

dravya n. building material or

element. 20.02a; 20.03a(2); 24.34a; 28.01c; 48.59c; 48.62a; 48.63a; 48.64a; 48.75a; 48.83c; 48.108b; 48.109d; 48.124c; 48.127a; 48.132a; 48.137c

dvār f. door. 19.128b; 48.69a; 48.96b

dvāra n. door. 18.27c; 18.28b; 18.32c; 18.42c; 18.43b; 18.52c; 19.30a; 19.79a; 19.91a; 19.91d; 19.93b; 19.97c; 19.98c; 19.109c; 19.110a; 19.124b; 19.125a; 19.126a; 19.127a; 19.129a; 19.131b; 19.132a; 19.133b; 19.134a; 19.135a; 19.136b; 19.139a; 19.140a; 19.141b; 19.142a; 19.143b; 19.145b; 19.146b; 19.148b; 19.152a; 19.154d; 19.160a; 19.161a; 19.162b; 19.171a; 20.01a; 20.01c; 24.18c; 24.27c; 24.28c; 24.30c; 24.35b; 24.37b; 24.39b; 24.41b; 24.45a; 28.02a; 28.07d; 28.08a; 28.20a; 39.02d; 39.03c; 39.04d; 39.05d; 39.08a; 39.09a; 39.12b; 39.17b; 39.19c; 48.19a; 48.23c; 48.26b; 48.33c; 48.41a; 48.41c; 48.42a; 48.58a; 48.58c; 48.59a; 48.59a; 48.60d; 48.61d; 48.65c; 48.67d; 48.69c; 48.70c; 48.73a; 48.74a; 48.80b; 48.82d; 48.85c; 48.90b; 48.92d; 48.94a; 48.94a; 48.95b; 48.117b; 48.122a; 48.122d; 48.124b; 48.126a; 48.128a

dvārakoṣṭhaka m. gate house. 18.27d

dvārapakṣa m. door-leaf. 18.31a

dvārapedyā f. *a part of the threshold. 28.09cd

dvāramūṣā f. a kind of small door. 19.77b

dvārasaṃvaraṇa n. door-leaf. 18.31d

dviguṇa n. a type of > *catur-bhadra*. 19.56a; 19.143a

dvibhadra n. a house with two > *mūṣās*. 19.43d; 19.47c; 19.72a; 19.90b

dvibhaya n. a type of > *tri-bhadra*. 19.51a; 19.112d

dvimandira n. a type of > *tri-bhadra*. 19.49b; 19.101b

dvirgata n. a type of > *catur-bhadra*. 19.68b; 19.163d

dviśasta n. a type of > *tri-bhadra*. 19.51a; 19.112b

dviśāla, -ka n. edifice with two wings and an open courtyard. 18.18d; 19.02c; 19.05c; 20.27c; 20.28a; 20.31b; 20.36c 22.01a; 22.02d; 22.10d; 22.21a; 22.52(1)b; 22.52(2)c; 48.17a

dvīpa n. a type of > *dvibhadra*. 19.45b; 19.83d

DHA

dhanādhīśa/dhaneśa n. a type of > *siddhārtha*. 22.14d; 22.27d

dhānyapūraka n. a type of > *su-kṣetra*$_{I}$. 21.12b; 21.37b

dhāman n. ABODE. 19.21c; 19.131a

dhārāgāra n. a type of water pavilion. 18.50d

dhārāgṛha n. a type of water

pavilion. 18.50c

dhārāsāra n. a type of > *sukṣetra*$_1$. 21.11b; 21.34c

*dhārmika*n. a type of > *ṣaḍbhadra*. 19.66b; 19.206b

dhāvana n. a type of > *caturbhadra*. 19.59d; 19.173d

dhiṣṇya n. ABODE. 18.08c; 24.41a

dhūmra n. a type of > *daṇḍa*$_1$. 22.17c; 22.39b

dhauma n. a type of > *ṣaḍbhadra*. 19.67a; 19.211d

dhruva n. a type of > *tribhadra*. 19.53b; 19.121d

dhvāṅkṣa n. a type of > *halaka*. 24.02c; 24.12a

dhvāntasaṃhāra/dhvāntasaṃghāta n. a type of > *pakṣaghna*$_1$. 21.16a; 21.48b

NA

nakula n. a type of > *cullī*$_1$. 21.13b; 21.39d

nagara n. city. 18.01a; 18.02a; 18.03b; 18.07a; 18.07c

nata n. a type of > *caturbhadra*. 19.56c; 19.148d

nandana n. a type of > *halaka*. 24.02c; 24.10b

nandapīṭha, -ka n. a type of house. 24.37d; 24.38a; 24.43a

nandinī f. a part of the door frame. 28.14b

nandyāvarta n. a type of > *catuḥśāla*. 19.78a

nala n. a type of > *caturbhadra*. 19.57b; 19.155d

navaśāla n. a building consisting of nine wings. 19.10a

nāga n. a type of > *sukṣetra*$_1$. 21.09c; 21.28d

nāgadanta, -ka n. ivory; *a kind of ornamentation. 48.70a; 48.105d; 48.120a; 48.122c; 48.125a; 48.128c

nāgapāśa, -ka m. a kind of ornamentation. 48.120b; 48.122b

nāgendra n. a type of > *tribhadra*. 19.50a; 19.106d

nāḍī f. hose; pipe. 18.47a

nādya n. a type of > *caturbhadra*. 19.56a; 19.144a

niketa m. ABODE. 18.08b; [21.58a]

niketana n. ABODE. 19.136b; 39.03b

nigama m. small market town. 18.03d; 18.04a

nigraha n. a type of > *daṇḍa*$_1$. 22.17c; 22.38d

nidhana n. ABODE. 18.08c

nirānanda n. a type of > *pakṣaghna*$_1$. 21.17a; 21.52c

nirghṛṇa n. a type of > *pakṣaghna*$_1$. 21.17b; 21.54a

nirjīva n. a type of > *cullī*$_1$. 21.13a; 21.38c

nirdhūma n. a type of > *daṇḍa*$_1$. 22.17d; 22.39d

niryūha, -ka m. protrusion of the joists; beam head. 18.17a; 19.38d; 28.43a; 28.45b

nilaya m. ABODE. 18.09c

nivāsa m. ABODE. 18.01c

niveśa m. ABODE. 19.25c;

24.44b; 39.11d; 39.19c

niveśana n. ABODE. 19.219b; 19.223b; 21.32b; 21.38d; 21.50d; 22.12d; 22.47d

niveśyadvāra n. front door. 39.10c

niḥśreṇi f. ladder. 18.11c

niṣadha n. a type of > *ṣaḍbhadra*. 19.66b; 19.206c

niṣkalaṅka n. a type of > *siddhārtha*. 22.14c; 22.27b

nistoṣa/-ya n. a type of > *cullī*$_1$. 21.14b; 21.43d

nīḍa n. ABODE. 18.09a

netra n. a type of > *ṣaḍbhadra*. 19.68a; 19.217a

nairṛta n. a type of > *dvibhadra*. 19.45d; 19.85b

PA

pakṣa m. door-leaf. 18.31c

pakṣaghna$_1$ n. a type of > *triśāla*. 20.26d; 21.02d; 21.05a; 21.15c; 21.18a; 21.47b; 21.56c

pakṣaghna$_2$ n. a type of > *pakṣaghna*$_1$. 21.17c; 21.55b

pakṣadvāra n. side-door. 18.52

pañcabhadra n. a house with five > *mūṣās*. 19.60c; 19.72d

pañcaśāla n. a building consisting of five wings. 19.04a

paṭṭa n. a kind of moulding. 24.28d; 24.31b; 24.32c; 28.19c; 28.41a; 28.43a; 28.44c; 48.133b

paṭṭakoṭi f. *a kind of moulding. 24.31d; 24.33a; 24.34c

paṭṭapiṇḍa m. *a kind of moulding. 28.41b

paṭṭasandhi m. *a kind of moulding. 48.95a

pattana n. city with a royal residence. 18.05b

patra n. *a kind of moulding. 28.25c; 28.26b

patrajāti f. *a kind of moulding. 28.39

pada n. a type of > *pañcabhadra*. 19.64b; 19.197d

padmakastambha m. a particular type of pillar. 28.27c

padmapatrī f. *a kind of moulding. 28.40b

pannaga n. a type of > *cullī*$_1$. 21.13b; 21.40b

parigha m. a horizontal beam for locking the city gate. 18.33c

paridhāna n. a particular type of > *saptaśāla*. 20.34c

parisara m. *latrine. 18.44d; 19.33b

parka n. a type of > *caturbhadra*. 19.58c; 19.164d

pallava m./n. *a kind of moulding. 28.30b; 28.32c

**pallavikākula* m. *a kind of moulding. 28.29d

pallī f. tribal village. 18.06d

pallikā f. small tribal village. 18.06d

pavana n. a type of > *vāta*$_1$. 22.18c; 22.41c

pāpa n. a type of > *halaka*. 24.02b; 24.09a

piṇḍa m. a kind of base or moulding. 28.10b; 28.10c; 28.24c;

28.40d; 28.42b

pidhānāvaraṇa m. door-leaf. 18.31c

pināka n. a type of > *caturbhadra*. 19.59a; 19.168b

pīṭha n. base, pedestal. 24.19a; 24.26a; 24.26c; 24.45a; 39.29a

puṭabhedana n. market place. 18.05d

pura n. city; fort. 18.33c; 18.52d; 48.08c

purīsaṃvaraṇa n. city wall. 18.54b

puṣkara₁ n. *reservoir, tank; well. 18.01b

puṣkara₂ n. a type of house. 24.41c; 24.42c; 24.43b

puṣkariṇī f. well. 18.20b

puṣpatoraṇa n. a type of gate. 18.39a

puṣpamālā f. a kind of decoration. 28.30a

pūrṇabāhu m. a constellation of the doors within a dwelling. 39.11b; 39.15d; 48.25a; 48.26d; 48.29a

pṛthu n. a type of > *caturbhadra*. 19.54d; 19.135b

pedyā f. *a part of the threshold. 28.10c; 28.12a

pedyāpiṇḍa m. *a part of the threshold. 28.08c; 28.10a; 28.11a

pedra m. *a kind of moulding. 28.40c

paitra n. a type of > *tribhadra*. 19.48c; 19.95b

pauṣṇa n. a type of > *caturbhadra*. 19.54a; 19.126a

prakara n. a type of > *sukṣetra₁*. 21.11d; 21.36d

prakāśa n. a type of > *tribhadra*. 19.48c; 19.94d

pragāla n. a type of > *pañcabhadra*. 19.61b; 19.178a

pragrīva/prāggrīva m./n. a kind of fence around the dwelling. 19.38c; 22.04c

pracaṇḍa n. a type of > *daṇḍa₁*. 22.17a; 22.34c

praṇālī f. rainpipe; gutter. 18.41d; 28.48a

pratāna n. a type of > *saptabhadra*. 19.68d; 19.222b

pratipālanā f. *a kind of moulding. 28.22d

pratimoka m./n. *a kind of moulding. 28.44b

pratiśraya m. ABODE. 18.09d

pratīkṣa, -ka n. a type of > *pañcabhadra*. 19.62c; 19.186d

pratīcya₁ n. a type of > *ekabhadra*. 19.43a

pratīcya₂ n. a type of > *caturbhadra*. 19.57a; 19.152a

pratolī f. gate tower. 18.25a

pratyakṣāya m. a constellation of the doors within a dwelling. 39.11c; 39.17c; 48.25c; 48.27b; 48.31a

pradvāra n. space outside the door. 18.42d

prapālaka n. *a kind of moulding. 28.21b

prabha n. a type of > *pañcabhadra*. 19.62b; 19.186a

prabhañjana n. a type of > *vāta₁*. 22.18d; 22.43a

pramoda n. a type of > *tribhadra*. 19.49d; 19.103d

pralaya n. a type of > *vāta*$_1$. 22.19b; 22.44d

praveśa m. entrance. 39.13a; 39.15a; 39.15c; 39.17d; 48.25d; 48.27d; 48.28a; 48.31b

praveśana n. entrance. 18.28a; 28.36d?

prasabha n. a type of > *caturbhadra*. 19.59b; 19.169d

prasādhaka n. a type of > *tribhadra*. 19.48d; 19.97b

prastha n. a type of > *saptabhadra*. 19.68c; 19.221b

prahīnavāstu
v. *hīnavāstu*

prākāra m. wall. 18.35c; 18:42a; 18.52c; 18.53b; 18.54a; 18.54c; 18.54d; 20.33b

prāgāyata n. a type of > *ekabhadra*. 19.42c; 19.79d

prāggrīva
v. *pragrīva*

prāgvilagna n. a type of > *ekabhadra*. 19.42c; 19.80a

prāta/prānta n. a type of > *pañcabhadra*. 19.64c; 19.199b

prānta n. a type of > *tribhadra*. 19.48d; 19.96d

prāsavinyāsa n. a type of > *ekabhadra*. 19.43a

prāsāda$_1$ m. a kind of raised platform. 18.22a; 28.13c

prāsāda$_2$ m. a temple. 48.08c; 48.10d; 48.37b; 48.63c; 48.66a

prāsādikā f. a small raised platform. 18.22b; 18.22c; 18.35d

priyānanā f. a type of jamb. 28.14d

PHA

phalaka n. board; plank. 18.34c; 18.36b

phaliha m. a horizontal beam for locking the city gate. 18.33d

BA

bāhyamaṇḍalā f. a part of the door frame. 28.12d

bāhyasūtra n. *a kind of moulding. 28.29b

BHA

bhaktaśālā f. kitchen. 18.27a

bhagandara n. a type of > *cullī*$_1$. 21.13d; 21.42b

bhadra$_1$ n. a type of > *tribhadra*. 19.48d; 19.96b

bhadra$_2$ n. a type of house. 24.35d; 24.36a; 24.36d; 24.43a

bhadraka n. a type of > *halaka*. 24.03b; 24.18a

bhadrā$_1$ f. synonym for > *mūṣā*. 19.30c; 19.33a; 19.44b; 19.69d; 19.73b

bhadrā$_2$ f. a type of > *jamb* 28.15a

bhaya n. a type of > *tribhadra*. 19.49c; 19.102b

bhaya(pra)da n. a type of > *halaka*. 24.02b; 24.09d

bhava n. a type of > *ṣaḍbhadra*.

19.67b; 19.213a

bhavana n. ABODE. 18.08d; 18.29a; 19.01b; 19.112b; 19.138b; 20.07c; 21.43b; 22.52(2)d; 39.04c; 39.07b; 39.08b; 39.24a; 39.25d; 39.26d; 39.33a; 48.64b; 48.133b

bhavanājira n. courtyard of a dwelling. 18.29c

bhasman n. a type of > *cullī*$_2$. 22.20a; 22.48b

bhāṇḍīra n. a type of > *sapta-bhadra*. 19.68c; 19.219a

bhāra n. a type of > *tribhadra*. 19.51c; 19.115c

bhāratulā f. a type of beam. 48.101a

bhārapaṭṭa n. a kind of moulding. 48.102d; 48.103b

bhāraśākhā f. a part of the door frame. 28.13d

bhāsvara n. a type of > *ṣaḍ-bhadra*. 19.67c; 19.214a

bhitti f. wall. 18.14a; 18.26d; 18.41a; 18.44c; 18.51c; 20.35a; 24.19b; 24.22d; 24.23a; 24.23d; 24.45b; 28.53c; 48.44a; 48.47b; 48.52a; 48.57c; 48.70b; 48.76a; 48.102a; 48.117b; 48.133a; 48.138a; 48.138b

bhīma n. a type of > *dvibhadra*. 19.46d; 19.88c

bhujaṅgama n. a type of > *cullī*$_1$. 21.12d; 21.38b

bhūta n. a type of roof. 28.49a; 28.51d

bhūti(a)bhūṣaṇa n. a type of > *hiraṇyanābha*$_1$. 21.08d; 21.27d

bhūmi/-kā f. floor; storey. 28.47c; 28.47c; 39.21a; 39.22b; 39.24b; 39.33b; 39.33c; 48.77b; 48.78a; 48.78b; 48.80b

bhūṣaṇa n. a type of > *hiraṇya-nābha*$_1$. 21.08d; 21.27b

bhrama$_1$ n. a type of > *ṣaḍ-bhadra*. 19.68a; 19.217c

bhrama$_2$ n. a watercourse. 48.34a; 48.34c

bhrānta n. a type of > *catur-bhadra*. 19.56b; 19.146a

MA

makha n. a type of > *ṣaḍbhadra*. 19.67d; 19.216b

magadha n. a type of > *catur-bhadra*. 19.58a; 19.160d

maṇicchandas n. a particular type of > *saptaśāla*. 20.33d

maṇitoraṇa n. a type of tympanon. 18.38d

maṇḍapa n. pavilion. 24.01b

maṇḍala$_1$ n. circle; realm. 18.07d

maṇḍala$_2$ n. a type of roof. 28.49b; 28.53b

mata n. BUILDING; ABODE. 18.08b

mattada n. a type of > *pakṣa-ghna*$_1$. 21.17a; 21.52

mattavāraṇa, -ka n. a type of > *sukṣetra*$_1$. 21.09d; 21.29d

mandira$_1$ n. BUILDING; ABODE. 18.01a; 18.08b; 18.58c; 19.222b; 21.15b; 21.24d; 21.28d; 21.31b; 21.46b; 21.52b; 22.12b; 22.40d; 22.48d; 24.45a; 39.33d; 48.10d;

48.52d; 48.97b; 48.109d

mandira$_2$ n. a type of > *ṣaḍ-bhadra*. 19.67b; 19.212c

marālapālī f. a kind of cornice or moulding; a water spout? 18.41c

marut n. a type of > *vāta*$_1$. 22.18c; 22.41a

malaya n. a type of > *tribhadra*. 19.51b; 19.113d

masūraka m. lintel. 28.23d

mahādvāra m. front door. 18.52b

mahānasa n. kitchen. 18.27b

mahiṣa n. a type of > *yama-sūrya*$_1$. 22.16d; 22.34b

mahiṣī f. a type of > *śālā*. 22.07a; 22.08a; 22.09c; 24.37c

mahodara n. a type of > *su-kṣetra*$_1$. 21.11b; 21.35b

mātaṅga n. a type of > *catur-bhadra*. 19.58d; 19.166d

miśra n. a type of > *catur-bhadra*. 19.54b; 19.127d

muṇḍa n. a type of > *catur-bhadra*. 19.58d; 19.166b

muṣṭika m./n./f.? *a kind of moulding. 28.50c

mūtrabhūmi f. latrine. 18.44a

mūla n. a type of > *pañca-bhadra*. 19.65b; 19.203d

mūladvāra n. front door. 48.80a; 48.82c; 48.80a; 48.82c

mūṣā f. a kind of small door. 19.27c; 19.29d; 19.30b; 19.30c; 19.32d; 19.34a; 19.38a; 19.40d; 19.70c; 19.74c; 19.75a; 19.77c; 19.78c; 19.79a; 19.79c; 19.82c; 19.91b; 19.106d; 19.107a; 19.107c; 19.110d; 19.111d; 19.115a; 19.118b; 19.120d; 19.123c; 19.128d; 19.129d; 19.131d; 19.134d; 19.138d; 19.140d; 19.157d; 19.161d; 19.166d; 19.170b; 19.171c; 19.172b; 19.174d; 19.181c; 19.194a; 19.204c; 19.219a; 19.221a; 19.222a; 19.222d; 19.223c; 21.06a; 21.19b; 21.29b; 21.39d; 21.57b; 22.03c; 22.05c; 22.13a; 22.22b; 22.29a; 22.40c; 22.48c; 22.50c; 22.51a; 22.52(2)a; 48.17c; 48.32a; 48.34a; 48.38c; 48.70b

mr̥taka n. a type of > *yama-sūrya*$_1$. 22.16b; 22.33b

meghamāla n. a type of > *su-kṣetra*$_1$. 21.11a; 21.34a

YA

yamasūrya$_1$ n. a type of > *dvi-śāla*. 20.29c; 22.02a; 22.08b; 22.16c; 22.28c

yamasūrya, -ka$_2$ n. a type of > *yamasūrya*$_1$. 22.15c; 22.29d

yama n. a type of > *yamasūrya*$_1$. 22.15d; 22.31a

yāma n. a type of > *pañca-bhadra*. 19.61c; 19.180d

yāmya n. a type of > *halaka*. 24.03a; 24.16a

yukta n. a type of > *pañca-bhadra*. 19.62c; 19.187d

RA

raja n. a type of > *caturbhadra*.

19.59b; 19.170a

rasanā f. *a kind of moulding. 28.26b; 28.26d

rākṣasa n. a type of > *pakṣaghna*$_1$. 21.16a; 21.47c

rājadhānī f. capital of a realm; royal residence. 18.02b

rāṣṭra n. realm. 18.07d

ripusaṃhada n. a type of > *pakṣaghna*$_1$. 21.17c; 21.54d

rukma n. a type of > *hiraṇyanābha*$_1$. 21.06d; 21.20b

rucaka$_1$ n. a type of > *caturbhadra*. 19.54d; *19.59c; 19.133a; 19.170d

rucaka$_2$ n. a type of > *catuḥśāla*. 19.78c.

rūpa n. *a kind of moulding. 28.45a

rūpakarman n. a kind of ornamentation 28.44d

rūpaśākhā f. a part of the door frame. 28.11cd; 28.12c

roga$_1$ n. a type of > *caturbhadra*. 19.56d; 19.150b

roga$_2$ n. a type of > *cullī*$_2$. 22.20a; 22.46c

roga$_3$ n. a type of > *halaka*. 24.02b; 24.08b

roga$_4$
v. *ambhudavidhvaṃsa*

LA

lakṣmīvāsa n. a type of > *saptabhadra*. 19.69a; 19.223d

lagha n. a type of > *pañcabhadra*. 19.65a; 19.202a

layana n. ABODE. 18.09c

lambana n. a type of > *pañcabhadra*. 19.63d; 19.194b

lambikā f. *a kind of moulding. 28.38d

lāṅgala, -ka n. synonym for > *hala,-ka*. 24.11c; 24.12d; 24.15d; 24.16d

lātavya n. a type of > *ṣaḍbhadra*. 19.67d; 19.215b

lābha n. a type of > *pañcabhadra*. 19.65a; 19.202d

liha n. a type of > *caturbhadra*. 19.58b; 19.164b

līna n. a type of > *pañcabhadra*. 19.63c; 19.192d

lolupa n. a type of > *pañcabhadra*. 19.61a; 19.177b

VA

vakra n. a type of > *pañcabhadra*. 19.65a; 19.201c

vadha n. a type of > *tribhadra*. 19.48b; 19.93a

vana n. a type of > *tribhadra*. 19.51c; 19.114d

vanājira n. *clearing in the forest. 18.29c

vara n. a type of > *pañcabhadra*. 19.62a; 19.183d

varcaska m. latrine. 18.44b

varta n. a type of > *dvibhadra*. 19.47a; 19.89a

vardhana/vardhamāna$_1$ n. a type of > *caturbhadra*. 19.54d; 19.59d; 19.133d; 19.172d

vardhamāna$_2$ n. a type of

> *catuḥśāla*. 19.76c; 19.77a

valabhā f. *a kind of raised platform. 18.23d

valabhī f. *a kind of raised platform; balcony. 18.22d; 18.23a; 18.23c

valīka n. protrusion of the purlins. 18.17c

vasati f. ABODE. 18.08d

vasu n. a type of > *ṣaḍbhadra*. 19.66b; 19.207b

vasudhāra n. a type of > *siddhārtha*. 22.13c; 22.22c

vājin n. a type of > *ṣaḍbhadra*. 19.68a; 19.216d

vāta$_{1}$ n. a type of > *dviśāla*. 20.30c; 22.02b; 22.09a; 22.19c; 22.40d

vāta$_{2}$ n. a type of > *vāta*$_{1}$. 22.18c; 22.42a

vātayana

v. *vātāyana*

vātāyana n. window. 18.14a; 18.14c; 48.122c; 48.125b

vāpikā f. well. 28.45d

vāpī f. well. 18.20b; 48.87c

vāma n. a type of > *caturbhadra*. 19.59c; 19.172a

vāmana n. a type of > *ṣaḍbhadra*. 19.66c; 19.208b

vāraṇa n. a type of > *cullī*$_{1}$. 21.14c; 21.44d

vāliśa n. a type of > *ṣaḍbhadra*. 19.67a; 19.211b

vāsa m. sleeping chamber. 39.19d

vāsava n. a type of > *sukṣetra*$_{1}$. 21.10b; 21.30c

vāsula n. a type of > *saptabhadra*. 19.68d; 19.222d

vāstu m./n. plot. 19.220b; 20.04c; 20.21a; 20.30d; 20.31b; 20.32b; 24.09a; 24.12a; 24.18a; 24.26d; 39.06a; 39.07a; 39.08a; 39.09a; 39.12b; 39.13a; 39.13c; 39.15a; 39.16d; 39.17b; 39.19c; 48.09b; 48.10c; 48.14d; 48.21a; 48.21c; 48.26b; 48.27d; 48.29d; 48.63a; 48.63b

vikarāla, -ka n. a type of > *yamasūrya*$_{1}$. 22.16a; 22.32b

vikṛta n. a type of > *halạka*. 24.02d; 24.13a

vigraha n. a type of > *daṇḍa*$_{1}$. 22.17c; 22.38b

vighāta n. a type of > *tribhadra*. 19.49a; 19.99b

vighna$_{1}$ n. a type of > *caturbhadra*. 19.54c; 19.130b

vighna$_{2}$ n. a type of > *pakṣaghna*$_{1}$. 21.17b; 21.53c

vicitra n. a type of > *pañcabhadra*. 19.63d; 19.193d

vijaya n. a type of > *pañcabhadra*. 19.61c; 19.180b

vitardi f. a terrace in the inner courtyard. 18.16a

vidruta n. a type of > *pañcabhadra*. 19.63b; 19.190d

vidhāraṇa n. a type of > *caturbhadra*. 19.56b; 19.147a

vina n. a type of > *dvibhadra*. 19.45d; 19.85d

vinoda, -na n. a type of > *pañcabhadra*. 19.62d; 19.189a

vipakṣa n. a type of > *catur-*

bhadra. 19.54c; 19.131a

viparīta n. a type of > *halaka*. 24.03a; 24.17a

vipaścima n. a type of > *dvibhadra*. 19.46b; 19.87b

vipāsa n. a type of > *dvibhadra*. 19.46a; 19.86b

vipradoha, -ka n. a type of > *pañcabhadra*. 19.63a; 19.190b

vibudha n. a type of > *pañcabhadra*. 19.64a; 19.195c

vibudhāgāra n. temple. 18.57d

viyat n. a type of > *tribhadra*. 19.49d; 19.104d

virodha/-in n. a type of > *kāca*$_1$. 22.20d; 22.51c

vilaya n. a type of > *hala, -ka*. 24.02d; 24.14a

viloma$_1$ n. a type of > *tribhadra*. 19.48a; 19.92a

viloma$_2$ n. a type of > *caturbhadra*. 19.58c; 19.165b

vivara n. a type of > *ṣaḍbhadra*. 19.67a; 19.210c

viśikha$_1$ n. a type of > *caturbhadra*. 19.59b; 19.169b

viśiṣa/viṣikha$_2$ n. a type of > *pañcabhadra*. *19.62b; 19.185a

viśo(e)ṣaṇa$_1$ n. a type of > *caturbhadra*. 19.56d; 19.151a

viśoṣaṇa$_2$ n. a type of > *pakṣaghna*$_1$. 21.16d; 21.51d

vihaṅga, -ma n. a type of > *cullī*$_1$. 21.13a; 21.39b

vihārabhūmi f. sporting ground. 18.56c

vīthī/-ikā f. a kind of footpath around the building. 19.38c; 22.04b

vīra n. a type of > *tribhadra*. 19.51d; 19.117b

vr̥ṣabha$_1$ n. a type of > *dvibhadra*. 19.45d; 19.85c

vr̥ṣabha$_2$ n. a type of > *halaka*. 24.02a; 24.06c

vedikā f. *a kind of moulding. 28.45a; 28.47a; 48.134c

vedī f. * a kind of moulding. 24.29b; 24.30a

veśman n. ABODE. 18.09c; 18.45b; 19.02a; 19.03a; 19.08a; 19.12b; 19.17d; 19.19b; 19.19d; 19.22d; 19.23d; 19.26b; 19.26d; 19.31a; 19.34b; 19.73d; 19.74d; 19.79b; 19.80c; 19.92a; 19.97b; 19.99b; 19.104b; 19.105d; 19.140d; 19.153a; 19.153d; 19.222d; 19.224(2)a; 20.09c; 20.27c; 21.42b; 22.07b; 22.50a; 22.51c; 22.52(2)c; 24.18d; 24.37a; 28.15b; 28.16d; 28.31c; 28.51c; 39.02c; 39.12b; 39.21b; 39.29a; 48.06a; 48.16c; 48.19b; 48.19d; 48.20c; 48.31b; 48.51b; 48.52b; 48.54a; 48.61d; 48.72d; 48.77c; 48.107b; 48.130d

vaira n. a type of > *pañcabhadra*. 19.62a; 19.184c

vairipūraṇa n. a type of > *pakṣaghna*$_1$. 21.17d; 21.56b

vaivasvata n. a type of > *yamasūrya*$_1$. 22.15d; 22.30c

vaisana/-ha n. a type of > *saptabhadra*. 19.68c; 19.220a

vyartha n. a type of > *caturbhadra*. 19.57c; 19.157c

vyākula n. a type of > *pañcabhadra*. 19.63c; 19.192b

vyākośa n. a type of > *dvibhadra*. 19.45c; 85a

vyāghra n. a type of > *pakṣaghna*$_1$. 21.16c; 21.50b

vyāpta n. a type of > *caturbhadra*. 19.57c; 19.156c

vyāyata n. a type of > *tribhadra*. 19.49d; 19.104b

vyāyāma n. a type of > *tribhadra*. 19.52a; 19.117d

vyāsakta n. a type of > *pañcabhadra*. 19.64b; 19.196d

vyāhṛta n. a type of > *tribhadra*. 19.52b; 19.118d

ŚA

śaṭha n. a type of > *dvibhadra*. 19.47a; 19.89c

śatacchidra n. a type of > *cullī*$_1$. 21.13c; 21.40c

śayanāgāra n. sleeping chamber. 48.105c

śaraṇa n. ABODE. 18.09b

śarala/sarala n. a type of > *caturbhadra*. 19.56a; 19.141d

śava n. a type of > *yamasūrya*$_1$. 22.16b; 22.33c

śastottara n. a type of > *tribhadra*. 19.50c; 19.108d

śākuna n. a type of > *pakṣaghna*$_1$. 21.17b; 21.53b

śākhā f. door-post, jamb. 24.29d; 24.20b; 28.11b; 28.14a; 28.15a; 28.15c

śākhānagara n. a city that is not the capital of the realm. 18.02c; 18.03a

śātakumbha n. a type of > *hiraṇyanābha*$_1$. 21.08b; 21.25c

śānta$_1$ n. a type of > *pañcabhadra*. 19.62d; 19.188a

śānta$_2$ n. a type of > *siddhārtha*. 22.14c; 22.26d

śārdūla n. a type of > *pakṣaghna*$_1$. 21.16c; 21.50d

śālā f. cottage; shed; room. 18.19d; 18.20a; 18.23a; 18.23c; 18.58b; 19.22a; 19.22c; 19.25b; 19.26a; 19.27a; 19.27d; 19.28a; 19.28c; 19.29c; 20.02b; 20.26b; 20.35a; 21.03b; 21.04d; 22.07b; 22.08d; 24.11c; 24.12d; 24.13c; 24.15d; 24.16d; 24.22c; 24.25a; 24.35c; 24.37c; 24.39c; 24.41c; 28.18b; 39.10a; 48.18c; 48.32b; 48.33a; 48.34b; 48.34c; 48.35a; 48.36b; 48.79a; 48.138c

v. *sīmāśālā*

śāśvata n. a type of > *siddhārtha*. 22.14a; 22.24d

śiva n. a type of > *siddhārtha*. 22.14b; 22.25a

śīrṣaka n. head; *capital. 18.48a; 48.133b

śuddhānta m. innermost chamber; female apartments. 18.24d

śekhara n. a type of > *pañcabhadra*. 19.64a; 19.195a

śobhana n. a type of > *tribhadra*. 19.50b; 19.107d

śoṣaṇa n. a type of > *pakṣaghna*$_1$. 21.16d; 21.51b

śrīdhara m. a particular type of pillar. 28.33a

śrīvaha n. a type of > *dvi-*

bhadra. 19.46c; 19.87d

śliṣṭa$_1$ n. a type of > *dvibhadra*. 19.46c; 19.88a

śliṣṭa$_2$ n. a type of > *tribhadra*. 19.49c; 19.102d

ṢA

ṣaṭśāla n. a building consisting of six wings. 19.04c

ṣaḍdāru, -ka n. *a kind of wooden construction associated with the > *alinda*. 23.21b; 23.25b; 23.27d; 23.31a; 23.41b; 48.121a; 48.124a

ṣaḍbhadra n. a house with six > *mūṣā*s. 19.65d; 19.72b

SA

saṃyamana n. *footpath along the estate boundary. 18.40a; 18.40d

saṃyamanapriya n. a type of > *ekabhadra*. 19.42d

saṃśraya m. ABODE. 18.08a

saṃsthāna n. ABODE. 18.08c

saṃhāra n. a type of > *yama-sūrya*$_1$. 22.15c; 22.29b

sukukṣa n. *a house with an interior courtyard. 20.08a; 20.09b

v. *kakṣā*.

saṃgraha m. 28.46

saṅghaṭṭa m. synonym for > *gṛha-mālā*. 19.13a

sacchatra n. *a house with a continuous roof. 20.08a; 20.09a

satata n. a type of > *pañca-bhadra*. 19.63b; 19.191b

sadana n. ABODE. 18.01c; 18.08a; 39.05c

sadman n. ABODE. 18.01c; 18.08a; 19.20d; 22.16d; 24.39a

saṃtāpa n. a type of > *hiraṇya-nābha*$_1$. 21.07c; 21.23b

saṃdoha n. a type of > *pañca-bhadra*. 19.63a; 19.189c

sandhi m. 18.37c; 48.103c

sandhipāla m. 28.42d; 48.119c; 48.134b

saṃnyāsa n. a type of > *cullī*$_1$. 21.14a; 21.43a

sapakṣa n. a particular type of > *saptaśāla*. 20.34d

saparikrama n. *a house with an uninterrupted > *alinda*. 20.08b; 20.09d

saptabhadra n. a house with seven > *mūṣā*s. 19.68b; 19.71d

saptaśāla n. a building consisting of seven wings. 19.08a; 20.33c

saprabha n. *a house with an > *alinda* on the outside. 20.08c; 20.10c

sabhā f. assembly hall. 18.58b

saṃpada n. a type of > *pañca-bhadra*. 19.64b; 19.197b

saṃparka n. a type of > *pañca-bhadra*. 19.65b; 19.203b

saṃpuṭa m. one leaf in a double door. 18.32a

sarala

v. *śarala*

sarpa n. a type of > *cullī*$_1$. 21.13c; 21.41b

sarva(to)bhadra$_1$, *-ka* n. a > *catuḥ-śāla* with eight > *mūṣā*s. 19.69c; 19.224(1)b

sarvatobhadra$_2$ n. a type of > *catuḥśāla*. 19.79b

saha n. a type of > *caturbhadra*. 19.59d; 19.174b

sāṭika/sāṭīka n. a type of > *ṣaḍbhadra*. 19.66c; 19.207c

sādhāraṇa n. a type of > *caturbhadra*. 19.56c; 19.148a

sāṃparāyika n. a type of building related to defence. 18.01b

sāra n. a type of > *hiraṇyanābha*$_1$. 21.07c; 21.23d

sārasa n. a type of > *sukṣetra*$_1$. 21.10c; 21.32d

**sālā* f. wall. 18.45a

sālina n. a type of > *pañcabhadra*. 19.61b; 19.178d

siṃhakarṇa m. a decoration of the gate. 18.39d; 28.55a; 48.106c

siddhārtha n. a type of > *dviśāla*. 20.29a; 22.02a; 22.07c; 22.15a; 22.23d; 22.25a

siddhārthaka n. a type of > *siddhārtha*. 22.13d; 22.23b

sīmāśālā f. *a > *śālā* on the edge of the compound? 48.37a

sukṣetra$_1$ n. a type of > *triśāla*. 20.26c; 21.02c; 21.03d; 21.04a; 21.11d; 21.12a; 21.28a

sukṣetra$_2$ n. a type of > *sukṣetra*$_1$. 21.11d; 21.36b

sukha n. a type of > *caturbhadra*. 19.57d; 19.158d

sugandhānta n. a type of > *saptabhadra*. 19.69a; 19.224(1)a

sugāra n. a type of > *tribhadra*. 19.51c; 19.116b

sujaya n. a type of > *pañcabhadra*. 19.61c; 19.179d

sutaghna n. a type of > *pakṣaghna*$_1$. 21.17d; 21.55d

sudakṣiṇa n. a type of > *tribhadra*. 19.49c; 19.101d

sunāga n. a type of > *tribhadra*. 19.50a; 19.105d

sunītha/-ta n. a type of > *dvibhadra*. 19.45a; 19.83b

sundarī f. a part of the door frame. 28.14c

supratīka n. a type of > *caturbhadra*. 19.57b; 19.155b

suprabha n. a type of > *pañcabhadra*. 19.62b; 19.185d

subhadra n. a type of > *ekabhadra*. 19.43b

suraṅgā f. an underground passage. 18.25b

suradāruṇa/devadāruṇa n. a type of > *pakṣaghna*$_1$. 21.16b; 21.49b

surasthāna n. temple. 18.57a

suvarṇa n. a type of > *hiraṇyanābha*$_1$. 21.07b; 21.22c

suvarṇatoraṇa n. a type of tympanon. 18.38c

suṣira n. hole, opening. 18.48c

susaṃyama n. a type of > *dvibhadra*. 19.45b; 19.84b

susthita n. a type of > *pañcabhadra*. 19.64d; 19.199d

susvana n. a type of > *ṣaḍbhadra*. 19.67d; 19.215d

sūryaprabha n. a type of > *sukṣetra*$_1$. 21.09c; 21.29b

sevya n. a type of > *caturbhadra*. 19.60a; 19.175b

saiphala n. a type of > *catur-bhadra*. *19.59c; 19.171d

sopāna n. staircase. 18.10d; 18.11d

saudha n. house with a rooftop terrace. 18.12d

saubha n. a type of > *dvibhadra*. 19.46b; 19.87a

saurabha n. a type of house. 24.39d; 24.40a; 24.43b

stambha m. post, pillar. 18.16c; 18.48a; 19.21a; 24.23d; 24.30d; 24.31b; 24.31c; 24.32b; 28.21c; 28.22d; 28.23a; 28.25a; 28.31b; 28.33d; 28.34a; 28.35a; 28.35d; 28.41c; 48.70a; 48.76a; 48.85a; 48.118a; 48.122a; 48.125b; 48.133a; 48.138b

stambhakoṭi f. *a kind of moulding on the pillar. 28.20b

stambhapaṭṭa m. *a kind of moulding on the pillar. 28.46a

stambhapiṇḍa m. *the base of a pillar. 28.24b

stambhasūtra n. *a kind of moulding on the pillar. 28.28b

strī(pra)da n. a type of > *siddhārtha*. 22.14c; 22.26b

sthala n. brick-paved section of floor near the door. 18.43b; 28.23b

sthita n. a type of > *pañca-bhadra*. 19.64d; 19.200c

sthira n. a type of > *catur-bhadra*. 19.55d; 19.141a

sthūṇā f. post, pillar. 18.11b

svarṇa n. a type of > *hiraṇyanābha*$_1$. 21.07a; 21.22b

svastika$_1$ n. a type of > *catur-bhadra*. 19.55b; 19.139d

svastika$_2$ n. a type of > *catuḥ-śāla*. 19.75b

svaira n. a type of > *catur-bhadra*. 19.57a; 19.154a

HA

haṃsa n. a type of > *sukṣetra*$_1$. 21.10c; 21.32b

hari m. a type of > *sukṣetra*$_1$. 21.10c; 21.31d

harmya$_1$ n. topmost storey. 18.10b; 18.12c; 18.15a; 18.17a; 18.41c

harmya$_2$ n. a type of > *ṣaḍ-bhadra*. 19.66a; 19.205d

harmyatala m./n. rooftop terrace. 18.15d

harmyadvāra m. door of the topmost storey. 18.35a

harmyaprākāraka m. parapet of the rooftop terrace. 18.15c

harmyāvalokana n. window of the topmost storey. 18.35b

hala, -ka n. a type of > *catuḥ-śāla* with protruding corners; the protruding portions of such a building. 19.12d; 24.01d; 24.03c; 24.04d; 24.05d; 24.07b; 24.08a; 24.08d; 24.10d; 24.14c; 24.15b; 24.17c

halakālinda m. an L-shaped > *alinda*. 20.15a; 20.16a; 20.17a; 20.18a

hastinī f. a type of > *śālā*. 22.07a; 24.25c

hiraṇya n. a type of > *hiraṇya-*

nābha$_1$. 21.06c; 21.19d

hiraṇyanābha$_1$ n. a type of > *tri-śāla*. 20.26c; 21.02c; 21.03a; 21.09a; 21.18c; 21.58a

hiraṇyanābha$_2$ n. a type of > *hi-raṇyanābha*$_1$. 21.08c

hīnabāhu m. a constellation of the doors within a dwelling. 39.11a; 39.13c; 48.25b; 48.27a; 48.30ab

hīnavāstu n. a building with less than four > *śālā*s.24.25b; 24.45d

hīragrahaṇa n. *a kind of moulding. 24.32a; 28.35c; 28.36a

hīraśākhā f. *a kind of moulding. 48.134a

hema n. a type of > *hiraṇya-nābha*$_1$. 21.06d; 21.20d

Appendix

Concordance of Br̥S 52.02-41, 68-73 with MP, VP, and SAS

NB: This concordance is based on the text of Br̥S, i.e. only those text passages from MP, VP, and SAS have been entered that have a parallel in Br̥S 52.02-41; the only exception to this rule are the regulations concerning the number of storeys in VP 02.157-159ab and SAS 39.21-25, which do not have a parallel in Br̥S and MP.

Stanzas with a considerable degree of congruence but with different wording are quoted in < >; stanzas that exhibit a certain degree of similarity, but express a different idea are given in [ ]; verbatim correspondence of stanzas is indicated by !; stanzas that deal with the same general topic, but give widely different rules, are marked with ~.

Br̥S	**MP**	**VP**	**SAS**
<52.02-03>	<252.05ab-19>	<01.06-23>	—
	– the houses of *karmopajīvins* –		
<52.04>	<254.14cd-16>	<02.135-136>	[19.16]
<52.05>	<254.18cd-19>	<02.137>[1]	[19.15cd]
<52.06ab>	<254.20-21ab>	<02.138>	—
<52.06cd>	—	<02.139>	—
[52.07]	<254.17-18ab>	<02.140>	—
<52.08ab>	[254.21cd-22]	[02.141]	?[19.17ab]?
<52.08cd>	[254.23-24ab]	<02.142>	—

[1] One half-stanza seem to have been lost here, since the dimensions of the house are given without mention being made of the *senāpati*.

<52.09ab>	—	<02.144>	—
<52.09cd>	[254.24cd-25]	<02.143>	—
<52.10>	<254.26-27>	<02.145>[2]	~19.15cd
	– height of houses –		
<52.11>	—	<02.116cd>	—
—	—	<02.157-159ab>	<39.21-25>
	– the houses of *varṇins* etc. –		
<52.12>	<254.28-29ab>	[02.146-147]	[19.15ab]
<52.13>	[254.29cd-30ab]	—	<19.19>
<52.14>	[254.30cd-31]	<02.148-149ab>	[19.17-18]
<52.15>	[254.32ab]	<02.149cd-150>	—
<52.16ab>	~254.32cd	[02.151ab]	—
<52.16cd>	—	[02.151cd]	
<52.17-19>	<254.33-36>	<02.152cd-153>	[19.22-26]
	– the *vīthikā* –		
<52.20-21>	<254.37-39ab>	<02.154-155ab>	?[20.08-12]?
	– the height of the storeys –		
<52.22>	<254.39cd-40>	<02.155cd-165>	<28.16, 47>
	– thickness of walls –		
<52.23>	<254.41>	<02.161>	<24.22cd>
	– dimensions of doors, pillars etc. –		
<52.24>	~254.42-43ab	~02.162	~24.26cd-28ab

[2] The dimensions of the house are not given; presumably one stanza was lost.

<52.25>	——	~02.163	——
<52.26-27>	<254.43cd-255.02ab>	<02.164-166ab>	~28cd-34
	– the five types of pillars –		
<52.28-29>	<255.02cd-05ab>	<02.166cd-168>	——[3]
52.30	<255.05cd-06>	02.169[180]	[24.34]
	– five types of *catuḥśāla* –		
52.31-36	[254.01cd-04ab]	02.170[4] <02.191-197>	[19.75-79][5]
	– four types of *triśāla* –		
<52.37-38>	<254.04cd-08ab>	<02.186-190>	<20.24-27ab> <21.02-05ab>
	– six types of *dviśāla* –		
<52.39-41>	<254.08cd-14ab>	[02.171-185]	<20.27cd-32>
	– position of living area and doors –		
<52.68>	——	~07.12	<39.02-10>
<52.69-73>	[254.07cd-09]	<07.56-65ab>	[39.02-10]

3 SAS 28 contains a description of five different pillars which differs widely from that given in the other three texts.

4 VP 02.169-170 are verbatim reproductions of BṛS 52.30-31; cf. KERN (1872:285 fn.2).

5 They are also alluded to in 24.44.

Bibliography

A. Primary Sources

Amarasiṃha

The Nāmaliṅgānuśāsana Amarakośa of Amarasiṃha. With the Commentary (Amarakośodghāṭana) of Kṣīrasvāmin. Edited [...] by Krishnaji Govind Oka. Poona 1913. [Reprint Delhi 1981]

Bhaṭṭotpala: see Varāhamihira

Bhāskara

The Līlāvatī. A Treatise on Mensuration by Bhāskarāchārya. Edited with Exhaustive and Critical Notes by Pandit Muralidhar Thakur [...] . Benares 1928

Bhoja

Nāmamālikā of Bhoja. Critically edited by Ekanath Dattatreya Kulkàrni [...] and Vasudeo Damodar Gokhale [...] . Poona 1955. (SIAL. 18)

Samarāṅgaṇa-Sūtradhāra of Mahārājadhirāja Bhoja, The Paramāra Ruler of Dhārā. Orignally Edited by Mahāmahopādhyāya T. Gaṇapatiśāstrī [...] . Revised and Edited by Vasudeva Saran Agrawala [...] . Baroda 1966. (Gaekwad's Oriental Series. 25)

MahārājādhirājaśrīBhojadevaviracitam Samarāṅgaṇa-Sūtradhāra-Vāstu-Śāstram, (mūlamātram.) Bhavana-niveśaḥ. Mahāmahopādhyāyaśrī Gaṇapati-śāstrisampādita-pūrvaṃ Ḍā. Dvijendranātha Śuklena [...] *punassampāditaṃ* [...] . *Naī Dillī* 1965. [Reprint New Delhi 2001] [= SHUKLA 1965a]

Samarāṅgaṇa-Sūtradhāra-Vāstu-Śāstra. (Bhavan-niveś – pratham bhāg.) vistr̥t adhyayan, hindī-anuvād tathā vāstu-padāvalī. Ḍā. Dvijendranāth Śukla [...] . *Naī Dillī* 1965. [Reprint 2003] [= SHUKLA 1965b]

The Saraswatī Kaṇṭhābharaṇa by Dhāreśvara Bhojadeva. With Commentaries of Rāmsinha (I-III) and Jagaddhara (IV). Edited by Paṇḍit Kedārnāth Śarmā and Wāsudev Laxmaṇ Śāstrī Paṇśīkar. Bombay [2]1934.

Śṛṅgāramañjarī Kathā of the Paramāra king Bhojadeva of Dhārā. (Containing thirteen Tales pertaining to the life of the courtesan in Ancient India, narrated in the rich Kāvya style.) Critically Edited [...] by Kumari Kalpalatā K. Munshi [...] . Bombay 1959. (Singhi Jain Series. 30)

Yuktikalpataruḥ. Mahārāja-ŚrīBhoja-viracitaḥ. Edited by Paṇḍit Isvara Chandra Sāstrī [...] . With a Foreword by Narendra Nath Law [...] . *Kalikātānagaryyām* [...] *Khrīṣṭābdāḥ* 1917.

see KULKARNI, E. D.

Bhojadeva see Bhoja

Bhuvanadeva

Aparājitapṛcchā of Bhuvanadeva. Edited with an Introduction by Popatbhai Ambashankar Mankad. Baroda. (GOS. 115)

Buddhaghosa

The Sumaṅgala-vilāsinī. Buddhaghosa's commentary on the Dīgha Nikāya. Part I. Edited by T[homas] W. Rhys Davids and J. Estlin Carpenter. London 1886. [Reprint London 1968]

Cullavagga

The Vinaya Piṭakaṃ: one of the principal Buddhist holy scriptures in the Pâli language. Edited by Hermann Oldenberg. Vol. II. The Cullavagga. London 1880.

The book of the discipline (Vinaya-Piṭaka). Volume V (Cullavagga). Translated by I.B. Horner [...] . Oxford [6]1997. (SBB. 20)

Dhāreśvara Bhojadeva see Bhoja.

Halāyudha

Halāyudha's Abhidhānarathamālā. A Sanskrit vocabulary, edited with a Sanskrit-English glossary by Th[eodor] AUFRECHT. London 1861.

Haribhaṭṭa

Jātakamālā. Unpublished typescript by Michael HAHN.

Harṣadeva

see NARIMAN, WILLIAMS JACKSON and OGDEN

Hemacandra

Hemak'andra's Abhidhānak'intāmaṇi, ein systematisch angeordnetes synonymisches Lexicon. Herausgegeben, übersetzt und mit Anmerkungen begleitet von Otto Boehtlingk und Charles Rieu. St. Petersburg 1847.

The Deśīnāmamālā of Hemachandra. Edited with critical notes, a glossary, and a historical introduction, by Professor R. Pischel and Dr. G. Bühler [...] . Bombay 1880.

Jātaka

The Jātaka together with its commentary. Being tales of the anterior births of Gotama Buddha. For the first time edited in the original Pāli by V. Fausbøll. Vol.II. London 1879. (Reprint London 1963)

Jātaka Stories. Or stories of the Buddha's former births. Translated from the Pāli by various hands under the editorship of Professor E.B. Cowell. Vol. II. Translated by W. H. D. Rouse [...] . London 1895. [Reprint London 1957]

Kauṭilya

R.P. KANGLE. *The Kauṭilīya Arthaśāstra.* Part I. A critical edition with a glossary. Bombay 1960. Part II. An English translation with critical and explanatory notes. Bombay 1963. Part III. A study. Bombay 1965.

Mahāpātra, Sthāpaka Nirañjana

SthāpakaśrīNirañjanaMahāpātraviracitaḥ Śilparatnakośaḥ. A Glossary of Orissan Temple Architecture. [...] Sanskrit Text critically edited with English Translation and Illustrations by Bettina Bäumer and Rajendra Prasad Das. New Delhi 1994. (Kalāmūlaśāstra Series. 16)

Mahāvagga

The Vinaya Piṭakaṃ: one of the principal Buddhist holy scriptures in the Pâli language. Edited by Hermann Oldenberg. Vol. I. The Mahâvagga. London 1880.

The book of the discipline (Vinaya-Piṭaka). Volume IV (Mahāvagga). Translated by I.B. Horner [...] . Oxford 1951. [Reprint 1996] (SBB. 14)

Mahāvaṃsa

The Mahāvaṃsa. Edited by Wilhelm Geiger. London 1958.

The Mahāvaṃsa or the great chronicle of Ceylon. Translated into English by Wilhelm Geiger [...] . London 1964.

Mānasāra

Prasanna Kumar Acharya: *Manasara on Architecture and Sculpture*. Sanskrit Text with Critical Notes. London 1934. (Manasara Series. 3) [Reprint New Delhi 1995].

Manuṣyālayacandrikā

see ACHYUTHAN, A. and PRABHU, Balagopal T.S.

Matsyapurāṇa

The Matsya-Mahāpurāṇa. With introduction and verse-index. Edited by Dr. Pushpendra. New Delhi 1984.

Mayamata

Mayamata. Traité Sanskrit d'Architecture. Édition Critique, Traduction et Notes par Bruno Dagens. Première Partie [Ch. I-XXV]. Pondichéry 1970. Deuxième Partie. Ch. XXVI-XXXVI et Index-Glossaire général. Pondichéry 1976.

Mayamatam. Treatise of housing, architecture and iconography. Sanskrit text edited and translated by Bruno Dagens. 2 Vols. New Delhi 1994 [Reprint New Delhi 2000]

Meruтuṅga

Prabandha Cintāmaṇi of Merutuṅgācārya. Critically edited [...] by Jinavijaya Muni [...] . Part I. Text in Sanskrit with variants, an appendix and indices of stanzas. Śāntiniketan 1933. (Singhi Jaina Series. 1)

Utpala: see Varāhamihira

Varāhamihira

Bṛhat Saṃhitā. By Varāhamihirācārya with the Commentary of Bhaṭṭotpala. Edited by Avadha Vihārī Tripāṭhī [...] . Varanasi 1968 (Sarasvatī Bhavan Granthamālā. 97)

Varāhamihira's Bṛhat Saṃhitā. With English Translation, Exhaustive Notes and Literary Comments. [Edited and translated by] M. Ramakrishna Bhat. Delhi 1981 [Reprint Delhi 1986]

– see KERN, H[endrik]

Vātsyāyana, Mallanāga
Śrīvātsyāyanapraṇītaṃ Kāmasūtram. Yaśodharaviracitayā Jayamaṅgalākhyayā ṭīkayā sametam. Jayapuramahārājāśritasya Paṇḍitavrajalālasūnoḥ Mahāmahopādhyāyapaṇḍita-Durgāprasādadārakasya Kedāranāthasya kṛte Mumbayyāṃ Nirṇayasāgarayantrālaye mudritam. [Mumbai [2]1900]

Viśvakarman
Viśvakarmaprakāśaḥ. bhāṣāṭīkāyutaḥ. Khemarāja Śrīkṛṣṇadāsa Prakāśana, Bambaī-4. [Reprint Mumbai 2004]

Yaśodhara: see Vātsyāyana

B. Secondary literature

ACHARYA, Prasanna Kumar
1928 *Indian Architecture according to Mānasāra-Śilpaśāstra.* London. (Manasara Series. 2) [Reprint New Delhi 1996]
1934 see *Mānasāra*
1946a *An Encyclopaedia of Hindu Architecture.* London. (Manasara Series. 7) [Reprint New Delhi 1993]
1946b *Hindu Architecture in India and Abroad.* London. (Manasara Series. 6) [Reprint New Delhi 1996]

ACHYUTHAN, A. and PRABHU, Balagopal T.S.
1998 *An engineering commentary on Manuṣyālayacandrika of Tirumangalat Nīlakanṭhan Mūsat.* Calicut 1998

AGRAWALA, Vasudeva Saran
1966 see Bhoja: *Samaraṅgaṇasūtradhāra*

ALSDORF, Ludwig
1933 'Die Pratyayas. Ein Beitrag zur indischen Mathematik,' in: ZIi No. 9, pp. 97-157.

APTE, Vaman Shivram
APTE *The Practical Sanskrit-English Dictionary.* Containing Appendices on Sanskrit Prosody and important Literary & Geo-

graphical names in the ancient history of India. [...] By [...] Vaman Shivram Apte [...] . Second Edition, Revised & Enlarged. Bombay ^{2}1912. [1st Edition 1890]

AUFRECHT, Theodor

CC I *Catalogus Catalogorum*. An Alphabetical Register of Sanskrit Works and Authors. [Part I]. Leipzig 1891

1874 'Zur Handschriftenkunde (Kommentare zum Amarakosha),' in: ZDMG 28, pp. 103-124.

see Halāyudha

BÄUMER, Bettina, and DAS, Rajendra Prasad

see Mahāpātra, Sthāpaka Nirañjana

BEAMES, John

1872 *A comparative grammar of the modern Aryan languages of India*: to wit, Hindi, Panjabi, Sindhi, Gujarati, Marathi, Oriya and Bangali. Book I. On sounds. Book II. The noun and pronoun. Book III. The verb. London. (Reprint in one volume: Delhi 1966)

BHATTACHARYYA, Tarapada

^{2}1963 *The canons of Indian art or a study on vāstuvidyā.* Calcutta.

BÖHTLINGK, Otto

pd *Sanskrit-Wörterbuch in kürzerer Fassung.* Theile 1-7. St. Petersburg 1879-1889.

see Hemacandra

BÖHTLINGK, Otto, and ROTH, Rudolf

PD *Sanskrit-Wörterbuch.* Herausgegeben von der Kaiserlichen Akademie der Wissenschaften. Theile 1-7. St. Petersburg 1855-1875.

BÜHLER, Georg

1892a The Udepur Prasasti of the Kings of Malva, in: EI Vol. I, pp. 222-238.

1892b New Jaina Inscriptions from Mathura, in: EI Vol. I, pp. 371-393.

BURROW, T[homas], and EMENEAU, M[urray] B[arnson]
DET *A Dravidian Etymological Dictionary.* Oxford 1961.

COOMARASWAMY, Ananda K.
1928 Indian architectural terms, in: JAOS Vol. 48, pp. 250-275.
[2]1965 *History of Indian and Indonesian art.* New York. [First published in 1927]

DAGENS, Bruno
1970 see *Mayamata*
1994 see *Mayamata*

DEVA, Rājā Rādhākānta
ŚKD *Śabdakalpadrumaḥ. Syāra-Rājā-Rādhākāntadeva-Bahādureṇa viracitaḥ.* [...] Part 1-5. 1821. (Reprint Vārāṇasī 1961. Chowkhamba Sanskrit Series. 93)

DHAVALE, D. G.
1968 The date of Varāhamihira. In: ABORI No. 48/49, pp. 347-352.

DHAVALIKAR, M. K.
1969 Śrī Yugadhara – A Master Artist of Ajanta, in: Artibus Asiae, Vol. XXXI, pp. 301-308.
1971 Sūtradhāra. In: ABORI No. 52, pp. 215-220.
2004 *Satavahana Art.* New Delhi.

ELIZARENKOVA, T. Y.
1992 To the meaning of the Ṛgvedic *harmyá-/harmia-*, in: ABORI No. 72/73, pp. 573-582.

GABORIEAU, Marc
1991 The Indo-Nepalese House in Central Nepal: Building Patterns, Social and Religious Symbolism, in: TOFFIN (1991:33-53)

GANGULY, D. C.
[3]1979 Northern India during the eleventh and twelfth centuries: The Paramāras, in: *The struggle for empire.* Bombay. (The history and culture of the Indian people. 5), pp. 66-74.

GEIGER, Wilhelm
1964 see *Mahāvaṃsa*

GONDA, Jan
HIL *A history of Indian literature.* Wiesbaden, 1979-.

GRAY, Louis H.

1950 *The narrative of Bhoja (Bhojaprabandha) by Ballāla of Benares*. New Haven, Connecticut. (AOS. 34)

GUPTA, S[warajya] P[rakash] and ASTHANA, Shashi Prabha

2002 *Elements of Indian Art*. Including Temple Architecture, Iconography and Iconometry. New Delhi. (Perspectives in Indian Art and Archaeology. 4)

GUTSCHOW, Niels; KÖLVER, Bernhard; and SHRESTHACHARYA, Ishwaranand

1987 *Newar Towns and Buildings. An Illustrated Dictionary Newārī – English*. Sankt Augustin. (Nepalica. 3)

HAHN, Michael

1982 *Ratnākaraśānti's Chandoratnākara*. Edited by Michael Hahn. Kathmandu. (Nepal Research Centre, Miscellaneous Papers. 34)

see Haribhaṭṭa

JAIN, Kailash Chand

1973 *Malwa Through the Ages*. From the Earliest Time to 1305 A.D. New Delhi.

JEST, Corneille

1991 How I Built My House. An Account by Sarkiman Majhi, Fisherman, in: TOFFIN (1991:155-160).

KANSARA, N. M.

1998 The Vāstu-vidyā of Varāhamihira, in: Sambodhi Vol. XXII, pp. 108-118.

KEITH, A[rthur] Berriedale

^{2}1928 A history of Sanskrit literature. London. (1st edition 1920).

KERN, H[endrik]

1872 The Bṛhat-Saṅhitā; or, Complete System of Natural Astrology of Varāhamihira, Chapter LIII, in: JRAS, New Series, Vol. VI, pp. 279-300.

KÖLVER, Bernhard

1985 Kauṭalyas Stadt als Handelszentrum: der Terminus *puṭabhedana-*, in: ZDMG Vol. 135, pp. 299-311.

see GUTSCHOW, Niels, KÖLVER, Bernhard, and SHRESTHACHARYA, Ishwaranand

KOEPF, Hans
[3]1999 *Bildwörterbuch der Architektur.* 3. Auflage. Überarbeitet von Günther BINDING. Mit englischem, französischem und italienischem Fachglossar. Stuttgart.

KRISHNAMACHARIAR, M.
1937 *History of Classical Sanskrit Literature.* N.p. 1937. [Reprint Delhi 2004]

KULKARNI, E. D.
1953 *Śālihotra of Bhoja.* Critically edited by E.D. Kulkarni [...] . Poona. (Sources of Indo-Aryan Lexicography. 11)
1970-1972 Contribution of Bhoja to lexicography, in: JORM XL-XLI, pp. 75-81.

KULKARNI, R. P.
1987 Specifications for brick masonry according to Samarāṅgaṇasūtradhāra, in: IJHS Vol. 22 No. 4, pp. 328-331.

MANKAD, Popatbhai Ambashankar
1936 Samarāṅgaṇasūtradhāra and Yuktikalpataru. Whether these works are productions of one and the same king Bhoja of Dhārā Nagarī, in: ABORI Vol. XVII, pp. 358-370.
1950 see Bhuvanadeva

MARÉCHAUX, Pascal
1991 Two Houses in the Tibetan Cultural Tradition. In Pisang (Nyi-Shang) and in Stongde (Zanskar), in: TOFFIN (1991:209-224).

MAXWELL, T. S.
1989 Śilpa versus Śāstra, in: *Shastric traditions in Indian arts.* Edited by Anna Libera Dallapiccola in collaboration with Christine Walter-Mendy, Stephanie Zingel-Avé Lallemant. Vol. 1. Texts. Vol. 2. References and documentation. Stuttgart 1989. (Beiträge zur Südasienforschung Südasien-Institut Universität Heidelberg. 125).

MAYRHOFER, Manfred
EWA *Etymologisches Wörterbuch des Altindoarischen.* Vol. I-III. Heidelberg 1986-2001. (Indogermanische Bibliothek. II. Reihe, Wörterbücher.)

KEWA *Kurzgefaßtes etymologisches Wörterbuch des Altindoarischen. A Concise Etymological Sanskrit Dictionary.* Vol. 1-4. Heidelberg 1956-1978.

MISHRA, S.C.
1992 Archaeological testimony of *suruṅgā* and the Mauryanism of the *arthaśāstra* of Kauṭilya, in: ABORI No. 72/73, pp. 295-306.

MISHRA, Vibhuti Bhushan
1973 *Religious beliefs and practices of North India during the early mediaeval period.* Leiden/Köln. (Handbuch der Orientalistik. 2, Ergänzungsband III)

MITRA, Debala
[2]1980 *Buddhist Monuments.* Calcutta. (1st Edition 1971)

NARIMAN, G. K., WILLIAMS JACKSON, A. V., and OGDEN, Charles J.
1923 *Priyadarśika.* A Sanskrit drama by Harsha king of Northern India in the seventh century A.D. Translated into English by G.K. Nariman [...] A. V. Williams Jackson [...] and Charles J. Ogden [...] . New York. (Columbia University Indo-Iranian Series. 10)

PARAMAHANS, S. A.
1984 Units of measurements in medieval India and their modern equivalents, in: IJHS Vol. 19 No. 1, pp. 27-36.

PINGREE, David
1981a *Census of the exact sciences in Sanskrit.* Series A, Volume 4. Philadelphia.
1981b *Jyotiḥśāstra.* Astral and mathematical literature. Wiesbaden. (HIL. 6.4)

PISCHEL, Richard
PISCHEL *Grammatik der Prakrit-Sprachen.* Strassburg 1900. (Grundriss der indo-arischen Philologie und Altertumskunde, I. Band, 8. Heft)

RAGHAVAN, V.
1963 *Bhoja's Śṛṅgāra Prakāśa.* Madras.

RAHMAN, A. et al.
1982 *Science and Technology in Medieval India.* A Bibliography of

Source Materials in Sanskrit, Arabic and Persian. A. RAHMAN with the research assistance of M. A. ALVI (Persian), S. A. KHAN GHORI (Arabic), K. V. SAMBA MURTHY (Sanskrit). New Delhi.

RAU, Wilhelm
1957 *Staat und Gesellschaft im Alten Indien.* Nach den Brāhmaṇa-Texten dargestellt. Wiesbaden.

RHYS DAVIDS, Thomas W.
1898 Aṅgaṇa, in: JRAS NS Vol. XX, pp. 191-194.
1903 *Buddhist India.* London. (Reprint: New Delhi 1997)

RHYS DAVIDS, T[homas] W., and STEDE, William
PED *The Pali Text Society's Pali-English Dictionary.* Edited by T[homas] W. Rhys Davids [...] and William Stede [...] . London 1921-1925. (Reprinted 1986)

REDDY, E[mani] Siva Nagi
1998 *Evolution of Building Technology.* Early and Medieval Period. Volume I. Introduction. The context. Secular space. Political space. Volume II. Burial space. Religious space. The human facade. Delhi.

ROCHER, Ludo
1986 *The Purāṇas.* Wiesbaden. (HIL. 2.3)

SAHNI, K. C.
1998 *The book of Indian trees.* Mumbai.

SARMA, Shreekrishna
1958 The Maṇḍapadruma of Mahādevasūri. Edited with Introduction by Dr. Shreekrishna SARMA, in: ALB No. 22, pp. 119-157.

SARMA, S. R.
1986 The Sources and Authorship of Yuktikalpataru, in: AJOS Vol. III No.1, pp. 39-54.

SCHARFE, Hartmut
1968 *Untersuchungen zur Staatsrechtslehre des Kauṭalya.* Wiesbaden.

SCHLINGLOFF, Dieter
1967 Arthaśāstra-Studien II: Die Anlage einer Festung (durgavidhāna), in: WZKSO XI, pp. 44-80.

1969 *Die altindische Stadt. Eine vergleichende Untersuchung.* Wiesbaden. (Akademie der Wissenschaften und der Literatur. Abhandlungen der geistes- und sozialwissenschaftlichen Klasse, Jahrgang 1969 Nr. 5)

SHETH, Hargovind Das Trikam Chand
PSM *Pāia-Sadda-Mahaṇṇavo.* A comprehensive Prakrit-Hindi Dictionary with Sanskrit equivalents, quotations and complete references. (Reprint of 2nd edition Vārāṇasī 1963) Dillī 1986. [1st edition 1928]

SHUKLA, Dvijendra Nath
1956a see Bhoja: *Samarāṅgaṇasūtradhāra*
1956b see Bhoja: *Samarāṅgaṇasūtradhāra*
1958 *Vāstu-Śāstra Vol. I: Hindu Science of Architecture.* (Engineering, Town Planning, Civil Architecture, Palace Architecture, Temple Architecture and an anthology of Vāstu-lakṣaṇas). Lucknow. (Reprint New Delhi 1998)

SINCLAIR, W.F.
1898 Angaṇa as now used in Western India, in: JRAS NS Vol. XX, p. 623 sq.

SIRCAR, D. C.
1958 Mahudi Plates of Paramāra Bhoja, V.S. 1074, in: EI Vol. XXXIII, pp. 215-218
1960 Three Paramara Inscriptions, in: EI Vol. XXXV, pp. 185 sq.

STEIN, Otto
Kl. Schr. *Kleine Schriften.* Herausgegeben von Friedrich Wilhelm. Stuttgart 1985.
1925 Syrinx und Suruṅgā, in: ZII 3, pp. 280-318 (Kl. Schr. pp. 1-39).
1935 Arthaśāstra and Śilpaśāstra, in: ArchOr VII, pp. 473-487 (Kl. Schr. pp. 366-380).

STEINER, Roland
1996 Die Lehre der Anuṣṭubh bei den indischen Metrikern, in: *Suhṛllekhāḥ.* Festgabe für Helmut Eimer. Herausgegeben von Michael Hahn, Jens-Uwe Hartmann und Roland Steiner. Swisttal-Odendorf. (Indica et Tibetica 28), pp. 227-248.
1997 *Untersuchungen zu Harṣadevas Nāgānanda und zum indischen Schauspiel.* Swisttal-Odendorf. (Indica et Tibetica 31)

STRAUCH, Ingo

2003 STEINER, Roland: Untersuchungen zu Harṣadevas Nāgānanda und zum indischen Schauspiel (Indica et Tibetica 31). Swisttal-Odendorf 1997, in: OLZ 98/1, coll. 176-182. [book review]

TOFFIN, Gérard

1991 *Man and His House in the Himalayas: Ecology of Nepal.* Edited by Gérard Toffin. New Delhi. (First published in French under the title *L'homme Et La Maison En Himalaya: Écologie du Népal*, 1981.)

TRAUTMANN, Thomas R.

1971 *Kauṭilya and the Arthaśāstra.* A statistical investigation of the authorship and evolution of the text. Leiden.

VAJPEYI, R.

1972 On the meaning of the term "pratolī", in: ABORI No. 53, pp. 221-227.

VIJAYARĀJENDRASŪRI

ADhR *Śrīmad Vijayarājendrasūrīśvara-viracitaḥ Abhidhānarājendraḥ Kośaḥ.* [...] *Bṛhatbhūmiko pādghāta-Prākṛtavyākṛti-Prākṛtaśabdarūpāvalyādi-pariśiṣṭasahitaḥ.* [...] *Dīpavijaya-*[...]*Yatīndravijayābhyāṃ saṃśodhitaḥ. Bhāgaḥ* 1-7. Ratlām 1910-1934.

VOGEL, Claus

1979 *Indian lexicography.* Wiesbaden. (HIL. 5.4)

VOGEL, J.Ph.

1903 Sanskṛt *pratolī* – hindī *paulī*, in: *Album Kern.* Opstellen geschreven ter eere van Dr. H. Kern. Hem aangeboden door vrienden en leerlingen op zijn zeventigsten verjaardag den vi. April MDCCCCIII. Leiden, pp. 235-237.

Illustrations

Fig. 1 – The *vāstupuruṣamaṇḍala* according to SAS 11

1. Brahman
2. Aryaman
3. Savitṛ
4. Sāvitra
5. Vivasvant
6. Indra
7. Jaya
8. Mitra
9. Yakṣman
10. Rudra
11. Pṛthvīdhara
12. Āpa
13. Āpavatsa
14. Agni
15. Parjanya
16. Jayanta
17. Indra/Mahendra
18. Sūrya
19. Satya
20. Bhṛśa
21. Nabha
22. Anila
23. Pūṣan
24. Vitatha
25. Gṛhakṣata
26. Yama
27. Gandharva
28. Bhṛṅgarāja
29. Mṛga
30. Pitṛgaṇa
31. Dauvārika
32. Sugrīva
33. Puṣpadanta
34. Varuṇa
35. Asura
36. Śoṣa
37. Pāpayakṣman
38. Roga
39. Nāga
40. Mukhya
41. Bhallāṭa
42. Soma/Kubera
43. Caraka
44. Aditi
45. Diti

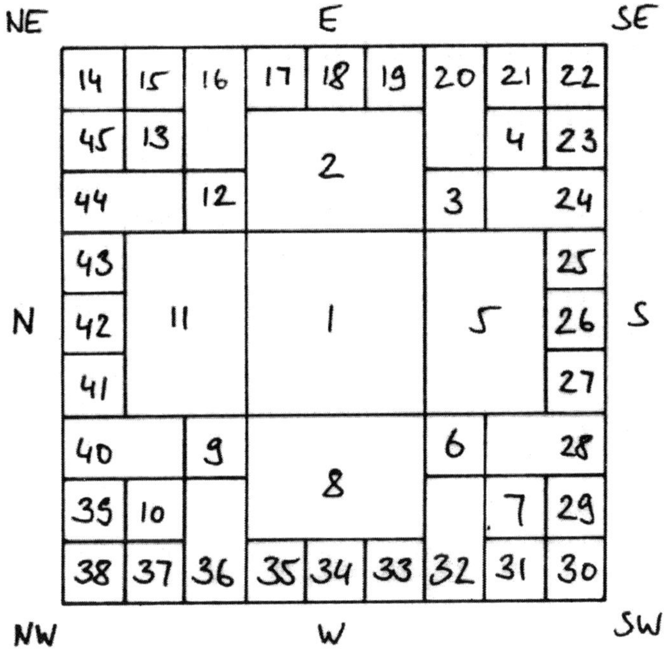
NE
E
SE
14 15 16 17 18 19 20 21 22
45 13 4 23
2
44 12 3 24
43 25
N
42 11 1 5 26
S
41 27
40 9 6 28
8
39 10 7 29
38 37 36 35 34 33 32 31 30
NW
W
SW

Fig. 2 – Relative position of main living area, sleeping area, and main entrance

Arrangement suitable ...

1) ... for a Brāhmaṇa   2) ... for a Kṣatriya

4) ... for a Sūdra   3) ... for a Vaiśya

Shaded area – main living area

S – sleeping area

D – front door

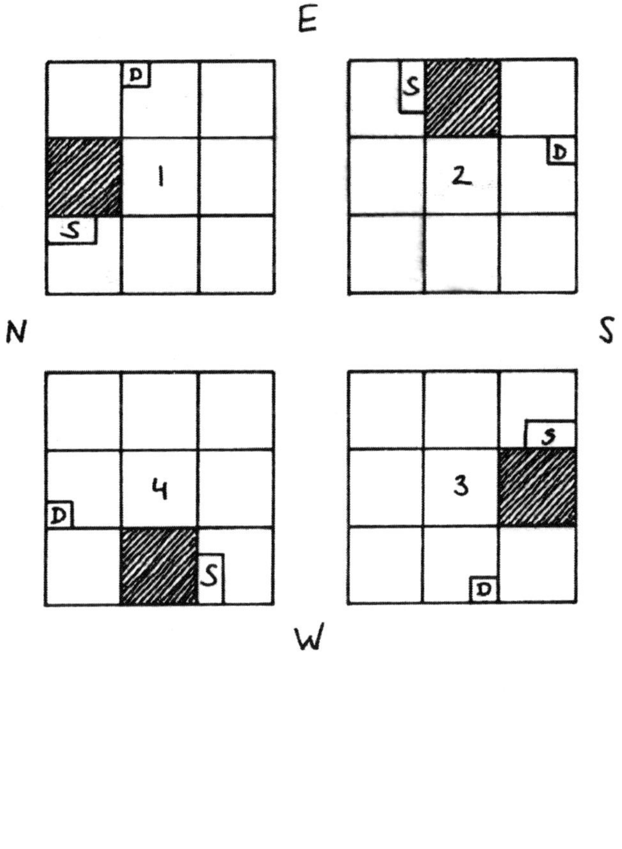
E
D
S
D
1
2
S
N
S
S
D
4
3
S
D
W

Fig. 3 – The *padas* of the *vāstupuruṣamaṇḍala* on which the front door may be situated

According to:

1) *Bṛhatsaṃhitā*

2) *Matsyapurāṇa*

4) *Viśvakarmaprakāśa*

3) *Samarāṅgaṇasūtradhāra*

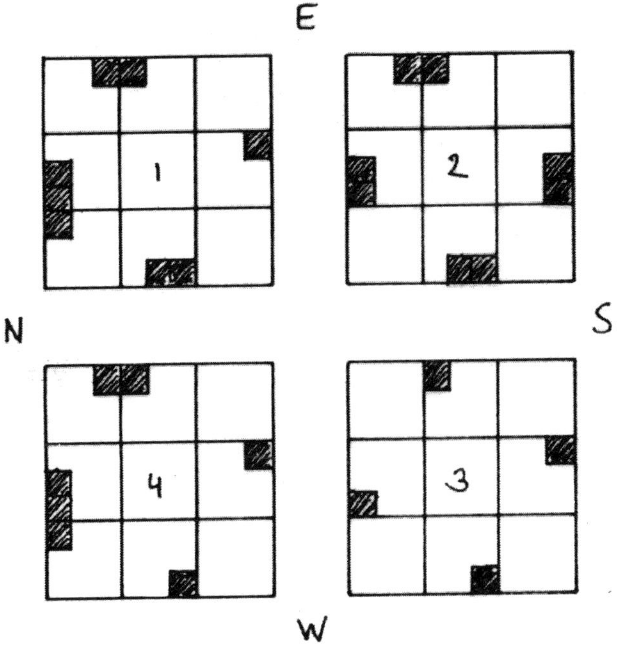

E
1
2
N
S
4
3
W

Fig. 4 – The four possible constellations of main entrance and *śālā* entrance

1) Utsaṅga 2) Pūrṇabāhu

4) Pratyakṣāya 3) Hīnabāhu

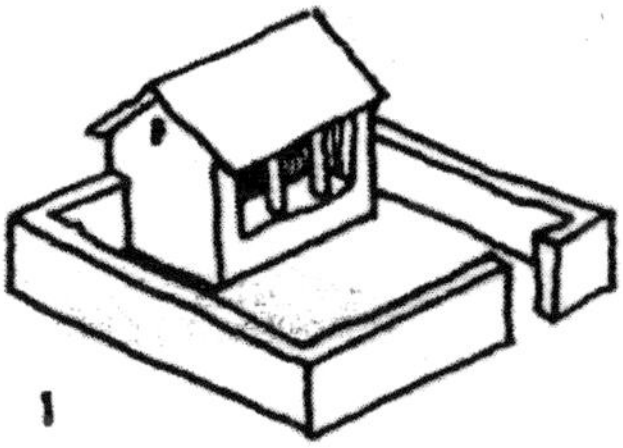

1

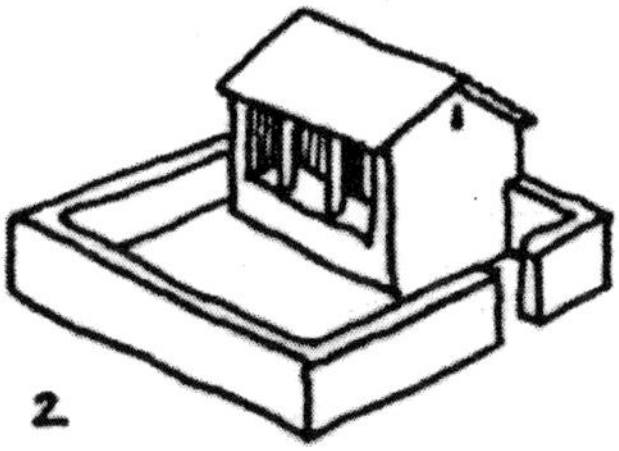

2

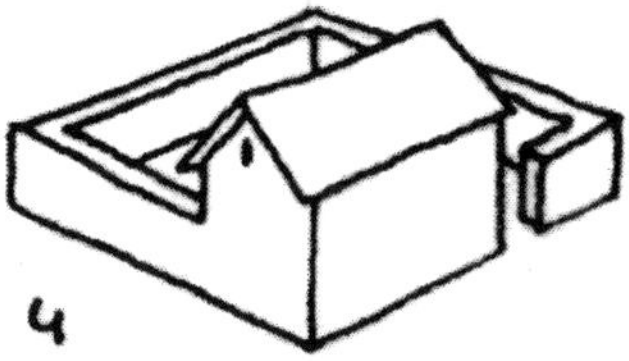

4

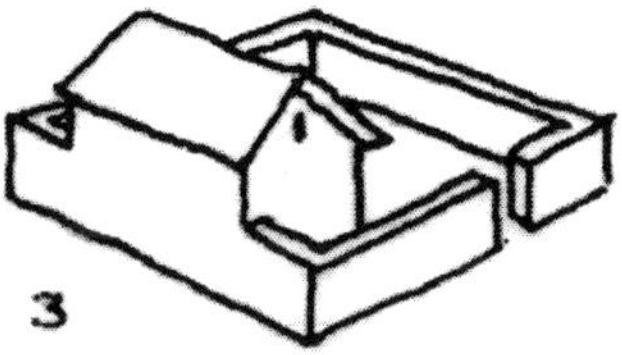

3

Fig. 5 – The five basic types of dwellings

2) Ekaśāla

3) Dviśāla

1) Śālā

5) Catuḥśāla

4) Triśāla

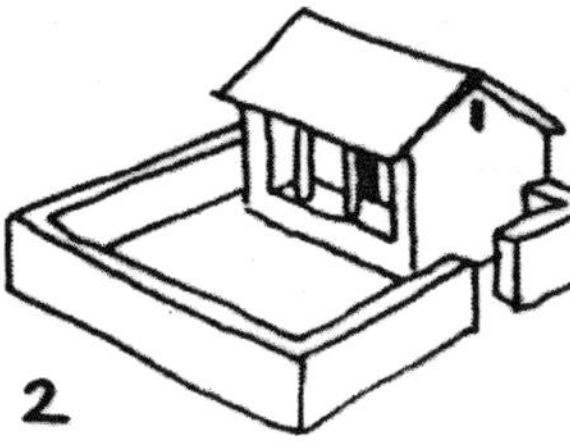

2

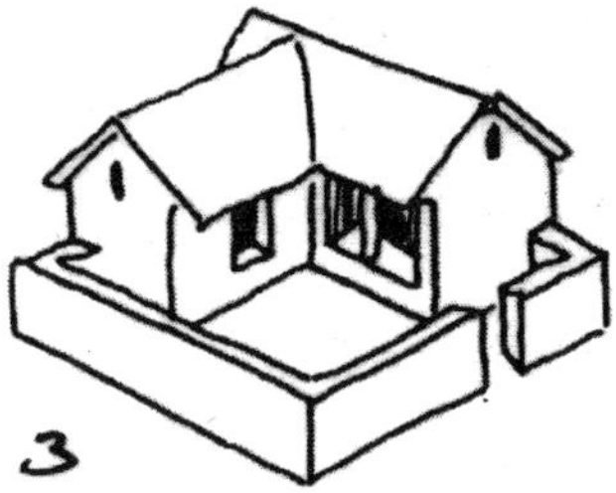

3

1

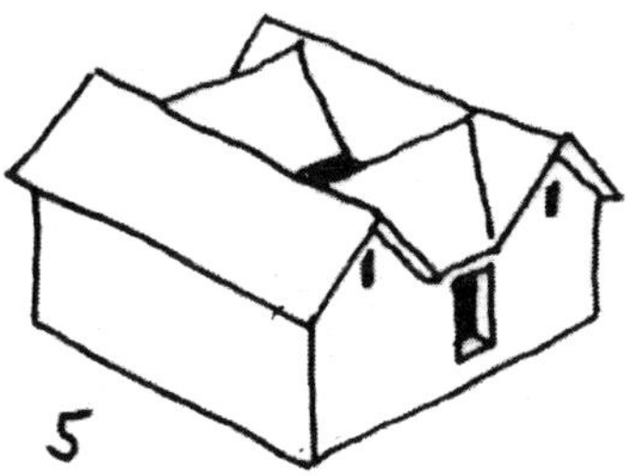

5

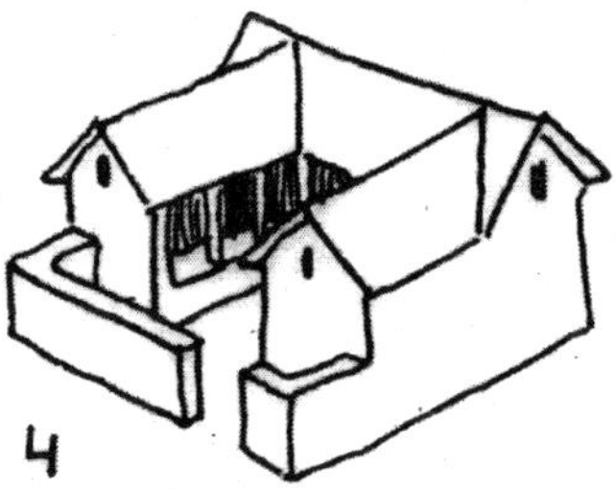

4

Fig. 6 – The four types of *triśāla*

1) Hiraṇyanābha

2) Sukṣetra

4) Pakṣaghna

3) Cullī

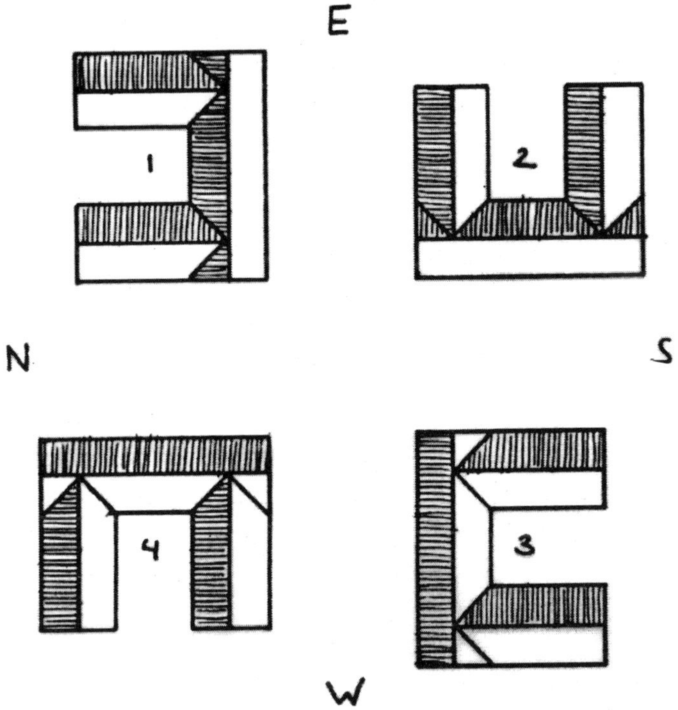
E
1
2
N
S
4
3
W

Fig. 7 – The six types of *dviśāla*

1) Siddhārtha

2) Yamasūrya

Daṇḍa

4) Vāta

5) Kāca

6) Cullī

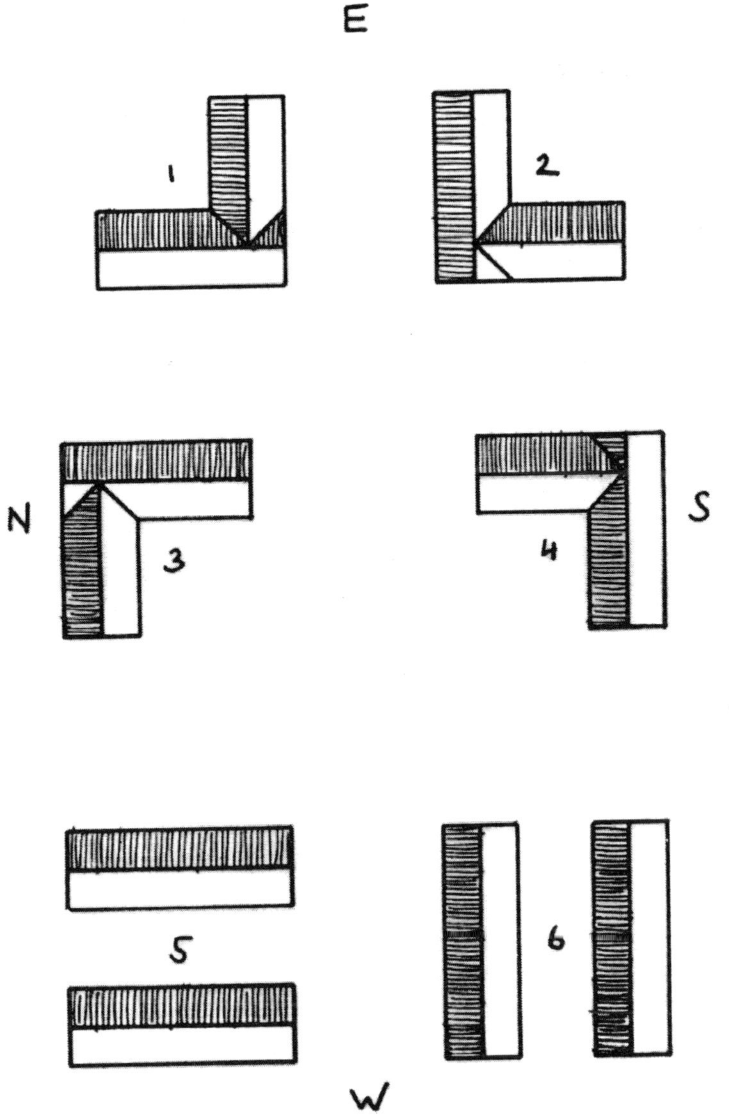
E
1
2
N
3
4
S
5
6
W

Fig. 8 – The sixteen basic types of *śālā*

1) Dhruva

2) Dhānya

3) Jaya

4) Nanda

5) Khara

6) Kānta

7) Manorama

8) Sumukha

1
2
3
4
5
6
7
8

Fig. 8 (cont.)

9) Durmukha

10) Krūra

11) Supakṣa

12) Dhanada

13) Kṣaya

14) Ākranda

15) Vipula

16) Vijaya

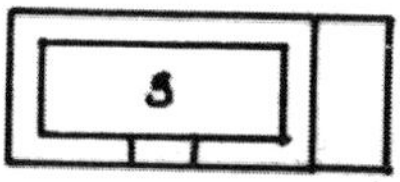
9
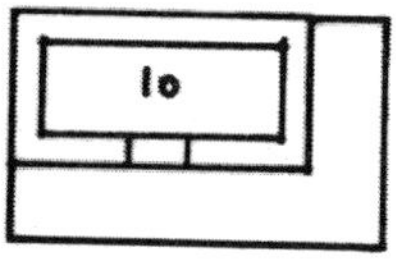
10
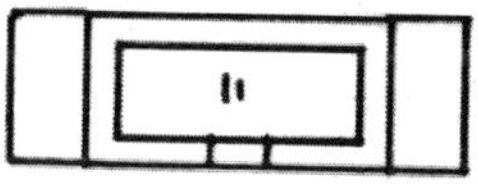
11
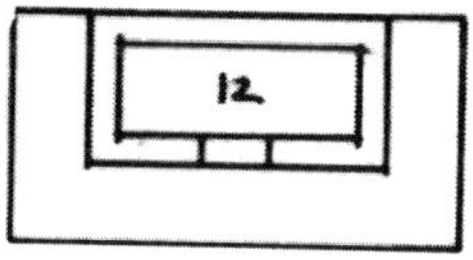
12
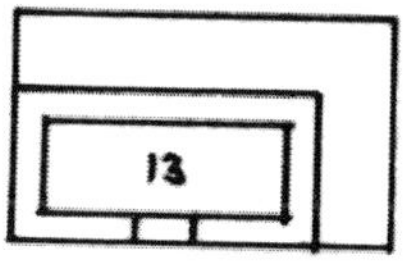
13
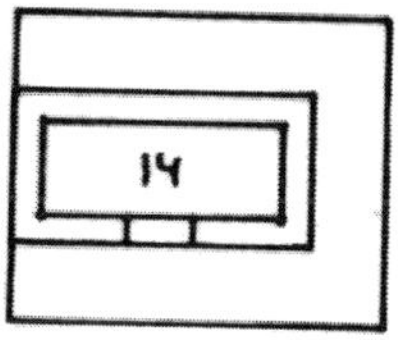
14
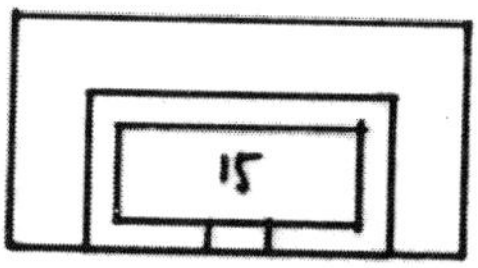
15

16

Fig. 9 – The fifteen types of *halaka*

1) Īśvara
2) Vṛṣabha
3) Candra
4) Roga
5) Pāpa
6) Bhayada
7) Nandana
8) Khādaka

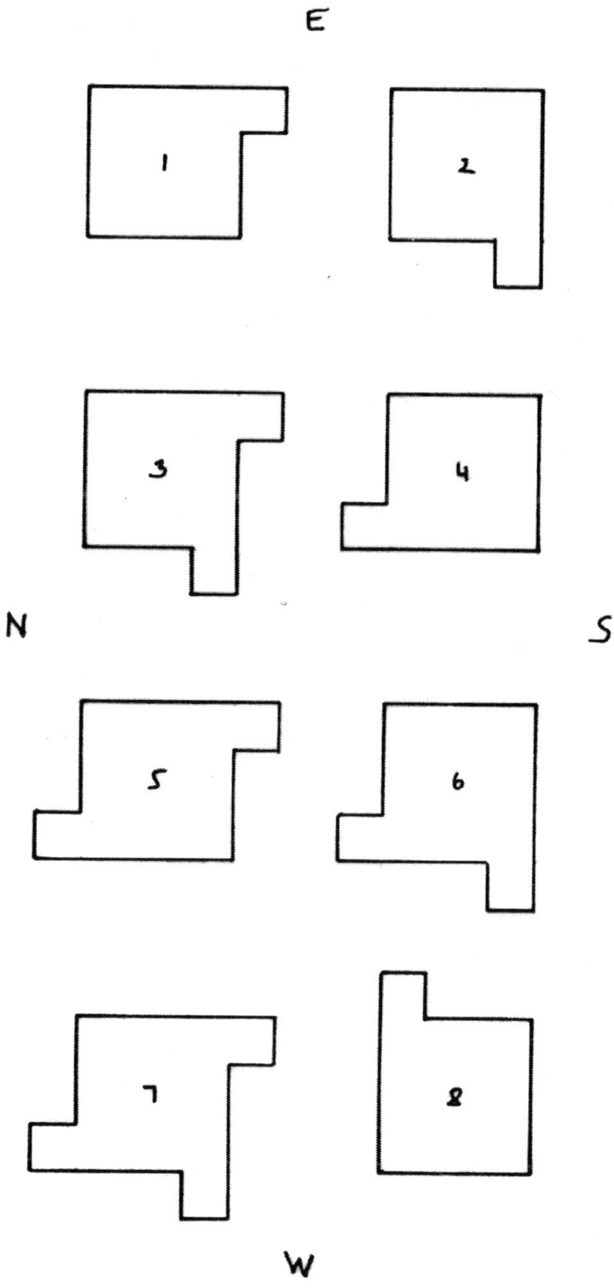
E
1
2
3
4
N
S
5
6
7
8
W

Fig. 9 (cont.)

9) Dhvāṅkṣa

10) Vikṛta

11) Vilaya

12) Kṣaya

13) Yāmya

14) Viparīta

15) Bhadraka

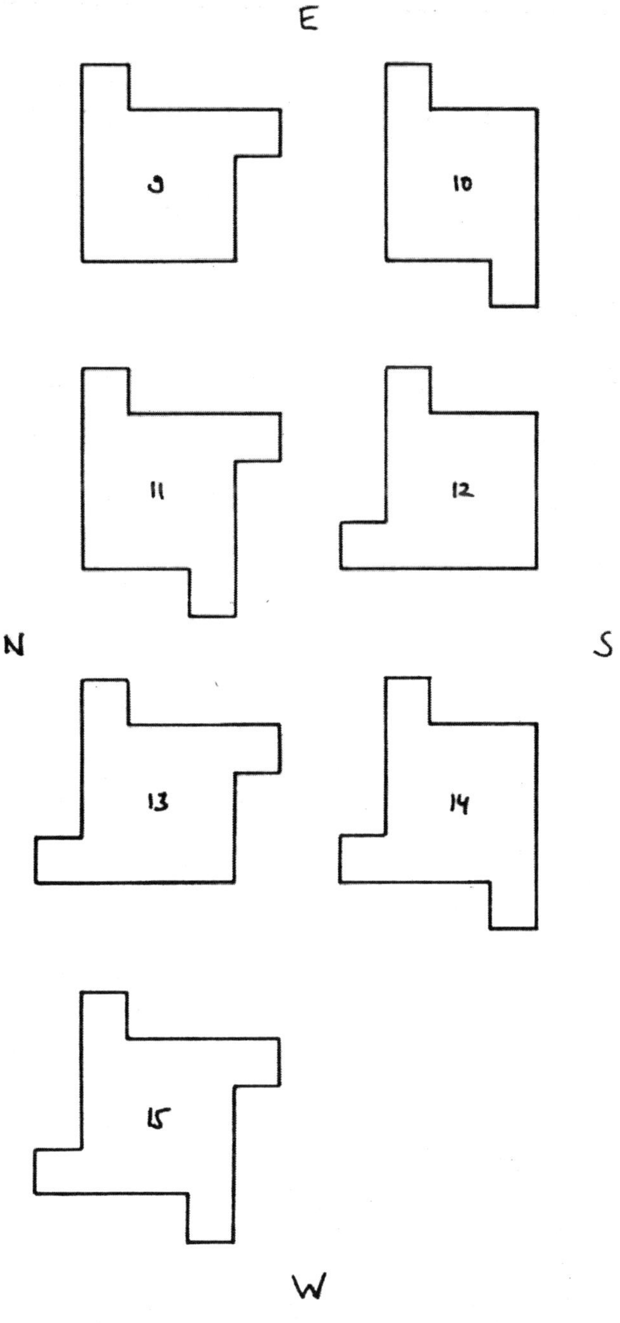
E
9
10
11
12
N
S
13
14
15
W

Fig. 10 – The plot sizes suitable for the four *varṇa*s (in cubits)

1) – 5) Brāhmaṇa	6) – 9) Kṣatriya
1) 32 x 35 2/10	
2) 28 x 30 8/10	6) 28 x 31 1/2
3) 24 x 26 4/10	7) 24 x 27
4) 20 x 22	8) 20 x 22 1/2
5) 16 x 17 6/10	9) 16 x 18

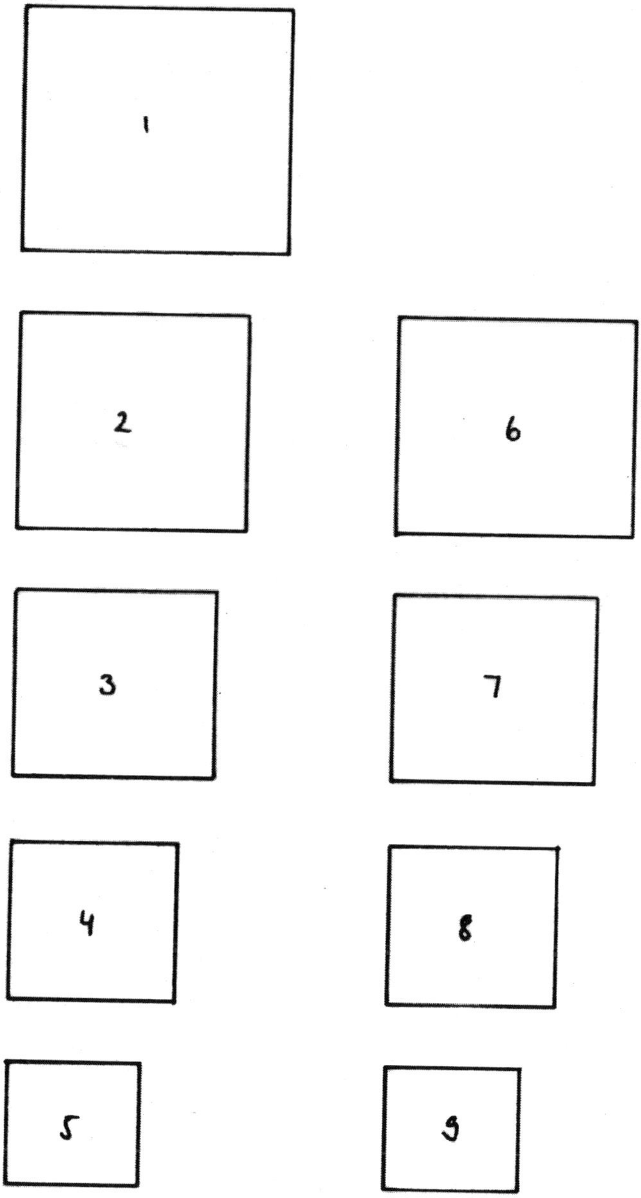
1
2
3
4
5
6
7
8
9

Fig. 10 (cont.)

10) – 12) Vaiśya	13) – 14) Śūdra
10) 24 x 28	
11) 20 x 23 1/3	13) 20 x 25
12) 16 x 18 2/3	14) 16 x 20

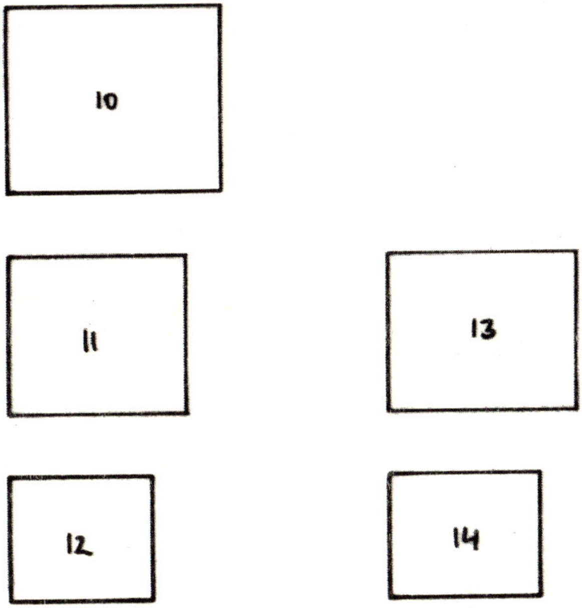
10
11
12
13
14

Fig. 11 – The increment of the length of the plot against the width prescribed for the four *varṇa*s

1) Brāhmaṇa: + 1/10	2) Kṣatriya: + 1/8
4) Śūdra: + 1/4	3) Vaiśya: + 1/6

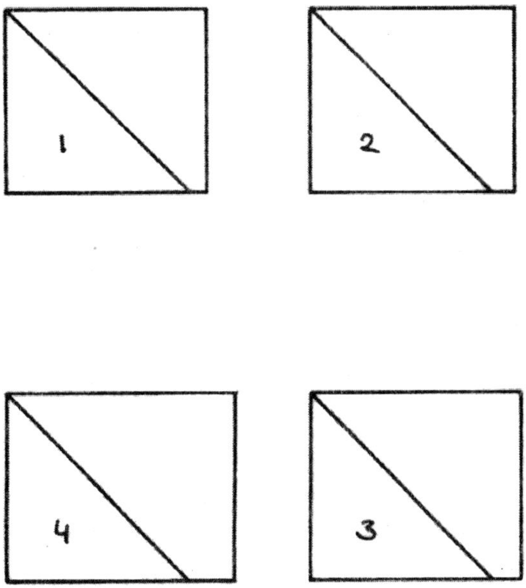
1
2
4
3

Fig. 12a – The ground plans of a *catuḥśāla* with a width of 32 cubits:

According to *Samarāṅgaṇasūtradhāra*

According to *Bṛhatsaṃhitā*

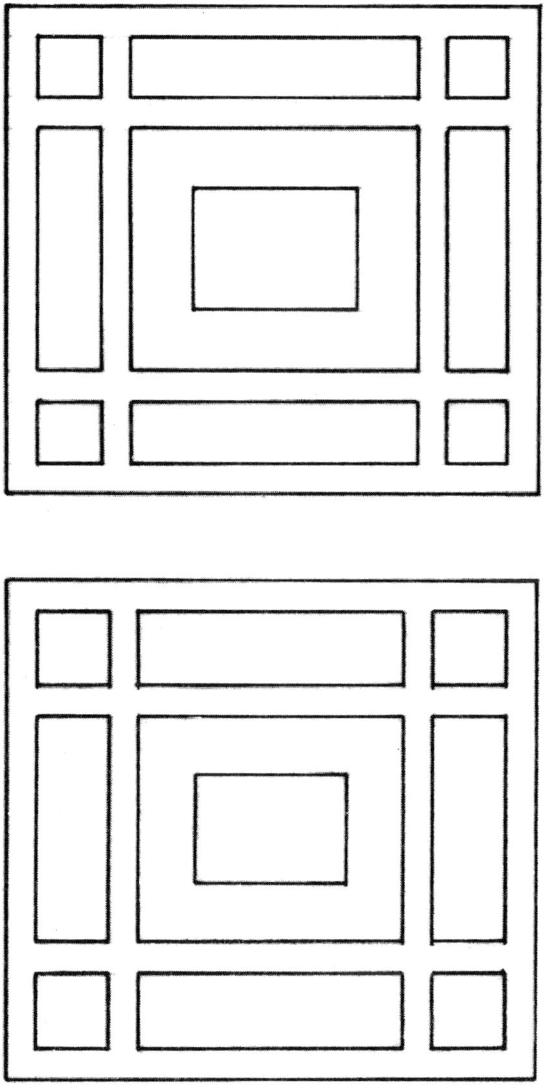

Fig. 12b – The ground plans of a *catuḥśāla* with a width of 16 cubits:

According to *Samarāṅgaṇasūtradhāra*

According to *Bṛhatsaṃhitā*

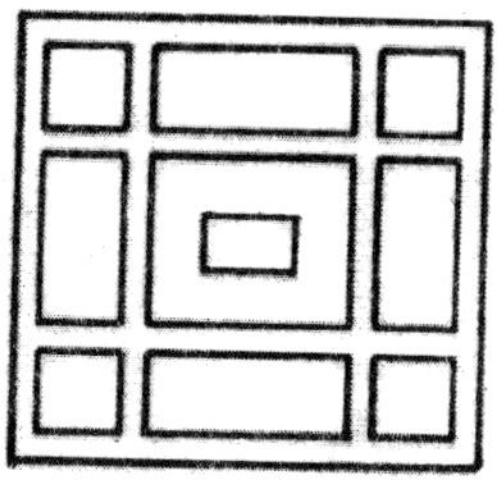